For my parents, my children, and my love:
The warmth in my life comes from the inspiration and
encouragement you have provided and still provide.
I am truly grateful to each of you.

And for all the imaginary and real characters who have significantly
influenced me and played an integral role in this journey.
Thank you for your profound love and impact on my life.

And for my real Mara… who generously offered her time and expertise
without asking for or anything in return. Your assistance and our
reconnection felt like reaching the fifth level of Jungle King.

Until We're Forty-Something

Kim Mazzei

Until We're Forty-Something

Chapter One

I am what you call an imperfect dichotomy. My friends would tell you they've heard me say, "I'm not like the other colors." As an adult, I've said it out loud, jokingly. As a little girl, I used to say it quietly to myself. I mostly lived in my imagination. I played outside and had friends, but I still scheduled alone time as an everyday event. I spent countless hours creating photo album collages and listening to 45 RPMs. I often stared at my face in my mirror, sitting cross-legged on my bedroom floor, playing music on my Musi-Center. I received it one year for Christmas from Santa, which even at ten years old, I knew was my parents. It cost $249 retail back then, but my Dad, Franco, "got a good deal." He installed a handicapped steel ramp at a store that sold stereos, Crazy Nate's. One day, I heard Franco telling my Uncle Pete about "the deal" which meant free. A barter, Franco often made.

I didn't care if it was free to my mom and dad; it was the most extraordinary Christmas gift ever, and I loved it! It had two speakers that produced sound from a radio, a turntable for 45s, and an 8-track cartridge player. It was a three-in-one. I played and paused 45s, lifting the needle with a tiny black lever in the back of the needle's arm, and all it needed was a slight push forward. I was careful to place it down gently on the spinning turntable to replay a chosen song over and over. It was challenging to jot down every lyric playing from vinyl in 1976. I kept repeating the verses to make sure I wrote down and memorized every word. It became easier once cassettes were introduced. Cassettes had a pause button. 8-tracks did not and were on a path to extinction.

iTunes was non-existent. There was no Google with answers to everything and no Apps like Shazam. I hand-wrote every word to the then doleful 1970s Bread hit. I was eight years old, pondering the meaning of David Gates lyrics, "If a face can launch a thousand ships, then where am I to go?" I would silently ask myself, in my bedroom mirror, what does that mean? Can't he just go wherever with whomever, and how can a face launch towards anything? I had no idea what it meant, but I wanted to find out.

It took a great struggle to finally arrive at my actual, authentic self, a simpler state of being. The transformation was sometimes ugly, and I haven't always been proud of myself. In retrospect, I am not precisely graceful; I have learned that grace is not usually a gift given but rather a learned behavior. I'm still not proficient.

In the meantime, I owned an equal number of those little yellow gizmos that fit inside the middle hole of my 45s. My mother, Vivien, told me they used to call those devices spiders when she was a teenager in the 50s.
When I was twelve, my 6th-grade teacher, Mrs. Thurman, assigned an essay: What would you like to do when you grow up? My reflection went like this:
Whatever I do, I want to make people laugh and cry, and I think whatever I do, I want to do it from my house in a pair of Levi's. There was more to my essay. Still, it was one run-on sentence I believed deserved an A. Mrs. Thurman gave me a D. However, I have spent many hours alone in my studio, often in a ripped pair of Levi's. I was born to be a storyteller, a mom, and a teacher. Creativity was my greatest gift. It is worth noting that I am not in the camp of looking back on how things used to be. I consciously try to stay present in my time and space.

Being present, in the now is also a learned behavior, and I wonder if others learn these truths without the struggle. Occasionally, I do daydream and anticipate the future but plan less and enjoy more. I spent much time in my *forty-something* days looking back. It was around that time, though I produced many happy snapshots to prove otherwise; I knew I wasn't living the best version of my *forty-something* self.

Some people, who knew me before the great transformation, liked the old version of me better. Change is hard for most people. But it wasn't a choice, I chose. It chose me. Essentially, something was missing in the everyday grind of my middle-aged years. I never felt like I was living the dream, no matter how flawless and enchanting it may have looked. The dream is still my perpetual goal.

I have always been a little bit of everything combined, which has created contradicting emotions that feel like waves rippling toward the shoreline in my veins. My soul is a variety of mixed ingredients that I have accepted and accept that I will always be a work in progress.

Thirteen years after I was born, history was made when MTV launched. It was the first 24-hour music/video channel. The first aired was "Video Killed the Radio Star" by The Buggles. I didn't realize the irony of that back then. After seeing MTV, I wanted to create videos with music and began researching how to do so. The following summer, I attended a camp program at a university, about half an hour from my home — *Imagery* and *Editing* for *Youths*.

Vivien drove me in the mornings and picked me up in the evenings. I was fourteen years old and every day in July, from 9-5, I learned about television production. I loved the studio and my counselor Reb, was equally fascinating. The following summer, the program was discontinued due to insufficient enrollment. Seemingly, most young teens were interested in something other than spending their summer inside a cold building to learn about almost anything. When Vivien told me the program went bust the following year, I was delighted to be free of any summer obligations, yet I thought of my counselor Reb. I truly felt sad that I would probably never see her again. I never did. Her sun-visor always worn to its side, etched in my mind.

As a young teen, I easily swayed into long summer days having almost nothing to do but much to anticipate. One day while I was sitting on the front porch with a popsicle, my brother Michael pulled into the driveway in his 1972 turquoise Nova. Four years older, Michael was hardly home. School, work, and his girlfriend, Audrey, kept him busy. He parked and merely grunted as he headed inside. I knew Audrey would be soon to arrive. An hour later, pressing my ear up against the pine pocket door, eavesdropping on their conversation or hopeful that they were making out to use for bribe material later, a loud and sudden bang catapulted me off the door by the object thrown at it from the other side. That was usually the pillow from Michael's arm's reach on the couch. A deep, explosive voice called out, "Vivien, she's annoying us! Get her away from us! Oh My God, Mom! Mom!" My mother dashed to my location, stared at me on the floor, and said, "Really, Em? Please come help me set the table and leave your brother alone!" I unwillingly popped up to insist, "Mom, I don't understand why he gets to kick me out of a room in my own house, and I don't get why he still calls you Vivien." She winked and whispered, "Core-four," and followed me into the kitchen.

Actually, I did know why Michael called Mom, *Vivien*. Michael, then 16, and Vivian were grabbing breakfast before his lacrosse game at Brian's Luncheonette.

Brian's was our go-to place around the block with a menu of comfort. Vivien was chatting with Brian when she noticed a woman walk up to Michael, but being far away, she couldn't quite make out what the woman was saying. Half listening to Brian, my mother watched the interaction between Michael and the stranger. Later that evening, Vivian couldn't finish telling the story at our dinner table because she was laughing so much, so Michael interjected. He looked at my father, still chewing on a mouthful of food, and blurted out, "Oh my God, Dad. This hot woman says, what's your name, honey? My eyes popped out of my skull, but Dad, I was so sophisticated, and in my manly voice, I said, *Mikal*." He continued, "The woman pointed to Mom, and Mom was glaring back, still next to Brian." Then she asked, "What is your girlfriend's name?" Michael was still chewing and talking, "Dad, I answered again in my lower register, *Vivien*." The woman grabbed Michael's forearm, pulled him close, and said, "She is way too old for you, young man," and put a piece of paper in his hand with a phone number.

Laughter burst from the table, and one silly joke after another ensued. We had to stop because our stomachs hurt. Mom had tears rolling down her cheeks and said, "Oh, Michael, I think I heard your voice crack like Peter Brady's. Maybe you aren't ready to be the ladies' man you fancy yourself to be." Laughing harder, Michael finally replied, "Vivien, you are way too old for this stud!" In his egocentric manner, he continued with two thumbs pointing at himself, "I can do better! Vivien, we're breaking up!" Michael could hardly get the sentence out, doubled up with tight fists harnessing his stomach. From that day on, Michael called mom, Vivien. Some short time later, I did too. Sometimes in public, people would look stunned when they heard my brother call our mom by her first name. It was as if my mother had allowed him to be disrespectful.

Mom never cared what others thought. She called it a
"core-four" share. That meant it was between us, and
nobody was better or worse off for not understanding. She
would smirk, look at Michael and me, wink and whisper,
"Core-four, my peeps. *Core-four."*
Michael sometimes threw pillows at the pine pocket door.
He occasionally opened my bedroom door and tossed one
of his favorite jerseys right at me and would say, "Here,
they won the bowl three years ago. It's yours because it
doesn't fit on my huge muscular arms. It's lucky!"
Sometimes he gently knocked and would peek his head in
and ask, "Hey, you want ice cream?" Those were the
moments I eagerly anticipated. His offer of ice cream was
always met with my enthusiastic response, "Um, yes,
please!" I loved when he was nice to me, and so did
Vivien.

Vivien was a golf mom, not to confuse that with today's
common term, "soccer mom." She played golf and enjoyed
long lunches with other stay-at-home-mom friends. After
school, she was my stay-at-home cook and chauffeur. Her
parents named her after Scarlett O'Hara's character
from Gone with the Wind. She was my best friend and a
great Mom. Her lasagna was my favorite among many
other dishes. There were always plenty of Vivien's
unforgettable blueprint originals, whether traditional
holiday meals or everyday dinners. Even better was the
familiar smell of my home. After a hard day of play and
imagination, in a big world of freedom and a tiny
neighborhood, there was no better scent than coming home
to Vivien's kitchen.
I remember cold winter afternoons, driving home from my
guitar lesson to our home on Haypath Lane. Vivien drove
up our long, blacktop driveway and carefully parked in our
oversized garage.

She knew I was the kind of kid who would stay in the car to listen to the rest of Melissa Manchester's "Don't Cry Out Loud." Mom would turn the ignition key just enough to shut off the engine allowing the radio to remain on. She taught me to notch it forward and pull the key out to completely turn the car off when the song ended. Since the car was garaged, the keys lived in the cup holder; where I'd leave them before heading inside. Most of my friends didn't know that ignition trick until they were much older. Vivien only stayed for the song length if it was one of her favorites: Barbra Streisand, Barry Manilow, Johnny Mathis, or the newest Air Supply hit. She usually scurried inside because dinner had to be made, and there was laundry to fold. I never thought of all my mother's hard work raising us, keeping a clean home, and juggling the schedules. I didn't know why Vivien was always in a rush. I just noticed she was.

It was easy to be around Vivien. She was hip and knowledgeable. She sported Liz Claiborne sweatsuits of many colors and designs on most days. I would call them classic vintage from the 80s. My Dad would go to one store and buy ten for her birthday. He never really knew what she liked. He just guessed she would like more of what she bought for herself.

Viv preferred gifts from him that meant something other than his customary, one-stop-shop for every color sweatsuit. I knew he meant well. He would ask me to wrap them for him when I was old enough.

I made her gifts. She liked that I put time and thought into her gift with a hand-made special card to go with it. She was my favorite fan, and I was hers. She would sit enthusiastically and listen to my guitar lesson. She drove me everywhere, cleaned my clothes, gave me money and told me to clean my room.

She lived for me and I didn't feel that was my burden. Childhood was good, even flawless sometimes. She was always in control of the household and everyone in it. I would cry when she and Dad vacationed, so afraid they would never return. When they were home, my father worked long hours. He came home to a clean house and a daily four-course dinner.

Franco and Vivien moved out of the Bronx a year after their vows. By twenty-two years old, my father was manufacturing and patenting mobility products in a business that would provide for his family long after his death. Franco was hard-working and completely blue-collar. He delivered dry cleaning in 1949 after elementary school at eight years old. Hours of work for a five, rarely a ten-cent tip, and perhaps enough to buy the fresh bread his Mama would expect him to have tucked under the arm of his hand-me-down parker upon his return home.

He hadn't changed much as I grew to know him. I knew he loved work, and I figured he loved us, too. I just thought that was what a man did - a man worked, and a woman cooked and folded too many clothes. That is how it was in nineteen-eighty-something, in my house anyway, and it all seemed normal, or at least the way I learned what normal was.

My father never complained about his long hours, nor did I. He made time to coach Michael's lacrosse games. I remember him cheering from the seats at all my band concerts. He used to take my brother on early Saturday mornings to ride a mini bike on the dirt roads behind a local golf course. After dinner on summer nights, he never said no when I asked him to have a catch. We spent countless hours on the greens, snatching a little white ball from a cup. He taught me how to play and how to replace the flag. I learned to tightly secure my bag on the back of the golf cart and plunge my putter back into the bag at the end of a hole. When I was too young to play golf, he took me anyway, and I steered the cart from his lap. He was a fan of Ronald Reagan, Carter not so much. He was fair, valid and no-nonsense. I liked him. He used to let me put clips and curlers in his hair, and his presence made me feel safe. Work and disparaging political declarations were his specialty. He wasn't too prejudiced, like my Grandpa. We didn't grow up hearing my mom or dad call people names that I would be too ashamed to admit I heard as a child. As for my grandfather, he would easily spill out derogatory words to tell a joke every so often at a family gathering. There was always his exception that made those words seem okay. Pop, as we called him, was over-the-top prejudiced, and it was allowed. My cousins and I were told that WWII Veteran Pop was entitled and that we should all do as we're told and not as he does. It was all good fun, and we mostly did what we were told. Despite his views, I didn't grow up to agree with; I loved him. Everybody loved him.

Sadly, he died when I was sixteen. By then, I knew I wasn't supposed to marry or date a brown or black boy. I was sure a Jewish boy would not have been a seamless choice either. I knew I was expected to date or marry a catholic boy, preferably of Italian descent. I learned not to call black people names, not out loud, at least. I knew that wasn't right. I may have known what my Pop meant when he would call a man a two-dollar bill, but it was as uninteresting to me as most of the snippets I heard from the adults' chatter.

Talk about generations of evolution and changes in lifestyles. I wonder what Pop's life was like as a boy and what made him so narrow-minded. At just three years old, I know Vivien would cry over the picture of him, her father, who bravely fought for our country as a marine.

My father was eight, hustling dry-cleaning for a 5-cent tip for his family's dinner bread. At nine, I was in my room, trying to figure out David Gates's lyrics. Decades later, my daughter was a preteen camper on trips to places I had never been and with a brand-new laptop.

But there were nights as a young girl I would sometimes sit on the top stair and listen to Vivien and Franco's loud talks in the kitchen when I was supposed to be asleep. Vivien would question Franco, "When will I come before business and your damn clients?" Sometimes he answered loudly, and sometimes he did not respond. I can picture a shoulder shrug and my father's facial expression silently conveying, "What do you want from me?"
When I was twelve years old, and later during college when I was twenty, I knew there was never any resolution to that conversation and the many others that followed. It became clear that my parents were stable life partners who may have missed the passionate love boat. Franco was her lifestyle provider, and Vivien kept his honey-do list full, belly full, and home full; Of life. They lived by the book their parents read to them when they were youngsters about what their roles should be. Sometimes it was exceptional, and sometimes it was really confusing.

Nevertheless, Franco, without fail, kissed my Mom and whispered, "Hello, Dear," every evening when he arrived home from work. Other than that, they weren't hugely affectionate in public or even in the confines of our home. Long after they passed, I learned to respect the parts of their sixty-eight-year union that were successful and beautiful. I learned to accept the parts that were not. I learned about loyalty in good times and in bad. My parents were a united front even when they weren't at their best together.

Growing up was comfortable and brilliant. There were home-cooked meals and traditional family functions. My parents threw fun parties and took Michael and me on many vacations. A schedule of some sort that made me feel loved and secure. It sure seemed impeccable.

Others peering in our bay window felt my family was clearly living the *American Dream*. In the upper-middle-class suburbs of Long Island, an affordable mortgage at thirteen plus percent for a four-bedroom colonial, pool, and Jaguar included. Life was good for the Netti family circa 1980.

We portrayed the vision of a nuclear family before social media portrayed it for us. We kept most things private rather than exposed, and we never aired the dirty laundry. Vivien just hung laundry outside in the backyard.

Most people never saw the laundry because she took those clothes in, folded them, and put them away before the company came over. Portrayals do not contain the heart. Between the excitement of new cars, vacations, and fine dining, I noticed that life is rarely as sweet as the cliché of the cherries.

Like most women who come to new mindfulness in their *forty-something* years, I watched Vivien change intensely after my grandparents died. She struggled through the grief, the ups and downs in her marriage, loss, change, and worry; showcasing feelings of regret that crept along her path while managing new emotions. I didn't process that then. I only figured that out when I turned *forty- something*.

I have thought a lot about why Vivien made her choices. I still think a lot about my chosen path and the *why* behind it. I think of all the routes we as a society decide to take, all the courses we do not take and the possible *why* that ignites these pre-set choices. I freely chose, what I was taught as a little girl to want. I thought it was my dream, and I knew it was my parent's dream for me. I managed to obtain the life I thought everybody wanted, even me.

By the time I turned *forty-something*, struggling to find true purpose had become real and arduous. I was forced to differentiate, assimilate who I had become, and hide from who I wasn't sure I was.

When I had children, I was forced to tumble back into my childhood while focusing on the future of my two miracles, Jude and Sami. Overall, Vivien enjoyed raising her two miracles, my brother and me. As we grew and needed her less, she kept busy redoing a room or adding a new deck, buying a car, and planning their next Saturday night out or a trip to Greece. Money never seemed an issue, and I felt rich enough as a kid. Through the years, Vivien made it clear to me that money wasn't everything, and Franco made it clearer that money was everything.

As a teen, I would and listen to Mom on the phone with her sister, Aunt Sophia, "Oh please, Soph I asked him ten times to fix the pool cover, and it was like waiting for paint to dry. If he's not at work, he's here sleeping with the damn loud television. It's enough to make my headache permanent." I guessed Aunt Sophia and my mother had much time to chat. I would lift the curled-up ten-foot, yellow phone wire over my head to cross to the cupboard bearing snacks.

Similar conversations would ensue between Michael's wife, Charlotte and me, decades later when we became wives and mothers. I would share some of the same feelings about Jesse. Charlotte and I chalked that up to the valid generalizations about men and women being built differently. Charlotte and I folded countless laundry baskets while on the phone for two hours or more and she would ask me, "Em, how bout I kick Mike out, and you, me, and the kids live together? I'll cook and food shop and we like the same sitcoms, right?"

The idea sounded much better than sharing my everyday life with a man I never understood.

Charlotte stuck by Mike through the hard times in their marriage, and Vivien stuck by Franco. For many years, I wondered why I couldn't stick by Jesse.

Before Vivien's fabulous five grandchildren arrived, there were many moments I knew she may have thought about leaving Franco. Still, they came from a generation that didn't entertain divorce.

I am sure the lifestyle change, after a divorce, scared Vivien and Charlotte into staying. When I was divorced, nearly as long as I was married, I began to understand why people remain for security or the children, even when they know they have fallen out of love. Vivien became a grandma in 2001 and four more times within five years. Her baby grandchildren would become the cornerstones of finally accepting her life as it was. They were the reward and the reason. When they arrived, life seemed to have a better feel all around.

Grandchildren do content the heart, and the fluff dissipates. Vivien and Franco were back to what I knew to believe in as a little girl. I saw some happiness again, and it felt good.

But the truth of my life was just starting to take form like a creeping vine twisting carefully, inflicting shallow scratches on the base of my neck. I noticed the itch some days, and I stretched and rubbed my neck slightly.

Some days, I noticed; others, I just tried not to notice.

Chapter Two

It was the beginning of summer, and life without homework had finally arrived. School had ended, and all the kids in the neighborhood were outside. There was a lot of calling for each other from mid-morning until dark. Ten of us played Ringolevio on the last day of school. There were two teams. In our version, each team had its own jail. The Maple Tree across the street and the light post in front of Dean's house. Whichever team could capture all of the other team's members, won. That night I told the others I would only play if I could be the guard. I was one of the oldest at almost fifteen, and although I enjoyed my neighborhood buddies, I was maturing and wanted to spend less time playing the same old games with the younger kids. That night, my job was to ensure a jailed player was not tagged free. Often the game would go on so long that we would call a time-out and run back to our houses in search of flashlights. We rarely called it because of darkness, but that night, when it was time to break for a flashlight, I told my friends I was tired and went to my room to be alone. There, I listed my favorite songs that would become my next custom-mixed cassette, a process that allowed me to express my evolving feelings.
After a lazy next morning of sleeping in, I was ready for my first summer day. I found my favorite matching red short-top ensemble, a quick hair shake, and my NY Yankee baseball cap, worn backward almost always. Not a stitch of makeup, even though all my peers at fourteen and fifteen wore makeup religiously. A thirty-second, teeth brush burden and cold water slapped my face to freshen up. My blue Puma kicks, last on the list, to aid me out the front door. Each step, a testament to my independence, my choice to wear what I liked, not what was expected. A small act that made me feel empowered and ready to face

the day.

I rarely had a plan other than bike riding around the block to the strip stores. I never looked at a clock. Those were endless, carefree days. Yet the warm summer evenings never lasted long enough. I had to be back before dark. That meant by eight-thirty, I would anxiously ride back from a friend's house or the strip stores as fast as I could before Vivien would get irate and come looking for me by car in her pajamas. It was usual for me to be around the hood or by the strip until the street lamps began to dim. That day was new, and I wasn't thinking of curfew. The sun shone, and high pressure was in control resulting in a flawless, clear blue sky above. I had my Sony Walkman in the handlebar basket of my ten-speed Schwinn. "Em, please don't use headphones while you're riding your bike! You won't be able to hear if a car is coming up behind you," Vivien talked to the back of my head, and my reply trailed off further as I slid out the storm door, "I only wear it in one ear, and I hear the cars with the other ear. K bye Viv's." Ah, I was finally free. My customary trek to the card store to buy gum, perhaps a magazine, especially if it had a fold-out poster of Blackie. He was gorgeous, and Matt Dillon was a close second. They were the two favorites in all the girls' school lockers. I definitely liked the way they looked.

I ran into Scotty and Dean three doors down from the Luncheonette at Mack's card store. The boys from the neighborhood were big into trading baseball cards, so they were always there. Max owned the place and set up a card table in the corner of his store to buy, sell, and trade cards. Max would sit with the boys and talk baseball for as long as the boys would listen. He was a baseball guru and he knew the answer to any question, past or present, about America's Favorite Pastime.

I sat with them, from time to time, and listened to stories

about how great George Brett was hitting, and other facts I have long since forgotten.

I spent most of my time before that summer of 1984 with my bestie Mara and Scotty, Dean, Lucy, Howie, and Davie from the neighboring area. I played Barbies with the girls, and we all played kickball and roller hockey on the street. Whiffle ball was on my front lawn or the park a few houses away with a real field. Ringolevio or a night swim at either Dean's pool or mine. Cozmo would come by with his blue and white truck at nearly 7:30 every evening, and we would sit on the curb, with our wet suits and towels draped on our shoulders. We all enjoyed an ice cream or rainbow snow cones as the sun still showed herself.

Scotty left Dean at Mack's with a new set of Topps Cards. Baseball talk was boring me to tears, so I walked out with Scotty and rode my bike slowly next to him while he headed home on foot. His house was directly across the street from mine, so we were constant companions.

"Can we all go to Brian's for lunch when you get back? I asked. "Ugh, after swim lessons maybe, but I think I have to go to my cousins," he replied. Scotty hated his weekly afternoon swimming lesson because the public pool was freezing. Michael taught me how to swim long before I was thirteen. I was four or five, and I was a quick learn. I was happy that Vivien never made me take lessons. I would have hated classes in the ice-cold, public pool.

Scotty and I briefly discussed how Mara and Howie had cheated during Ringolevio the night before. Scotty mentioned that Mara never really tagged Howie free from jail. I defended Mara, even though what Scotty said was true. It felt like a boys versus girls mentality, and above all, she was my best friend. I waved goodbye to Scotty just before he reached our block and then headed back toward the strip. I saw Lucy through the window of the Laundromat with her friend Diana from school but I

decided to pass by, hoping unnoticed, seven stores down
to the Luncheonette.

Usually, there would have been a bunch of us, but I was
alone that day. I walked in and set my headphones and
Walkman on the tabletop of my usual booth. Brian was on
the phone, and I could always tell when it was a big
catering order because he would write furiously on a big
white pad with yellow carbon. His usual staff was hard at
work coming in and out of the room behind the counter
with sandwiches to stay and other orders to go. A new girl
was at the register, and I wondered if Brian had hired a
cashier. I was mad he may have hired some stranger before
asking me if I perhaps wanted the job. I would have loved a
summer job, especially at the Luncheonette. I walked up to
the counter to place my order, and the new girl barely
looked up when asked, "What'll you have?" I stared at the
top of her head and said, "I'll take roast beef on toasted rye
with some mayo and a small lemonade with ice, please."
She scribbled my order on a small pad. She looked up,
smiled and handed me a number. I was rolling my eyes on
the way back to the booth. She treated me like an ordinary
customer. Louie would never give me a number. He would
call my name, and I would swipe my order off the counter.
She obviously didn't know that her boss, Brian and my
family had been friends for decades before she showed up.
Brian didn't notice me and disappeared with a sheet of
yellow carbon back to his office to make sense of his
scribble. The Luncheonette was busier than ever.

I sat in the booth alone, eating my sandwich and watching
the new girl take the money and write orders. I crumbled up
my sandwich wrapper, placed it in the trash, grabbed my
headphones and lemonade and decided to return home.

Mom was outside weeding as I fluttered into the backyard,
"Mom, Brian hired some girl, and I'm so mad. I want that

job," I whined and continued, "…all she does is take the money and write down orders. Oh my God, Mom, I'm so mad! Can you or Dad talk to Brian for me?
I don't want to play whiffle ball anymore, and I wish I worked at Brian's." Mom defended Brian and declared, "Brian cannot legally hire you until you are sixteen, Emmy.
Enjoy freeloading for one more year. You will have the rest of your life to work!" She pushed herself up and pulled off her gardening gloves, "I'm just about done. I'm going to take a dip; want to join me?" We both suited up and met poolside a few minutes later.

As applied to the average fourteen-year-old, I knew I was generally attractive. The mirror was mostly pleasing at that time when most of my friends were dealing with acne and awkward noses that seemed to grow as fast as their shoe size. I had a slim, athletic figure with just enough bosom to fill a 32B. I was a brunette with curls that hung just beneath my shoulders. By summer's end, natural blond highlights peaked out of my kinks, seared by the summer sun. My hair required such little preparatory measure. I never spent much time primping.
I was soulful, and my imagination was ever-present, even almost two years after turning an official teen. If I didn't prefer to be alone with music or books, I was that girl who enjoyed sports and other high-spirited activities traditionally associated with a boy. However, a girly tomboy who liked dresses but was also inherently competent with tools. I was especially good at Lacrosse, watching Michael play from boyhood. Although I never played in an official league, Michael and I were having catches and running drills in our yard by the time I was ten. Mike was a huge part of helping me develop coordination and cognitive skills I may have never acquired if I had not grown up with an older brother.

That summer, Michael spent most weekends at Audrey's house. Her Mom was divorced and loved having Michael around. He would often fix things around their house, and I guessed Audrey's Mom liked having a man around for that. Despite hearing Vivien tell Franco, she thought Audrey was too needy. They both liked Audrey enough. They did not want Michael sleeping over with his girlfriend on weekends and sharing a room. However, that topic was not discussed much in front of me.

One night Mom told Dad, "Hon, I feel like we're losing him to this girl. He's been there for the past four nights." It took Franco a few minutes to reply, and Mom just stared and rolled her eyes, waiting for his answer. When he finally answered, even I wished he could have said something to make Mom feel better. He said, "Guess we're supposed to lose him to a wife."

I put in my two cents, with hopes it would prevent Vivien from snapping at him, "Well, yes, Dad eventually marriage, but Audrey is like Mike's first real girlfriend, and it's like they're practically living together already." Dad said, "Maybe his first one is the right one. It could be worse; Audrey could be a drag queen." He chuckled and got up from the table. I stared into the distance, unsure what that meant, but I noticed my mother shaking her head in discontent.

Michael was almost nineteen and he did what he wanted. I liked waking up without Michael around sometimes. Having my parents to myself and making pancakes with Dad on Saturday morning was delightful. Vivien would laugh at the amount of powdered sugar all over the kitchen. I equally enjoyed it when Michael came home too. He wasn't always a jerk.

Franco woke me from a sound sleep at six-thirty the following day with a gentle knock. I saw him on the threshold of my bedroom doorway, and with blurry vision, I stared at him for a moment before saying with annoyance, "Um, Dad, it's Saturday; why are you waking me up?" He whispered, "Thought maybe you'd be up for nine? Let's go play in the grass, shall we?" While rubbing my eyes, I asked, "Can I drive the cart?" He chuckled, "Yes, you can chauffeur me, and it's your lucky day! No, Mike; he's still at Audrey's. I'll meet you downstairs in ten, caddy." He gave me a thumbs-up and pulled my door closed."

He grabbed a plain black coffee and a hot chocolate at Dunkin Donuts, and then we hit the road. We had a few hours together and memories that have lasted my entire life. Franco shot four under par, and I shot one over at our favorite nine-hole course. That day, my drives were impressive. The foursome playing behind us watched as I used my seven-iron to procure the perfect position to birdie the fourth. I did it with a chip in from the outskirts of the putting green. I felt like a world-class athlete, and the ones who witnessed it never knew my game wasn't always so memorizing and hardly consistent. My dads' high fives smacked the palm of my hand like an unyielding reinforcement of my abilities and as my father enjoyed the compliments from the group, I gazed at the scenic greenery. The morning sun warmed the dew and glistened in the distance of the fine-cut fairways. Taking a breath, I took a moment to reflect on our life. My parents' bank account was not the pinnacle of wealth, but they had the means to support and navigate us to any road we wanted to explore. I never doubted Michael or I would succeed in the years to come. Vivien and Franco would be essential in those results; how could we not?

I was bummed we played Skydrive nine instead of our usual Lightening Point eighteen, because Franco and Vivien had things to do later that day and their typical Saturday night dinner plans were also arranged. Franco and I arrived home a little before eleven in the morning. The house was quiet since Vivien and Aunt Sophia went shopping at the outlets, and Michael was still at Audrey's. My father settled in with a cigar and the newspaper on the shady part of the deck. I opened the slider, "Dad, I'm going to Mara's and probably end up at the Luncheonette." He looked from behind the newspaper, hiding his face, "What else is new? Have fun." *What else is new…* was just one of Franco's many over-used one-liners. It was not a question, and he had never expected to receive an answer. I gave him the peace sign from the edge of the door, "Good game, Dad! You still got it!" I closed the screen slider and headed out of the garage.

I called for Mara, who lived in the court just around the corner. Her Mom died six years before on a cold September day. Mara was only nine years old, and so was I. Her Mom had cancer for almost a year and was 46 years old. Her Mom worked as a nurse from three in the afternoon till three in the morning at least four nights a week. I didn't know her Mom, as well as I knew Mara's father. Once she became sick, I wasn't allowed in Mara's house. I wasn't a big part of the sadness that followed as the sorrowful news launched around the six-block radius of our suburb. Vivien heard the awful news and carefully told me after school in our kitchen. I was sad for Mara and cried before falling asleep that night. I faintly remember the details of the wake. We stayed downstairs in the funeral home while the parents sat upstairs with Mrs. Conti in a coffin. It wasn't my first wake, but I remember how creepy I thought it was. Everyone would whisper into each other's ear about how good Betty looked. I thought, she didn't look like Mrs. C, and the makeup was overdone. She was dead, and she was my best friend's mom. I couldn't imagine how Mara felt that day, so I ignored the awful feeling and played cards with her for two days straight in the smelly basement where everyone came crying to say goodbye and hug Mr. Conti.

Mara came over two days after her mom's funeral and stood at my screen door with the saddest face I had ever seen. Vivien waved her into our marble foyer and hurried to greet her at the doorsill. I just plopped down on the ninth step of the thirteen on my way downstairs when I heard the doorbell ring. Vivien got there first and opened the door wide.
"Oh, my Mara! I have no words to say, but I have arms to hold you, my sweet child. I am so sorry. You will be okay, and we are here for you." Vivien took Mara into her arms, and I watched as if it were myself in Vivien's arms on days when only my mom could solve all my problems. I wasn't sure how to navigate my fear of how Mara would push through such a tremendous loss. From that day on, death terrified me and I tried not to think of ever losing Vivien.

After Mara's mom died, I often found Mara at home folding her father's laundry rather than playing kickball with the other kids outside on the court. Mara effortlessly slid into her new role as keeper of the house and home. She didn't talk much about her mom, so it was easy for me not to either. Mara never complained about all the tasks, us other kids had our moms to do for us. I kept her company as she tackled her list of chores before her dad returned home from work. Sometimes, I would help her, but rarely because I was not fond of chores and didn't understand them. Mr. Conti owned a Wonder Bread Route and was one of the few distributors who owned the route and truck. He left obscenely early in the morning and was usually home at about three o'clock.

I met Mara only two years before her mom died. We were both seven. We discovered our bicycles had the same 1976 Bicentennial banana seat. We met in the cul-de-sac in front of her house. She wore purple-framed eyeglasses, a one-piece, red speedo bathing suit, and white tube socks with two red rings pulled all the way up to her knees. I wore an outfit far less becoming and I loved that neither of us cared. We became best friends instantly.
Over the next few years, we played with Barbie dolls in my pool or imaginary friend games in the branches of trees, called ourselves the Southern Sisters while trying to speak in our best down south accents.

Mara was part of my every day, and by almost fifteen, we knew quite a bit about each other. As little kids, we survived arguments over kickball and sharing our stuff. As adolescents, we overcame jealousies over clothes and boys. We were the kind of friends who figured out how tampons worked before we needed them. I stood outside the bathroom door for her play-by-play description of her first attempt to use one. Mara got her period five months before I did. She explained what it would be like, and I understood what she had told me after I got it. I wondered when mine would come; when it did, I wished it hadn't. We eventually figured out tampons and high-fived; We were happy we could go swimming when we had it.

I snuck around the side of her house up the redwood stairs leading to Mara's kitchen. She was standing over the sink, washing dishes. "Hey, wanna go up to the strip or park?" Mara looked up and, with her pointer finger, pushed her glasses up her nose. She lifted the bottle of Windex and sprayed the counter. She wiped it down with one piece of paper towel, and grinned, "Oh yeah! I'm done! Let's get outta here." She opened the cabinet above the sink and grabbed two of her Dad's Winston cigarettes from the soft pack and a white Bic lighter.

She dropped them into the front shirt pocket of her brother's flannel she was wearing, and I followed her down the stairs of her split ranch out to the garage.

We stopped at the Laundromat on our ten-speeds and popped a few quarters into one of the classic stand-up LED arcade games. Mara pressed the two-player button.

We played Jungle King while Dean and Davie played Asteroids to our left. The neighborhood kids were skilled at both games, but Dean was the best. He played Asteroids for up to four plus hours with one quarter. He monopolized the game, and the rest of us were sometimes annoyed. Mara and I usually made it to the third level of Jungle King. The second level was the most fun for me. On the second level, I used the joystick to move Tarzan around the screen to avoid the hungry crocodiles. I pressed the fire button to stab the enemies with the knife, but only when their mouths were partly or wholly closed. I had to avoid the ascending air bubbles and return to the surface periodically so Tarzan could catch a quick breath; otherwise, drown and game over. Mara's character got killed on the third level. She was bummed yet patiently waited for my last turn to end. I got past the fourth level and was psyched. My Tarzan jumped while spears were everywhere, ascending toward the woman when she was low enough for him to grab her. Mara was standing close by. I could smell the grape flavor of Bazooka bubble gum and hear her chewing in my ear. I didn't mind the smell of the gum; she was only standing so close to root me on.

I finally conquered the level, and the woman had been rescued. The screen read, "Congratulations!" Then a cute intermission played featuring Tarzan and the woman together along with a message saying, "I Love You!" Mara

and I stayed till the end after the woman kissed Tarzan. My
Tarzan guy died shortly into the next level, and we left. I
had my best score ever. What a perfect start to summer.
After Jungle King, we rode a mile up a winding hill on the
paved road to Lanes, the local bowling alley. It was about a
mile and a half away. We often found some of our school
friends there, usually not bowling but likely to be at the row
of arcade games in a small room to the left upon entering.
Lanes had a far more extensive game room than the two at
the Laundromat. Mara and I played a game each of
Centipede, Donkey Kong, and Ms. Pacman before we
headed downhill, riding with no hands back home. I never
forgot that day. Years later I found out Mara hadn't either.
Soon after, we headed towards the park and sat on our
favorite tree stump at the foot of the woods just behind the
handball courts. Mara grabbed the two cigarettes from her
shirt pocket. I said, "When are you quitting that filthy
habit?" She replied rather quickly, "When you do!" We
both laughed. She inhaled as she brought the flame to the
tip of her smoke. She handed the lit one to me and
immediately lit another for herself. She sat with knees up,
legs crossed over one another, and nestled her back against
a tree. I sat an arm's length away on the stump, leaning
forward with my elbows propped on my knees.
"Does your father ever notice some of his cigarettes
missing from his pack?" I asked Mara as I took a drag. "I
hope not; he'd kill me. I only take like one every week so it
doesn't look so obvious, and I always swoosh them around,
that way it looks like there is more in the pack."
She seemed to have it under control, and neither of us
smoked regularly. We felt cool while we sat in the woods
and caught up on the latest school or neighborhood gossip.
Mara blurted out, "I like Adam Bryon and Lucy's mom,
and Adam's mom are best friends, so do you think I should
tell Lucy?" I pondered momentarily, "If you want it to get

back to Adam, then *yeah*. But maybe you should see if you guys are in the same homeroom this September and try to become his friend, and then he will probably ask you out on his own." A couple of older kids arrived at the handball courts. We knew Matt, an older brother of one of the girls in our grade. He pretended he didn't know us. We sat and watched them play for a little while. The basketball court had a game going on too. Guys, our dads' ages had a regular afternoon five-on-five, and they were serious about winning. They always had a small boom box with cassettes of Kiss, Van Halen, or Aerosmith playing courtside. After we smoked and hardly inhaled Mara and I walked our bikes on the wide blacktop path leading to the park's back entrance/exit. She wanted to stop at home to pee, and I wanted to leave because I was getting hungry.

That was our last puff of Mr. C's stolen Winston in the park. Mara quit our occasional practice soon after; afraid Adam Byron wouldn't want to kiss her if he tasted smoke. As we turned our bikes into the court, her dad was hosing off his truck in the driveway. "Hey, Mr. C!" I declared. I hopped off my bike, setting its kickstand down. Mara ran inside the garage, holding her stomach and bellowing, "Be right back." Her Dad looked up, shaking his head. He knew she was in dire need of the facilities. I hugged Mr. C, and he placed his massive hand on the top of my head and tilted it up, "How's your summer going kiddo?" Mr. Conti was so tall. A gentle giant; my second Dad. He always appreciated my folks taking Mara on as their third child, and she often came with my family on vacations and many sleepovers at my house. I answered, "It beats homework, but I don't know what to do without Mara for the next few weeks. I'm gonna be bored. Please don't take her to Millie's this year." He started wrapping the hose in extended circles over his shoulder, "Sorry, Em," he sympathized, "We'll be back before you know it, and you can call Mara every day if you'd like." "Yeah, Mr. C? Franco is gonna hate my phone bill next month." He chuckled, "Better him than me... tell him I said that. Stay out of trouble; see you soon." He patted my shoulder and headed inside.

Mara was set to leave early the next morning for Maine, where her father's sister lived and a few cousins whom Mara loved spending time. I met them all when I joined them in Maine for a week, two years prior. It was a little, blue house on a dirt-dusted road. The home had few modern conveniences, but a vast, serene lake was out the side door. It reminded me of the movie On Golden Pond. We went canoeing and swam off their dock, and it was fun. I sometimes remembered being a little homesick and bored of board games by week's end. I declined the invite when Mara asked me to return to what I named *Little Blue House* the following year. I told Mara I was enrolled in a video class when she'd be gone, which wasn't true because the course was canceled by then. Either way, it was too long without television and too much togetherness in LBH, even with your best friend.

I waited a few minutes outside her stoop before Mara finally stepped outside. "My dad said I must go in now, pack and get the car loaded." I rose to my feet, "K, guess I'll head home for some eats. Have a great time at LBH. It won't be the same without you, Mars. Take care of you!" We hugged, and I waved to her on her driveway as I took a right out of the court and headed home.

Little did I realize, after that summer, the most valid friendship I had ever known would begin to shift. We would soon make more room for connections outside our neighborhood and our evolving selves, a change that was both exciting and bittersweet.

Vivien and Franco finally left at about six for seven o'clock dinner reservations. I left Michael and Audrey to themselves in the den and sat in the kitchen. I ate five of Viv's delicious chicken cutlets and left the corn and spinach untouched. I called Mara from the kitchen phone. "Hey, Mars, all packed?" Mara couldn't talk for long. "Yeah, we are all ready and my dad says we're leaving so early; at like three in the morning." She needed to sleep, so I told her I'd miss her, and we hung up the phone. Although I stood and stared out my front door for countless hours, I had never studied the Maple tree across the street in such depth before that moment. I noticed one of the limbs was bending slightly, making the familiar pavement we all skated on, or the jail we would protect playing Ringalevio look so different. It was a new perspective, and somewhere between my young conscience and more mature subconscious self, I noticed I liked the shift. I stayed in my room that evening to create a mixed cassette. I found the list I had written under some magazines scattered on my desk. I fit eight songs on one side of a 90-minute audiocassette. As I was dozing off to When Doves Cry by Prince, the Maple tree swayed outside, shifting and possibly making room for new buds with a reckless scent.

Chapter Three

I woke up and stared at the ceiling for a while. I was thinking about how Mara might have arrived at her Aunt Millie's, but I was barely awake. I sprang out of bed and hit rewind on the cassette player. The wheels turned fast, and I heard it stop. I pressed play, dialed up the volume and got myself dressed and ready for my Sunday.

It was around 11:30 when I ventured downstairs, making sure to avoid the open den pocket door. "Good afternoon," my dad's authoritative voice echoed, from his spot on the gray leather recliner. I peeked in, "It's still morning, Dad. And I'm not sure if you got the memo, but it is, in fact, summer." He pointed to the cable box, "I am aware it is summer, and I am aware it is lunchtime. See if golf is on channel seven, will you please?" I pressed the tan button with the number seven, and a Palmolive commercial was on. "No golf, just commercials all day." I said sarcastically, "Can I go now?" Franco waved his hand in the air, "Does your mother know where you are off to?" I replied, "Yup, going to tell her now. Bye, Dad."

Mom was out skimming the pool and had a big pot of gravy on the stove. Sunday dinners commenced at two-thirty in the afternoon, and it was expected that the four of us show up on time. The past few Sundays, Audrey joined us, and before the drive became a nuisance for them, Nanna and Pop came too.

I stood on the second stair of three, exiting our back door. Our backyard was pristine. It was the most oversized backyard on the street because our house was set back on a curve. The yard was private, with tall greenery on our neighbor's side of our fence.

Our L-shaped pool was heated by solar panels on our roof. The solar option wasn't standard in 1984, but Franco met a contractor who manufactured and installed solar panels on a job site. Franco bartered out the boards to help heat the pool water without using electricity, and he and Michael installed them on our roof.

I snuck up behind her, "Good morning, Viv." She replied, "Good afternoon, you mean?" I rolled my eyes as I approached the pool's edge, "Oh my God, Mom. Dad just said the same thing to me. Did you guys learn that in Parenting 101 on the same day?" My Mom smiled at my amusing sarcasm. After all, I learned it from her. She shook all the bugs off the skimmer into the nearby grass. "Okay, smart ass. Where are you off to now?" She posed. I didn't know who I wanted to call for, "Hmmm, I don't know, prob hit the strip, play Jungle King or whatever, and see who is around. Mara is probably in Maine by now." She hung the skimmer in the brackets Franco securely fastened to the fence years earlier. "Mara will be back before you know it," she answered. I started back in the house when she said, "Em, dinner won't be till 6ish. John and Sylvia are coming over around five to have dinner and discuss our insurance."

Even though I enjoyed our Italian dinner tradition on Sundays, I was happy to take a pass and not be obligated to come home so early. "Oh good, then maybe I'll end up at Lucy's and eat there." Vivien thought about it, "Well, let me know where you wind up and if you want to eat here later, maybe you can eat on the snack table in the den while we discuss our affairs with them." I nodded, "K, Mom later."

I took off on my red Schwinn into the hood. Free again! I coasted, standing on the wide left turn past Mara's house. She wasn't even gone for a day, and I was already beginning to feel like it was going to be lonely without her. I wondered why Mr. C left the outside yellow light on twenty- four hours a day when they left the house for vacation.

When they were home, that same light was never on.
It was like shouting to burglars, "Hey, if the side light is on,
we're in Maine for a few weeks, so come rob our house."
I smirked and thought upon their return, I would tell Mr. C
my thoughts about getting that light on a timer or
something. I pedaled a little faster making a left down
Corncrib Lane and off to my home away from home, the
Strip.
The new girl hadn't been at Brian's since I first saw her. I
was still disturbed by how she hardly looked up while
taking my roast beef order. I was still mad that Brian hired
her and not me. I hoped she'd quit and Brian would ask me
to replace her. However, as I walked further into
the Luncheonette, there she was propped up on her elbows,
sitting with one leg under her thigh and in *my* booth. She
was chatting it up with salty-haired Max from next
door. *Just great*, I thought. The Luncheonette was slowing
down after its usual early morning rush. On Sundays,
the Luncheonette smelled especially pleasing. It was a
wonderful aroma of fresh bread rising in hot ovens. "Smells
like heaven," Franco would say. "Give me a hunk of that
bread and my wife's pot of Sunday gravy, and I'm a happy
man," Franco told me it smelled like Arthur Avenue, and
he liked the familiarity. It reminded him of his childhood,
and years later, that same smell reminded me of mine.
Customers enjoyed the tasty cuisine and felt welcomed by
the whole vibe of the place. The deep blue colors on the
walls were cozy and inviting. Every booth had shiny,
colorful tabletops with twirled shades of blues and yellows.
Brian had an artist design the place, and she hand-painted
each tabletop. There was incredible artwork in frames, and
my favorite, was an Andy Warhol print of Marilyn Monroe.
Brian would always say it was the original. We all knew he
was fibbing about that. Marilyn was an original, but that
print on his wall was not. Still, the place was chic and way

ahead of its time.

Brian's long-time employee Louie placed a lemonade on the glass countertop for me, "Hey Emmy, I saved you a Subrosa. Got it in the back, in the safe, in the wall."

My eyes widened and a big smile swept my face, "No way, Louie, you're the best-est. Mm yes, that sounds perfect. Hope the Secret Service is surrounding the safe?"

Louie laughed heartily, gave me a wink and strolled toward the kitchen. Brian's Mom made Subrosas, only on Sundays. It was a freshly baked pocket of her homemade dough, filled with mouth-watering secret ingredients, and all the regulars knew they were sure to sell out well before noon. When they ran out; that was it. Customers formed a line, sometimes as early as six in the morning outside the door to get them.

As I passed the booth I would usually sit in, the new girl was conversing with Max. I surveyed the tables and slowly made my way to find a seat. The new girl's eyes met mine dead on, "Hey, kid, isn't this your booth?" I looked over my shoulder to ensure the question was directed to me, "Before you started to take my roast beef order, yep, that was my booth. Right, Max?" She smiled. Her smile made me smile. Max stood up, "You can have it, Emily. I'm returning to see if Mrs. Mack ate all the chocolate bars while watching the Yankee game. Have a good day, girls."

The new girl signaled with her hand to sit across from her, "What's your name, kid?" she asked. "Emily and... you must be the girl who stole my summer job?" She smiled again, "Ah, yes I heard there were thousands of applicants but didn't know you were one of them." I laughed. She stretched out her right hand. "I'm Alessandra, the girl Brian begged to help him with catering this summer."

Brian approached the table, "Alex, I got mounds of paperwork I must tackle. Can you hold down the fort?"

Alex looked up at him with a dumbstruck expression.

"Hmm, let me see?" She replied with a mocking tone. "Brian, there's not one customer in the joint," she said. Brian surveyed the eatery. "Well, here's one," and his hand presented me. Alex with quick wit replied, "She's not a customer; she's a groupie!" Brian winked at me, "My favorite Luncheonette groupie of all." He squeezed my cheek before walking through the kitchen towards his office. Alex sat back down.

"Okay, so tell me why you're rushing to get a job. I wish I could have said no when Brian asked, and been at the beach all summer." She paid close attention to my reply. "I'm just jealous and wish he had begged me. I'm tired and done with riding bikes and the same ole neighborhood crew. It would have been nice to make some money this summer, at least part-time. I'll need a car soon." I didn't want to sound whiny, so I took a breath and asked, "So, how old are you, and are you working here full-time?"

By now, she was more settled sitting with her back up against the wall in the corner of the seat and no longer hovering like she was when she was speaking with Max. She sat with one knee up, "I'm eighteen for two months. My birthday is coming up in September." I immediately wanted to be older.

I looked around the place and remained silent for a minute. Nick, another counter employee was playing solitaire with an old deck of cards, in the booth adjacent to Louie. Louie was reading the newspaper in the back booth, and the radio was playing a new Rod Stewart song I hadn't heard before called "Trouble." Alex answered my questions and asked me many more, in between popping up to take a phone call or help a customer that straggled in.

I left once for five minutes to get some Bazooka Bubble Gum at Mack's and ran into Lucy, who was thankfully going to her aunt's house for dinner. I was thrilled because if she wasn't, she would have expected me to go back to our block or worse she might have wanted to hang out in the Luncheonette with me. The minutes turned into hours, and I realized the Luncheonette was soon to close early on Sundays at six in the evening. Alex and I had been sharing bits and pieces of our lives for nearly six hours.

I watched Louie finish mopping the floor. When he was done, he threw on a light sweater and tipped his hat to us, "See you tomorrow, Alessandra and I guess I'll see you too, Emily." I chuckled, "Probs Lou, where else do I have to go? Hey thanks for saving me the last Subrosa!" He left, and Alex said, "They are good, those Subrosas!" And I interrupted. "They are phenomenal, and now that I have a friend on the inside, you can find out the secret ingredients Brian's mom puts in them?" She said, "Well, I will try to find out... now that I am your friend on the inside."

One by one, the staff punched out. The employees parked in the back, so the customers had convenient parking spaces in front. Brian had an army green duffle bag over his shoulder and a clipboard in hand with yellow scribbled carbon pages as he walked toward the light switch. "Hate to break up your coffee clutch, but it's quittin' time, ladies." I slid out of the booth's corner and rose.

"The front door is locked so come out the back with us, Emily and I'll drive you around to get your bike." Alex cordially insisted, "I'll drive her around Brian, get home and get some rest."

It was a cool summer evening, almost a crisp feel of fall in the air. The three of us walked out the back door together. Brian flipped the switch, pulled the door closed and locked it with the key as he juggled his bag falling off his shoulder and some paperwork in his teeth. He mumbled, "See you tomorrow girls."

Alex set down her Fendi bag on the hood of her car and pushed herself up to sit beside it with her two hands behind her. "Do you always sit on your car?" I asked. She smirked,

"You're a punk, huh? Actually, sometimes I sit up there," and she pointed to the roof of the Luncheonette. "Really?" I asked, "How do you get up there?" She leaped off the car, opened the door and threw her bag on the front seat then closed the door and started walking. "C'mon, I'll show you." I followed her to a small alley by the back of the Luncheonette door.

A big wooden breadbox with a padlock was positioned against the red brick building. Alex jumped on and reached her left hand down to pull me up onto it. The roof's edge was just about at my rib cage. I placed my hands on the rooftop ledge and skyrocketed up. Alex was right behind me. "Wow, love it up here!" I exclaimed. "Isn't it great?" She echoed. "I saw the sunset from right over here last week," she plunked down, "it was just so breathtaking." I sat next to Alex and picked at the weathered cracks on the rubber-like rooftop. I felt the black gravel sift through my fingers and fall on my thigh. I was chilly and wished I had a sweatshirt.

We sat there and talked about music and our families, laughing when telling each other our most embarrassing moments. I had learned that Alex's cousin and Brian, were best friends. She had known Brian since birth and they kind of behaved like siblings. Brian really needed help with the catering department and the mess of paperwork piled up on his desk. Alex had just finished her freshman year of college, majoring in Hotel and Restaurant Management. That sounded like a fancy major to me. She told me one day she wanted to own a restaurant that she imagined could be more high-end than Brian's.

She thought working for Brian would give her some experience and besides he practically begged Alex to spend the summer helping to organize and to take care of customers who were planning off premise parties. She worked hard and was a huge asset to Brian.

The sun was soon to set, and the sky was a majestic pink and orange. It suddenly dawned on me that Vivien would be driving around looking for me when it got dark, especially that I

hadn't popped in at home to let her know my whereabouts. I hoped that she and Dad's company distracted her from looking up at the clock. I even calmed down thinking she might I had figured I ended up at Lucy's and had forgotten to call her. I didn't want to tell Alex I had a curfew. She was eighteen and didn't seem to have to tell a soul where she was. After a few minutes of internal panic, I blurted out my thoughts. "Oh my God, Alex! My mom is definitely wondering where I am and if she comes up here and sees my bike in front of the now, closed Luncheonette, she's will freak out. And if she knows I was on this roof, she's going to freak out even more." Alex jumped up, "You should have called her before we locked up. Okay let's get down. I'll drive you around to get your bike and I will follow you home Em." As we made our way to the roof's edge looking down to the wooden breadbox, Alex tapped my shoulder. "Wait Em, look… this is the best part." I looked up and saw the sun's shimmering light fade into a mystic tint of pink and orange, like fire. I glanced at my Casio. It was precisely 8:13pm. The light dimmed and dusk was gone. It was not the first sunset I had ever seen, but it was the most beautiful I had ever seen. It was the first sunset I saw from the Luncheonette roof. It was spectacular. "Wow," I said to her, "It's surreal." I looked at Alex still gazing at the sky, "Hey, I gotta go!"
Alex and I jumped down to the breadbox and hurried to her car. She leaned over and popped the lock. The car was old and had a heavy door that made a loud screeching sound when I closed it. I looked at Alex mimicking the struggle to slam the door. "It's my brother's car, so he needed mine to impress a date; Whatever!" I laughed, "Sure, and you drive a Mercedes." She shook her head and said, "Not quite."

She pulled around the front and parked parallel to the curb. My bike was leaning against the front of the Luncheonette window, exactly where it had been since noon. Everything was closed on the strip, except the Laundromat, open from six in the morning until midnight, seven days a week.
Alex opened her window as I mounted my bike seat. She called out, "You live close, I presume?" I nodded yes, "Around the block and you don't have to follow me." I waved and took off. Alex yelled out the window, "I am following you. It's dark now!" I crossed the street out of the parking lot and was on Corncrib Lane, one block away from turning onto my street. Alex was slowly driving behind me, and I talked to her through her window. "Next right is my block."
As soon as I turned, Vivien's headlights shined into my eyes, and I felt like a fugitive that had just been captured after a prison break. I stopped my bike and put my feet down on the street. Alex stopped a few feet behind me. Vivien rolled down her window. Thankfully she wasn't in her pajamas, but she wasn't happy. "Emily Gerise, where in God's name have you been? I called Lucy, and nobody answered, and it's dark out and I still have company over." I interrupted her, "Lucy went to her aunt's for dinner, and I wound up eating at the Luncheonette and hanging with Brian and the new girl, Alex, who is in the white car behind me... Mom! She is following me home because I knew it got dark." I looked back at Alex in her car. Alex waved to both me and Mom. My Mom didn't wave back. "I'm sorry Mom, I lost track of time." Vivien was mad, "Get home, Em, you worried us." She turned into Mrs. Keller's driveway and backed out to turn around. She sped off back to our house. I was appalled that Alex had just witnessed me getting in trouble for missing a toddler's curfew.
I walked my bike to the driver's side window of her car. "Sorry she didn't wave. She's kinda pissed at me. This is

really awkward."

Alex spurted out a laugh, "Well, yep, she seemed pissed but really why didn't you think to call her from the Luncheonette before we closed. Probably would have been a good idea." I jumped on my bike seat, "Yeah, I guess. I gotta go. See ya around." Alex watched me hang a right into my driveway. She waved. I waved and I watched her drive away.

My parents still had company when I entered the dwelling, so I just said, "Goodnight all and headed upstairs." Vivien didn't ask me if I ate dinner and that's when I knew she was really pissed. My mom came up at eleven-thirty and slightly opened my door. I pretended to be asleep because I didn't want to hear *the not checking in all day was unacceptable* speech. I fell asleep shortly after she left my room. I knew I still had to deal with Vivien when I woke up. I knew since Michael and Dad were working, I would have to face her alone and eventually head downstairs. I was mad too and completely embarrassed. Vivien was folding laundry at the kitchen table.

"Good morning, Em." I dragged myself to the fridge and opened both doors, "Hi Mom." I grabbed the milk and placed it on the table. "Emily, I'm still very upset with your total lack of responsibility last night." I was standing by the cupboard looking for the Rice Krispies. "Okay Mom, I said I was sorry. I lost track of time." She turned to face me, my brother's white Hanes t-shirt in hand, "Emily, Brian closes at six and you lost track of time till after eight? What were you doing for two hours and with whom? And you didn't think to call me? You know I was hosting business associates so it was quite rude that I had to leave and come looking for you." My head was still buried in the cupboard pretending I hadn't spotted the Rice Krispies yet. "Mom! You act like I robbed someone's house or I stayed out past midnight. Lighten up." Vivien did not fancy my reply and sternly repeated her original question, and added another. "I asked you, where you were for two hours and why didn't you go to Lucy's for dinner like originally planned?" I set the cereal box on the table, "Mom, I ran into Lucy at Mack's, and she said she was going to her aunt's house for dinner, "Call Lucy's Mom and ask her! Then I played some video games and talked to Joe Luden. Remember him? He was Mike's eighth-grade lacrosse coach. Then, I ran into Mr. Keller. Then Louie saved me a Subrosa, and I wound up talking to the new girl, Alex, Brian's cousin, or whatever they are. They're not really cousins. Anyway, Alex and Louie, and Nick and all of them were just hanging out because the Luncheonette was so slow. I was there practically all day. I closed with Brian; you can ask him yourself." She took a deep breath and let it out. She whispered calmly, "Ok, Em, I'm not accusing of you of wrongdoing. I was worried and I'm still wondering what you did from after closing until almost nine o'clock?"

By now, I had a spoonful of cereal in my mouth, yet still managed to explain, "I was talking to Alex… the new girl who I wanted to hate for stealing my gig but now I think, is like my friend. She's really nice and is not Brian's cousin, but her cousin and Brian are best friends and they are so close that he calls her his cousin. They act more like Michael and me, and it's funny." Vivien was calmer now, "If you had called, I wouldn't have had to worry and I wouldn't have been so disappointed with you." I took hold of my cereal bowl with both hands and lifted the edge of the ceramic bowl to my lips. I drank the last bit of milk and stood up from my chair.

I wanted to tell Vivien to loosen the collar, trust me, and let me come home when I want. I wanted to tell my mom what had happened that day. I would have loved to tell her about the roof, the sunset and Brian calling me a groupie but I knew she wouldn't get it, so I didn't tell her.

I was a young teen and couldn't explain to my mom I just had a coming-of-age experience because I didn't know it was one. I just shrugged my shoulders and said, "Sorry, I should have called. I just lost track of time." I placed my bowl in the sink, returned the milk to the proper shelf in the fridge and said, "That's what Alex said after you, u-turned in Keller's driveway; that I should have called, and you were worried about me until you knew I was okay... then you were just mad at me." Vivien agreed, "Well then, Brian's cousin is brilliant, and you should listen to her more." I didn't answer as I fluttered back up the stairs to my room. I just thought, agreed and I intend to.

I figured I would arrive at the Luncheonette at about 2pm and see Alex again that day. I wanted to tell her that Vivien's wrath wasn't too tortuous. An hour and a half later, I returned downstairs and signaled to Vivien that I was off to the strip. Vivien abruptly stopped her telephone conversation, "...hold on, Soph," and she cupped the lower part of the phone receiver and looked me up and down. "Is that what you're wearing to Susan's party? Um, did you forget?" I looked at her with shock, horror, and disbelief. "Oh my God, Mom, it's like a thousand degrees and so humid, I don't want to go! Viv, please?" My mother raised her pointer finger in the air. It meant WAIT. "Soph, I gotta run. Call me tomorrow." She hung the receiver on its cradle and unraveled the curly yellow wire off her foot. "Emily! Dad and Michael are leaving work early, and I think Audrey is coming too. Yes, of course, you have to join us! It's a surprise, and besides, Lucy and all your friends will be there." I was distraught and moaned, "Mara won't be there, and Mom, I hate this weather. Why do I have to go? If Lucy will have all the other kids? Who has a birthday party at two o'clock on a Monday? Another thing, is that Lucy is a strange bird." My Mom was losing her patience with my rhetoric and considered it whining. "Emily, after last night, you're lucky you're not grounded but rather going to a party. Wear what you want, but you are going today. That's enough!" I stormed upstairs!

At two o'clock, my whole family walked four houses down to Lucy's house for her mom's forty-second surprise birthday barbeque on a Monday. Apparently, I had an attitude the size of Texas. I know that because as I dragged myself a few feet behind my folks, Franco whispered to Viv, "What's her size of Texas attitude about?" Vivien shook her head and didn't answer him, knowing I was an earshot away. That night I looked at a map and realized Texas was a big state, so that's why Franco used the analogy. Still, it was stupid I thought.
Lucy didn't have a pool, so it was boring. It was 97 sticky degrees, and I was sweating. The humidity felt like a thousand percent, and I didn't have to be a meteorologist to know it was best to be indoors, in a pool, or a cold shower. I kept thinking how much better it would be with Mara in our air-conditioned houses or sitting in air conditioning under Andy Warhol's Marilyn, talking to Alex.
We entered the yard and said our hellos to the guests, mostly the neighbors. I finally settled in at a picnic table with Lucy, Dean, Dave, and some of Lucy's cousins whom we had met a few times. Scotty's glasses fogged up when he returned to the table after using the bathroom. We were all bored, just looking at each other and letting out an occasional sigh. It was as if we were silently agreed that it was too hot to actually do any kind of activity, except maybe swimming in a pool, which Lucy didn't have. None of us wanted to be there.
They didn't play any music. The picnic table gave me a splinter and the guests were perspiring and wishing they

could leave too. Hence, the party ended early.

Lucy and I sat on the curb after everyone had left before seven o'clock. We talked outside for a bit about her boyfriend, being a jerk. He didn't even show up at her mom's party; instead, he chose to go fishing with his friends. Lucy was less than a year older than me and going into her senior year. I was about to start my junior year. She always had a boyfriend, and went to third base with more than one of them. I think she went further than that too. Mara thought she went all the way. That night I missed Mara tons. I never really felt comfortable hanging out with Lucy alone. In a group she was ok, but when it was just her and me, or even with Mara, all she ever talked about was boys and sex. She was excessively proud of her experience knowing Mara and I had little to none. She knew about things that Mara and I didn't know, and we often wondered if all her stories were true.

Hanging out with Lucy on the curb made me want to go home and call Mara. Only she would understand the waste of a summer afternoon at Lucy's horrible party. Surely, she would commiserate about the day I had to endure. I told Mara practically everything and vice-versa, but it was too late to call Millie's LBH. Even if I could have spoken to Mara that night, which I wanted to, I probably would not have told her about the sunset I saw with Alex.

We didn't talk about things like sunsets. We were almost fifteen and never really talked about anything profound. It had been five years since Mara's Mom died, and we hardly spoke about that. I never wanted to be the one who brought that up; And she never did.

I thought she would have been mad about me hopping onto the strip rooftop for the first time without her. Even worse, had I told her she probably would have wanted to go to the roof. I felt that it would be awkward to go back up without

Alex and I would not have wanted to tell Alex I told Mara about any of it. It was teenage turmoil, in a way. I needed clarification on how to handle these two very different friendships. I knew my experiences with Alex, while Mara was in Maine may have hurt Mara's feelings. I would have told her every other little detail that happened in my life if she had given me the time to listen, but I knew she wouldn't stand in Millie's hallway on a small cord for too long anyway.

Mara and I were too young to value our friendship when it existed, though it was a tremendous force of stability during our younger years. Our friendship was tilting like the arcade games we often played together, and the youthful fun didn't mean as much anymore. We were growing up and apart.

I never said goodbye to Mara, and she never said goodbye to me. We just paused for too long a while, becoming each our own. I tried to ignore I knew our friendship was fading away because, at that time, I still believed and felt that *that could never happen.*

I told Lucy I had to go and walked home. Mom was making fried eggs and cheese on Thomas' English Muffins. That was customary on a Sunday evening after our early dinner. Vivian never made them on a Monday, but everyone was hungry because the food at Lucy's was awful. I opened the front storm door and stepped out of my flip-flops. I meandered into the kitchen, "Hope there's one for me, Viv?"

Audrey opened the pocket door, "Need help? The boys are waiting to be served." I rolled my eyes at Audrey, and my mom, answered, "Thanks, Audrey, we're all set. Grab these and a few napkins for yourselves." Audrey took three sandwiches and a few napkins into our den. Vivien wiped the counter and placed the frying pan in the sink to the left.

She asked, "Do you think Susan was surprised today?" I supposed she was trying to make idle conversation. I didn't care about her question and was blasé with only a shoulder shrug. She continued, "It was a lovely afternoon barbeque." I disagreed, "Yeah, Viv, if you like sitting in a furnace… it was great. Oh, and the food was disgusting." I picked up my sandwich, "Coming?" I asked. Vivien was right behind me.

We all watched television and enjoyed our egg sandwiches. My Dad laughed out loud while watching Newhart, one of his favorite sitcoms. I never thought it was as funny as he did. I cleared everyone's empty paper plates, folded up the two snack tables, and stored them behind the den bar. During a commercial, Franco yawned loudly and said, "That hit the spot!"

I concurred, "Yeah, it did, and I think I'm going up." My father blew me a kiss. "Have a good sleep Em. By the way, I agree the food was terrible." Vivien shot him a look, and Dad smirked at me like he got in trouble too. Audrey and Mike sequentially mumbled, "Goodnight." Mom said, "Goodnight, Emmy. See you in the morning." I replied, "Goodnight, all."

I moved up each stair at a slow pace. I cleaned up my messy clothes all over the floor and organized my stuff. I washed up, brushed my teeth, and tucked myself in before eleven o'clock.

My Sony fifteen-inch black and white television provided the only shadows of light in my room. Thankful, I didn't have to get up and change the channel for two of my favorite shows back-to-back; The Odd Couple and directly after, The Honeymooners. I vaguely heard Vivien quietly enter and turn my television off before Honeymooners was over. My mom kissed my head, and I rolled over. I usually would be sound asleep, but I stayed awake in silence. I thought about Alex. I thought about Mara, who I did miss, and the rest of the neighborhood kids I hardly missed.

I was fully awake while trying to fall asleep to see images of sunsets with my eyes tightly closed. The awakening felt awkward because I thought I was changing and it felt uncomfortable. I eventually fell into a deep sleep and dreamed about a rotary phone in the hallway of a *Little Blue House*.

Chapter Four

I called Mara from my bedside phone shortly after my eyes opened. After four rings, her Aunt Millie said, "Hello?" I immediately replied, "Hi Auntie, it's Emily. How are you enjoying all the company?" Millie's high-pitched voice sounded off with a giggle that hurt my ears. "Hi, Emily; how I wish you were here with us. The more, the merrier at LBH." I replied, "Thanks, and I wish I could have come, um… but I have a summer camp program next week and um, maybe next year. Anyway, is Mara around?"
Aunt Millie's clear and vibrant voice called out, "Mara, sweetheart, Emily is on the telephone for you. Okay, Emily, she's coming so hold on. I have to put the phone down because I have a pot of soup that's just about to bubble over if I don't get to the stovetop to lower the burner. Take care, my love." I heard a big bang as Millie set the hand-set down.
I was still in bed with my phone wedged between my ear and shoulder. I waited for over five minutes. Finally, Mara was on the other end of the line. "Hey Em, what's up?" I knew she was standing in the hall on the only rotary phone in the entire house with a short two-foot cord.
"I'm good. Def miss you, Mars. I had an awful time at Lucy's yesterday. It was so hot, and the food was awful too." She quickly inquired, "Was Adam there with his family?" I was displeased with her lack of interest in any details regarding the awfulness of the party. Nevertheless, I answered, "Yeah, he was there for like an hour with his mother, but they… lucky them… left because they were picking up his little brother or some fake story." She wanted to hear more about Adam, "How did he look?" I was slightly angry, "He looked like… Adam. He was there for less than an hour and gone like the wind. I didn't talk to him at all.

Vivien made me go, and we stayed for five unbearable hours."

She didn't prompt any further conversation other than her unexpected goodbye. "Hey Em, sorry but my cousins are all waiting for me by the dock. Call me soon, though, okay?" I said, "Bye, Mars. Have fun." I hung up, rolled my eyes and pushed myself out of bed.

Finally, downstairs, there was a note from Vivien on the kitchen table. She always wrote in script, and her penmanship was beautiful.

Emily, please take the clothes out of the washer and hang them up before you disappear today. I am playing golf with the girls and should be home around 3:00 pm. Chicken cutlets in the fridge if you get hungry for lunch before I get home. Xoxo, your loving Mom, Vivien

I hated hanging clothes on the line when a perfect working dryer was next to our washer. It's not that Vivien was hell-bent on not using the dryer to save on our electric bill, although that was a bonus. She liked the fresh, outdoor scent of clothes coming off the line and hung them anytime the weather allowed. I wasn't asked to do it often. Still, it was a chore I didn't love.

I decided to tackle it before making myself some breakfast. It was a less humid July day, and the neighborhood was quiet. I stepped out my back door and hung all the damp clothes with the clothespins that belonged to my Nanna. Since Nanna stopped hanging her clothes, Vivien came home months earlier with a bag full of them. My Mom said they didn't make clothespins like that anymore.

I knew Viv would expect to get home and see that task incomplete, so I set out to prove her wrong. I hung the clothes carefully and a few inches apart, just as she liked them. I watched television while enjoying the pancakes I whipped up with Bisquick and lots of delectable butter, powdered sugar and syrup.

After a quick chat with Aunt Sophia who called to look for Vivien, I blasted music at an unhealthy decibel and enjoyed my shower in my empty house.

I left a note for Mom on the kitchen table next to hers. I never wrote in script, I hardly do, even today. Still my hand-writing was really neat. I wrote:

Viv, Please take the clothes in from the line before you disappear.

Ha-Ha Mom! I went to the strip on foot. I made pancakes, showered, and picked up every stitch of clothing from my bedroom floor. I hope you realize you are a slave driver. I'll be home before you embarrassingly look for me in your pajamas. Hah again! I will call you by 3:30 pm and tell you my whereabouts. Xoxo, your loving daughter, Em.

I decided to take the longer route to the strip to see if anyone from the neighborhood was at the park. Nobody was. I continued walking on the sidewalk listening in one ear to Pat Benatar, We Belong. It was a huge hit and even though it was overplayed by the local radio DJs, I still liked it. I looked both ways and crossed the street to head around another corner. There was a shiny red Chevy

Camaro blaring the same radio station out its opened windows. The bright sunlight and glare from the windshield made it hard for me to make out the driver. I took out my earphone and backed up on the street as the car stopped next to the curb in front of me.

"Hey kid, where were you yesterday?" Alex squatted in the driver's seat and leaned as much as she could towards the opened passenger window. "Alex, what are you doing here?" I walked over to her car and poked my head down into the window. She pressed the unlock button on her side, "Hop in. Want to go for a ride?" I opened the door, "Wow, Alex cool car without a squeaky door. What are you doing here? Are you on your way to work now?" Her right hand was tapping to the beat of the music on the stick shift in the middle console between the two black leather seats. Her left hand on the steering wheel. "Nope, Tuesday is my day off, but I had to drop something off to Brian, so I figured while I was in the neighborhood, I'd swing by now that I know where you live." I hopped inside and enjoyed the new car smell. I couldn't believe I was sitting in the coolest car ever with my new, coolest friend ever.

"Alex, I was listening to the same station as you. Gotta love... Pat Benetar, huh?" Alex nodded and started singing really loudly to the next song on the same station, Rod Stewart, Young Turks.

She quieted down to answer, "Yes indeed, love that song and this one too. Love summer music and love the beach! Wanna go?" Alex was cruising through the side streets. "Sure, I guess. Is this really your car?" Alex beamed, "I picked it up last night. It's my first new car." I was so impressed, "So it's brand new?" She was on cloud nine. "Yep, and you are my first passenger." I was honored. Before I knew it, we were on Ocean Parkway heading south.

We drove to the beach with the windows and sunroof open.

Summer never felt that good on my bicycle. The radio was turned up to drown out the wind pouring into the car and blowing our hair all about. Alex pulled into an almost empty, parking lot.

"What beach is this?" Alex stopped the car and put the stick shift in park. She turned down the radio, "It's a private beach, only residents allowed." I raised my eyebrows, "And so you live around here?"
Alex smiled, "Yup, that's my house." Her expression made me unsure if she was being truthful but part of me believed her. After all, I was sitting in a brand-new Camaro. "So, you live in that gorgeous house?" Alex busted out laughing, "I wish, nah... this is a private beach though. My Aunt Annie lives around the block. She doesn't drive, so she lets me put the sticker on my car. She's really sweet and I visit her often. She knows after our lunch I like to come here to decompress and smell the salt air." I chuckled, realizing that Alex's relaxed spirit was one of the things I enjoyed most about her.
We both exited the car. "It's really not crowded at all," I noticed. Alex opened the hatch and picked up a blanket. "It's a little more crowded on the weekends but hardly during the week. It's great for me because I usually come on Tuesday's if the weather cooperates. C'mon!" She stepped over a small wooden guardrail. I followed her down a narrow sandy path with shrubbery on both sides. It was a short walk and we were standing one hundred feet away from the Long Island Sound.
Alex shook the blanket, and I grabbed two corners. We set it down on the sand. She sat down with her arms wrapped around her upright knees. I kicked off my flip-flops and fell to my knees. I folded over the corner of the tie-dye blue cotton blanket.
Alex watched me while as we exchanged comments about

how the beach was our favorite place in the world. I took the sand in both hands and pulled it forward into a mini hill. I folded the blanket back. I set myself down and I laid my head on my newly made pillow sculpted in sand. "Make yourself at home," Alex said. I glanced away from the sky and looked over to her, "I just did. You're just jealous you don't have a pillow." I closed my eyes and listened to the water rippling. There were a few moments of silence until I quietly mumbled, "This doesn't suck Alex." She let out a deep breath of solidarity. I asked, "Hey, you want me to chisel a pillow for you?"

She stretched out her arms before dropping them into the sand. "Nope, I'm just fine without a pillow but thanks." We were both less talkative and equally enjoying the peace. I listened to the vibrating sound of the surf. I had never been to such a quiet and private beach.

There were only a handful of people. Six women sat closer to the water. They drank out of red plastic cups and their laughter was boisterous and nonstop. Alex didn't open her eyes when she said, "I wish I could hear what is so funny." I tried to listen too, but their laughter drowned out their dialogue. Hearing them laugh made me smile.

While Alex continued to rest, I watched a young couple walk together down the shoreline until they disappeared into the brush. The water gently splashed the sides of the rock jetties, and I noticed the vibrant green algae exposed at low tide. To the far right of the happy ladies, a toddler repeatedly wobbled toward the water until his big sister caught up and steered him back to their empty blanket. Their mom sat in a beach chair with a watchful eye behind her camera. Alex and I sat furthest away from the water taking in the scent of the salt in the air. It was peaceful, and it felt nothing like hanging out with the kids on my block. It was perfect. We stayed for an hour or two and time passed by quickly.

As we entered my township, I said, "Um, Alex maybe you should drop me off at the park because I don't feel like dealing with Vivien's two thousand questions about where I've been.

I'm not sure she would be pleased that I've been cruising around with someone she doesn't know in this hot rod. Alex echoed, "…hot rod, red, baby!" Alex drove through the open fences of the park and pulled over.

She understood, "I guess I can see your mom being taken off guard. I mean you getting out of a strange car with someone she doesn't know. I get it." I told her I had no friends who had their licenses yet, so I was a little unsure how she would react. I was allowed to drive with Michael but he was my brother, so it was different.

As I swung open the car door and planted my feet on the pavement, Alex' voice cut through the air, "Hey kid, wait!" She fumbled in her bag producing a pen and a scrap of a white envelope. "That's my number just in case you ever need a ride," she said, a mischievous glint in her eye as I leaned in to take it. Maybe I'll see you tomorrow, at Brian's? She added her voice filled with anticipation.

I shrugged my shoulders, "Probs! Alex thanks for the ride. By the way, I love that beach almost as much as the sunset from the roof. I walked out of that park gate a million times before, but never the way I did that day. I felt my heart beating and I skipped with a light step. I was on the same block heading home as usual but nothing was usual. I just felt different.

My Dad's charcoal gray Audi was in the driveway, and it wasn't even four o'clock. That was remarkably early for Franco to be home from work. I walked into the den, "Hey Dad, banker's hours?" He yawned, "Yes, I took half the day because your old man is tired." I kissed him on the check, "Where's the ball and chain, Franco?" My Dad laughed with his eyes, "Your mother is upstairs doing…

whatever it is she does." I walked through the pocket door into the kitchen. My dad called out, "Hey can you slide that shut, think I'd like to take a snooze before dinner." I shut the pocket door, "K Dad, have a good sleep. I'll be out front."

Dean and Stevie were skateboarding in the street. I walked over and sat on the curb and watched them. Lucy came outside too and sat beside me. "Hi, Em, where you been? Me and Davie had lunch at Brian's and Max gave us free Bazooka." I hardly cared about their same ole' day at the strip but replied, "Free gum is cool." Scotty's mom opened his front door, "Dinner soon, Scott." That was my cue to say, "Lucy, I have to go eat now too. See you tomorrow maybe." I jumped up from the curb said bye to the boys and went inside.

"Oh good," Vivien said, "I was just going to call you in. Were you supposed to call me at three-thirty?" I plunked my Walkman down on the edge of the steps. "Mom, I was on the block, really?" She let it go and later I found out that she didn't return home from golf until much later than she had expected so I was in the clear. I had dinner with my parents and Mom told us how she hurt her wrist playing golf earlier. Dad talked about his meeting in the city and the ramp and elevator job at Shea Stadium which took longer than expected.

Neither of them asked about my day, and I was glad I didn't have to lie about being in Alex's car or at the beach. I cleared my plate and skipped upstairs to suit up for a swim. I decided to dip in the pool while my parents sat on the deck, enjoying their wine and discussing upcoming plans and schedules. I hardly heard them because I wasn't interested in listening.

I was floating on my back, and the water flowed loudly in and out of my ears as I stared at the stars above. I thought about how I was in the right place at the right time when Alex pulled around the block earlier. It was so extraordinary to hang out with her.

She was older and more mature than the kids in the neighborhood. She told me about how things were in college and how she paid $1.83 a gallon for gas.

The kids in the neighborhood never talked about what things cost or what they wanted to do with their lives. Alex asked me how I felt about high school and my friends.

We loved the same music and we endlessly talked about lyrics. We both loved the sand in our toes and the sound of the ocean. We were both Italian and had early Sunday dinners with our family. I never connected on those levels with anybody, even Mara.

I was still floating on my back, carefully controlling my breathing. I exhaled from my diaphragm and felt my body sink. I inhaled and held my breath until my body floated to the water's surface. I tipped my head and noticed the water rippling over my bathing suit top and making a small puddle in my cleavage.

I liked how I looked and was thinking about some of the stories Lucy told Mara and me about having sex with boys. I would look at myself in the mirror after a shower, touch my breasts and wonder how it may feel to have a boy touch them and if I would like it. The thought was both, scary and exciting.

I floated around long before my dad meandered toward the pool's edge and asked, "You ever getting out?" I looked up, "Dad, it's so warm. The water is warmer than the air. You should come in." Franco declined my invite, "Emmy, I'm shot. Gonna jump in the shower and jump on the couch for a bit." As my dad turned to go inside, Vivien walked out of the sliding screen door with a towel and tossed it on the lounge chair. I didn't even realize I forgot to grab one from the hall closet before I jumped in earlier.

"Em, I'm going in and don't want you in the pool alone. Ready?" I was and started paddling to the steps, "Yep, getting out; thanks for the towel, Viv." I examined my wrinkled fingers and wondered why water made them look like that. I sat outside before going into the house. I was shivering.

Our house was always cool in the summer and warm in the winter. We had central air downstairs and individual air-conditioner units in our bedroom windows. Franco would freak out when I left it on during the day when I wasn't in my room. He preferred I use it only at night to sleep comfortably. When I was dry enough, I entered through the back door. The kitchen was cleaned and wiped down with only a dim light above the stove. I saw my parents' watching television in the den through the open pocket door. Vivien dozed off in her leather chair with her feet resting on the matching hassock. I walked over to my mom and whispered, "Mom, I'm going up."

Vivien opened her eyes, "I'm not sleeping, just relaxing. I'll be up soon and come to say goodnight." I kissed the top of her head and went to my room.

I tossed the wet towel down the laundry chute and watched it slide down on its way to the basement. It was one of the many genius ideas my mom thought of and my dad was able to execute. As I watched the towel drop, I suddenly remembered I had tossed my shorts into the chute earlier before my night swim. I immediately thumped down the stairs to get them.

"Oh my God, Em, what is going on?" I kept moving towards the basement door, "Sorry, Mom, I have to get something in the basement." I guessed my loud descent on the steps woke her, and she wasn't thrilled I did. I opened the chute door, and the dirty clothes came tumbling into the basket. I was relieved the torn envelope was still stuffed in the front pocket of my shorts. I gripped it with my left hand

and held the banister with my right as I skipped every other stair back up two flights. I took off my wet bathing suit and slung it over my chair. I slipped on a long-sleeved nightshirt, climbed into bed, and was hopeful about what would come. I wasn't sure why I was smiling so much, but I couldn't help it.

Chapter Five

Being a part of a New York Yankee fan club family,
particularly on my mother's side, was a given. I was born
into baseball. But that day, Franco told me to be ready by
eleven for the one o'clock Met's game at Shea Stadium.
The Shea Stadium general contractor gave Franco two
tickets. I had been looking forward to being Franco's date
for months. He had asked me to go when school was still in
session. Vivien had no interest in America's favorite
pastime, unless it was a Yankee game and Michael was
packing for his road trip to South Carolina. He was going to
Audrey's father's house to meet her father and, soon-to-be
step-mom for the first time.

Franco told Michael to take his work Caravan, which had
more room and was far more reliable than Michaels' Nova.
Audrey told me that she was nervous about meeting Carol
and glad Mike was accompanying her.

Audrey and I talked a lot because she always arrived earlier
than Michael wanted her to. Mike would get mad that he
never had time to shower and relax before she came over. I
would tell him, "Better early than super late, right though?"
He would just look at me and breathe an ugly sound from
his nose. "No Em, sometimes later is better. Sometimes a
person just needs a minute to themselves." I liked that
Audrey was early because we would pick up bread, soda or
anything else, Vivien may have forgotten to stock up on for
our dining event.

Audrey was way cooler when she wasn't in front of my

parents. She drove and sang loud, "What's love got to with it?" And repeating, "Got to do with it, got to do with it?" She wasn't the best vocalist, singing out loud to Tina Turner. Still, I liked to hang with her. When we arrived back at my house, she was more polite. I understood why she had those dual personalities.

Her parents divorced when she was two years old. She spent every summer with her father since then, and she seemed really close to him. It was difficult for me to understand Audrey's upbringing but it was interesting how normal she seemed even though her folks split up. My parents didn't consider a divorced family normal; therefore, Vivien wasn't convinced she was the right fit for Michael. They seemed pretty serious about each other and Audrey seemed normal to me. More importantly, I was glad I would have Michael entirely out of my hair for a few weeks.

The game was great even though the Met's lost one to three to the Cardinals. The Met's always seemed to blow it, making it easier to be a Yankee fan. Neither of us cared who won. There was a man ten seats away who caught a foul ball and handed it to a little girl a few seats away from us. We hoped the whole thing was captured on television. Franco and I wondered if we would be in the shot, plastered on the evening news or if we would be in a picture, in Newsday's sports section the next day. We talked on the way home about how it was an unbelievable happening and just yards away from us. We were so excited we saw a glimpse of us on the stadium screen in slow motion. We ate hot dogs and cotton candy, and Franco bought me a soft stuffed animal in a Met's uniform. It was a great day.

My Dad was always so generous. I think he offered to buy me the stuffed bear to commemorate the day. He said,

"Hey just put that thing away when Uncle Jerry and Pete come over. Who wants to hear them berate the Met's over and over?" My dad was right. Mom's brothers, loathed the Met's and we all thought they took the Yanks/Mets rivalry to over-the-top levels. I said, "Yeah, I think Uncle Jerry and Viv's would disown me if they saw this this guy, huh Dad?" He agreed, "Well, Em, I would hate if Mom disowned you so hide it under the mound of clothes on the floor in in your room." I pushed the bear into his shoulder. "Hey Dad, you're the one who will be disowned because Viv's will know you bought it for me." That made him laugh, and he replied, "I will have to deny that and tell Mom you must have stolen it as I am a true-blooded Yankee fan, just like her." I finished his sentence, "… and Uncle Jerry and Pete, huh?"

The rest of the car ride home, my dad told me about all the structural steel ramps he manufactured that helped people with disabilities get around the stadium. He also installed elevators and chairlifts that helped people in wheelchairs get to the VIP lounge. My dad was a huge part of that undertaking and the construction lasted several years. He said, "The permits were a bitch," I didn't understand most of what he was explaining. Nonetheless, I was so proud and I listened with both ears. Franco was a regular guy from an underclass upbringing but he was my giver. He was the person who gave and gave. Even more, he asked for very little in return. Every year for his birthday when I asked, "Dad, what do you really want? He would reply, "Respect!" He already had that from me constantly.

It seemed we were home for hours. That summer night was long-lasting. My parents ordered tons of Chinese food, and Dean and Scottie's parents came by to eat and play their wonted Trivia Pursuit board game outside on the deck. They were funny to listen to for a little while.

They were loud and I heard them poking fun at each other from the den. The men enjoyed scotch and the ladies sipped wine. Vivien always had chips, crackers and cheese out after dinner and I occasionally grabbed snacks and returned to the den to watch television. My parents and their friends always had fun.

Earlier, when Franco and I were at the game, Michael and Audrey hit the road. It was almost eight in the evening and the sun had not set. Usually on those nights, the kids from the neighborhood would come by and we would play a board game in the basement or take a swim but that evening I wasn't in the mood to see any of them and was glad they never came by. I sprawled out on the sofa and decided if anyone did call for me, I planned to say I had an awful headache.

I picked up the phone and dialed the number I almost memorized written on the torn envelope, Alex handed to me the day before. It rang three times, "Hello?" It was Alex. "Hey Alex, it's Em. Figured I'd say hey." Alex was out of breath, "Hey Em, I just came inside from washing my car. I'm glad you didn't lose my scribbled number. What are you up to?" I told her about the game and how my dad and I were hoping we'd make it on the evening news sports segment. She asked about the commotion radiating through the screen door and I explained the excitement of adult neighborhood Trivia night. "Hey Em, was thinking of getting ice cream with my sisters. Wanna get some ice cream with us?" I sprung to an upright position still sitting on the edge of the couch. "Um, well Alex, where and I don't think I could get a ride? My brother left and my parents have company."
She immediately replied, "Well silly, we would come and pick you up. I only live about ten minutes from your house and we can go to Friendly's, by you?" I was thrilled by the

invite but had to get clearance from Vivien and wasn't sure what she would say.

"Alex, let me ask my folks. Can you hold on for a minute?" I gently placed the receiver down on the oak coffee table, unlike Mara's, Aunt Millie who never did that gently. I scurried to the screen door.

"Mom, mom can I go to Friendly's with Alex and her sisters?" She didn't answer and so I slid open the screen door. I darted to Vivien's side and asked again, "Mom, can I go? Can I go to Friendly's with Alex and her sisters? They are waiting to see if I can go and they will pick me up." Vivien looked up, "Alex who?" She looked down at the board game and back up at me, "What? Emily?" I was getting impatient and was only worried that Alex was holding over a minute now. "Oh my God, Mom. Alex! You know, Brian's cousin! Whatever Mom, they are on hold. Can I go?" My mom threw the dice and inquired, "Alex drives and where? Friendly's? Emily, I don't even know this person and I'm not sure I want you in some eighteen-year-olds car." I answered her question and pleaded, "Yes, Mom she drives and her sisters who my age are going. She's a better driver than Michael. Please, Mom, please?" Thankfully, Dean's mom chimed in. "Oh Vivien, I've known Alex for years and she's lovely. Know her mom from that Mahjong game I used to play with Cecila and Maddie. Is very good to her sisters, always driving them to the mall." I agreed, "Yes Mrs. Seelie, she offered to take us to Friendly's and I really want to go." Finally, by the grace of God, Franco put his hand around my mom's left bicep and Vivien turned towards him, "I think it'll be okay." Vivien nodded in agreement mostly because Dean's mom said she knew Alex.

My Dad looked up, "Have Alex come in and say hello before you leave, okay?" I quickly headed back to pick up the receiver, "Alex, are you there?" She was. "Of course, I am. Did they say yes?"

I tried to sound calm, "Yeah, but can you just come in and say a quick hello?" I heard her smile through the receiver and she answered, "Sure, kid, I'll come meet the folks so they don't think I'm an axe murderer." I grunted an instinctive sound of amusement, "Ok, see you in ten then." I hung up the phone and ran upstairs to my room. I changed into denim cut-off shorts and lifted my shirt over my head. I threw it in the corner and picked up my green cotton jersey off the floor. I shook it out and slipped it over my head. I flew back down the stairs and waited on the steps outside my front door. It took twenty minutes before I saw her Camaro turn onto my street. I bounced off my stoop and met her in my driveway. Alex stepped out of her car while introducing me to her sisters. "Em, this is Sophie and that's Rae back there." I peeked into the window, "Hi," I said. They both waved from their respective seats.

"I'll be right back, stay put," Alex said to them. "Okay let's meet your mom and dad, yes?" I led the way through my front door foyer through the kitchen and left through the pocket door leading to our den. Alex followed. I opened the sliding screen door and Alex and I stepped out on the patio. "Mom, Dad, this is Alex." Alex approached the table, "Hi Mrs. Netti, it's nice to meet you." My mom half smiled, and my dad stood up and reached out his hand, "Hi Alex, thanks for coming in to say hello." They shook hands and I thought it was weird but okay. Then he reached into his front pocket and handed me ten bucks.

"Enjoy your ice cream." I was so anxious to leave but played it cool, "Thanks, Dad. Okay we're gonna go now." Mrs. Seelie prevented our departure, "Hi Alex, how's your mom?" They chatted briefly before Mrs. Seelie excused herself to the ladies' room. Vivien was still seated, "Where are your sisters, Alex?" Alex looked towards the door, "Oh

they are just waiting in the car, anxious for ice cream."
Vivien smiled, "Okay Em, have fun. See you guys in an
hour or two?" Alex responded, "Yeah, that sounds about
right. It was nice to meet you all."
Alex approached the car and told Sophie to hop in the back.
Sophie's expression was one of profound disapproval. I
immediately interjected, "I'll sit in the back, no worries."
Alex settled in her driver's seat, "Soph, c'mon let Em sit in
front and you can on the way home." Rae said nothing and
stayed crunched up in the back of the tall bucket seat.
Sophie stepped out, released the lever and pulled the seat
forward. She climbed in the back and I got in the front. I
immediately turned my body around to talk to them.
"Thanks for inviting me for ice-cream. My night was so
boring!"
Sophie was about to turn fifteen like me and Rae was
fourteen. Almost twins, I thought. I mentioned to Sophie
that I had an Aunt Sophia. She wasn't impressed by the
coincidence. She pointed out that her birth name, Sophie
was completely different than Sophia. I sensed she was
still annoyed Alex kicked her out of the front. Rae was
quieter of the two. She was about to start her freshman
year in high school and we talked about that a bit. Alex
turned up the radio and before I knew it, we were all
singing, "*You say I'm a dreamer, we're two of a kind. Both
of us searching for some perfect world we know we'll
never find. So perhaps I should leave here, yeah, yeah and
go far away. But you know that there's nowhere that I'd
rather be than with you here today.*" It was another overplayed, Thompson Twins summer song. We all loved it
anyway.
We enjoyed ice cream and idle chatter at our table. I liked
them all so much. The ice cream shop was packed and
freezing so we didn't stay long. Rae skipped to the car and
Sophie walked behind her. Alex and I were only a few feet

behind them, "Hey if you want, I was thinking of dropping off my sisters and then I'll drive you back home?" I was happy about that, "Yeah, I don't think we've been gone that long and Vivien is drinking wine and Franco is undoubtedly calling out crazy trivia answers. Sounds good!"

When Alex unlocked the car, I pulled open the door and immediately hopped in the back. Sophie graciously accepted and thanked me, "Aw, Emily I would have sat in the back." I replied, "No biggie." Alex gave Sophie a harsh look and started the engine. "I'm dropping you both off and then taking Emmy home. I have to stop at Brian's and pick up some paperwork anyway." She didn't wait for them to respond, and turned up the radio and opened the sunroof. I sat in the back diagonal to Alex and looked up at the stars. There were millions of bright stars in a clear, dark sky. It meant the next day was going to be perfect. Alex and Sophie stepped out onto the driveway and adjusted their seats so Rae and I could climb out. "Tell Mom and Dad, I had to go to the library to work on something." Rae nodded, "K." She turned her head towards me and said, "Nice meeting you, Em. You have to come to the San Gennaro Feast with us next month." Sophie added, "…and the festival." I thought that was so nice of them to say that. "Thanks guys that sounds like so much fun. Hope I can!"

Alex jumped back in the driver's seat and I settled shotgun. She opened the garage from her remote on her visor and her sisters went inside. We pulled up in my driveway. She turned off the engine and we just sat and chatted about the Met's game in full detail.

She told me more about her sisters and her brother who was seventeen and a senior. I was shocked how close they all were in age, "Wow, Alex! I can't believe you are all only about a year and a half apart in age. Your parents were busy, it seems." We laughed and she grunted, "That is gross! Can't even think of my parents in such an act. Ew." I ran inside to tell my parents I was home and back out to my driveway. They were cleaning up the deck and the table out back. Their company was gone. "Hi Mom, I'm just sitting in the driveway with Alex. Be in… in a few." Vivien answered, "You girls can come back here or hang in the basement. We're going inside shortly." I didn't mention that we already dropped off her sisters, "Um, yeah maybe or I'll be in soon. We're just listening to some of the mixed cassette tape I made in the car." I went back out to the driveway and Alex and I sat listening to the locust chirp, with the sunroof and windows open. That night I told Alex all about Michael. She wanted to see a picture of him but I didn't feel like running inside to get one. I promised I would show her the one I had in my wallet the next time I visited the Luncheonette.

"Hey, Em? There is a summer festival at the park on Saturday if you want to come? My sisters will be there and two or ten of my cousins." She laughed and continued, "Oh and my idiot brother will probably show up. We just walk around, shop and eat zeppole's." I knew Mara was coming home early Saturday afternoon but we didn't have any set plans. "Sure, I don't think I have any plans. I'll see what's going on." I was tired and figured it was time to head inside.

My mom was out cold while Johnny Carson stood in front of a blue curtain, reciting his nightly monologue. I didn't care much for the show though I had seldom seen it in its entirety. My Dad was sleeping upstairs. I left Viv's where she was on her chair and headed to my room. All I thought about until I fell asleep was how cool the festival on Saturday would be. I was praying Vivien would say it was okay too.

I was sitting at the kitchen table, still sleepy and in my nightshirt listening to Vivien. She told me she was trying to figure out when Aunt Sophia would come with my cousin Jack and her husband, John. I loved when they came for overnights. Jack was only three years old and he thought I was the funniest person ever. I loved taking him swimming and playing games with him. Aunt Sophia always thanked me for being so good to him.

Franco came in from yard work. "Are we ordering lunch from Brian's or do you have something else in mind?" My Mom looked at me, "Em honey, call in our usual order and ask if they have any fresh mozzarella too. I roasted peppers yesterday." Dad's expression lit up. I dialed the number. "Hi Louie, it's Emily Netti." I was bummed Alex didn't answer. "We want the usual Lou, and my mom also wants a fresh mozzarella." Louie knew precisely what to do, "Gotcha Emily, be ready in about twenty minutes." We left ten minutes later and Brian and Vivien got their usual chat in, while Alex packed up our to-go lunch. I stayed by the counter and told Alex I would ask about the festival. "What time would you swing by to get me and when should I tell my parents I would be home?" She quietly responded, "Do you think they would let you stay out till midnight or one because after the festival we may see a movie." I was cool and just said, "Yeah, I think they'll be fine with it." I knew my mom would think that was too late, but I planned to fight for a later curfew that summer.

My mom came back just as Alex served up our order. She was sure to add a few free extras that my parents surely recognized when we unpacked everything at home. It was a perfect afternoon to bring up the festival, "Mom, Alex and a bunch of people are going to the Festival in Greenlawn, this Saturday and I want to go with them."

My Dad watched the game on the small color television on the shelf directly above my head." Vivien said, "Please, honey can you lower the volume?" Franco immediately stood up and turned the dial to the left. "Who is a bunch of people, Em?" My Dad continued eating. I answered, "Ya know… Alex, her sisters and her brother and all her cousins go too. And Alex can pick me up and drop me off too so I wouldn't need you to drive me." Vivien was slightly blowing on her hot split pea soup.

"Well, I guess you can go but your father and I have that timeshare expo and then we are having dinner with the Lerner's." I was so happy to hear that. "So, I would be home alone anyway… so I can go, right?" She nodded yes. "I will probably get picked up at two but after the festival they all are going to the movies and so I'd be home at one." Of course, she thought it was too late, "One in the morning? I think eleven is late enough Em." I really wished my mom wasn't as strict with summer curfews. I argued, "Mom, most of the time people don't even go out till nine or ten and eleven is on the early side to come home. How do I say? Okay Alex, I can go but while your sisters who are younger than me can stay out, um, I have to go home at eleven." Vivien looked at Franco, "Hello, are you okay with her driving around at one in the morning?" Franco looked up, "If you are, then yes!" My mother was so annoyed with his five-word reply. "Mom, we won't be driving around. We will be at the festival and at the movies at night!" My mother finished the last of her soup and stood up. "I understand Emily but Alex is almost nineteen, and you are still fourteen." I reasoned, "But her sisters are my age and Mom, it's so annoying." Vivien was rinsing off her dish in the sink, "I get it but they are her sisters. I would let you stay later if Michael was there too. I was getting mad. "Mom, I can't always hang out with Michael and it's so stupid you don't trust me if Michael's not going to be there." She saw my frustration and gave in, "Emmy, I do trust you. It's not about trust it's about people making dumb decisions in the wee hours. Okay you can go but twelve the latest." I was hyped up for Saturday!

I sprung up with my dish and set it in the sink. "K, thanks Mom I really have to get over to the girls' now." Franco got up too, "I'll drive you because I have to pick up mulch. I ran upstairs to grab my sweatshirt. I was full and ready to babysit for two girls who lived a few blocks away. Jade and Jenna's mom, Lisa called me to babysit and she paid me six dollars an hour in cash. I liked babysitting and the money gave me a sense of independence. I always wished Lisa asked me more often.

The girls were two and four and a half years old. Other than my cousin Jack, they were the cutest kids I had ever seen and I loved them. When Jack was visiting, I would take him there and play with the three of them for free. When I entered their house, they would run and hug me so hard sometimes I would fall over. They liked to play dress up so I would gather my old clothes and dresses that were too small on me yet so big on them. I had a toy microphone and acted as the host of their fashion show. Timing was impeccable to land the gig before the festival. I felt bad to keep hitting up Franco for spending money and it felt good to have my own.

Chapter Six

I woke up Saturday morning happier than on any other day of the summer. My parents left at two o'clock, and Alex picked me up at 2:30 pm, and it could not have worked out better.

Alex pulled into my driveway and honked once. I walked outside my door with tremendous excitement. "Where are your sisters?" I asked. "Where are your folks?" she asked. "Oh, they left for some luncheon about a timeshare. Hey Alex, do you want to take the ten-cent tour? I would love to show you my house and my room." Alex eagerly consented.

We walked into my front door, and as I headed up the first step, she asked, "Can I see the laundry chute in the basement?" I stopped on the step and remembered I told Alex about her phone number in my shorts pocket plunging down the laundry chute. She couldn't understand how Franco built such a thing in the walls.

"Okay, I'll show you that first. Follow me," I said. We walked through the foyer and down the stairs of the basement. It was a finished room with beige tile and plywood walls. Alex noticed the Jacuzzi hot tub and the pool table, and I walked directly to the trap-ceiling door to demonstrate the laundry chute. Alex asked, "So your dad is a carpenter?" I said, "Well yeah, he's very handy, and here's the chute where your phone number was trapped in my shorts." I pointed to the ceiling. Alex opened the sliding chute door, and a few clothes tumbled down. "That's so freakin cool, Em." I was noble and worthy of the compliment. "Yeah, my dad is the bomb, Alex. He can build anything. He's amazing." Alex was impressed. "But it was your mom's idea, right?"

I answered, "Oh yeah, Vivien is the brains behind all the

functionality in this house. The woman should truly get paid to help design homes. Viv is a genius and Franco is the pure craftsman behind all her great ideas." Alex looked over the surroundings. "What is this?" She was standing by the timer my dad installed outside the bathroom. "It's a heat lamp, so if you leave the pool on a cool night and want to change, we run down here and the bathroom is warm. And if someone turns it on and never comes down here, the heater will turn off after twenty minutes so the electric bill is not through the roof." Alex was impressed. "Can I show you, my room?" We headed up the stairs through the hallway to my bedroom door. My room was spotless, and that was not usual. There were no clothes on the floor and my bed was made. I was hoping to show Alex my room which is why it was in pristine condition. I wanted her to feel how I felt when I saw her car. I was becoming more aware of the worldly and materialistic pressures of having name-brand jeans to wear to school, a car with a sunroof or living in a house my friends would think I was lucky to live in. But that day, I just wanted Alex to know more about me and wondered if she would like the color of the carpet or the posters on my walls.

She stood in the middle of the room. "Wow, cool room, Em. It's big! And wow, you have your own bathroom, huh?" She peeked into the attached door.

My Mom and I beautifully decorated my bedroom. My bedspread was an array of earthy gray colors and complimented my off-white furniture with warm, pastel green painted walls.

"Hey, so you like Blackie, huh?" I smiled and glanced at the poster on the wall over my bed. "Who doesn't, right?" Alex agreed and told me how Sophie was an avid General Hospital fan. I was never one for soaps, probably because Vivien and I never watched them but I still knew who *Blackie* was.

She glanced into Michael's room briefly, and I pointed out our extra guest bedroom, which we called Vivien's sewing suite. I gave her a quick tour of my parent's bedroom and showed her the custom shoe rack Franco built in their closet. He was so talented and it was hard not to show him off to Alex. As we headed downstairs, I asked, "So, Alex, where's Rae and Sophie? I thought they were coming today?" I locked the front door, "Follow me out the garage," I said. Alex told me her sisters had gone to the festival with their cousins earlier and we would surely meet up with them. I was happy to have Alex to myself for the ride and not have to feel bad about sitting shotgun. I said, "Well, I hope we see them there." She said, "We def will! C'mon, let's get out of here. It's a beautiful day!"

I felt independent roaming around the Sons of Italy Festival. Alex and I weren't there for more than twenty minutes when Rae snuck up behind us and put her hands over my eyes. "Guess who?" I wasn't surprised and turned to hug Rae. Sophie was a few feet approaching. They introduced me to their two cousins and we decided to make a left on Mulberry Street to check out some shops. The streets were transformed into a red, white, and green revelry. I smelled the sizzle of sausage, heard live music and witnessed vintage cars angled on display with Italian tassels and big gold horns hanging from the rear-view mirrors. I bought a headband. I immediately pulled my hair back and placed it around my forehead. We all shared sausage and pepper heroes along with frosty drinks. We strolled the decorative streets for hours. We followed and spied on two cute Italian boys, who we named Ernesto and Marcello, and every once in a while, they would stop and look back at us while we hid and laughed. They were handsome, and Sophie wanted to marry the one we named Marcello.

It was getting late in the evening, and Alex's sisters were meandering in the record store, buying up Italian cassettes and newer cassettes from some guy named Pupo. They were in there for what seemed like forever.

Alex and I popped on the sidewalk curb for a seat. I told her that it was by far, my best summer ever and it had just begun. She told me it was hers too. We were both at ease when Rae and Sophie appeared flashing their new cassettes. I knew we would be listening to that all the way home. In fact, we listened to that cassette for the rest of the summer. I learned to sing every Italian word to that album and understood the meaning behind every lyric.

Upon our arrival back to Alex's house, I called Vivien. "Hey, Mom." Vivien was glad to hear from me. "Hi Em, how was the festival? Where are you now? Your father and I just walked in and I think we will buy a timeshare in Aruba." She sounded excited, "Really? Cool! Hey Viv, think I can sleep over here tonight? Alex will drive me home tomorrow?" She didn't respond quickly but finally said, "Well, I don't know, Em. I don't know the parents and hardly know Alex or her sisters." I calmly replied, "Mom, they are nice; her parents. You will not meet every single parent of the kids I become friends with throughout my high school years. We got to the festival earlier than planned and back earlier than expected; I thought you'd be happy. Sophie is looking at the paper to see if there's a movie around the block at Loews." I heard Vivien sigh, "Okay, Em. I guess you can stay if it's okay with their folks. Should I speak with them?" I cackled, "Viv, they hardly speak English, so not sure how that phone convo would go." Vivien actually laughed, "So what movie are you girls going to see?" Sophie was calling out times and titles. "Not sure, Indiana Jones or Karate Kid, maybe? Want me to call you tonight when we get back?" Viv said, "Yes, I would." We hung up the phone and I was psyched!

I sat in the front on our way to the movie and on our way home to Alex's house, all while Sophie complained how the backseats were claustrophobic. Alex told her to stop her bitchin', or she could crawl up in the hatch next time. Rae busted a gut when Alex said that.

On the way home, it was the first I ever heard Rae talk so much. She loved Ralph Macchio. Sophie couldn't care less about him, and Alex and I thought he was too long, skinny and awkward. We called Rae, Mrs. Macchio for a while after that night. I phoned Viv to let her know we were all settled in back at Alex's and it was way before midnight so she was relieved.

Alex's parents were asleep upstairs. Rae grabbed a few nectarines from a wooden bowl on the countertop and we all went downstairs. She tossed a nectarine to me, sat in a saggy beanbag chair and handed one to Alex and Sophie as she sat on the sofa's edge. Alex got up and settled into the loveseat with a patchwork quilt. We ate our fruit. The basement was spacious. There was a circular brown couch and a loveseat recliner with time-established comfy indents. The floor was tan and brown squared tiles slightly covered with a shaggy area rug.

The television was on in the background though we were not paying attention. Sophie pulled the rope from her upright lounge on the couch and the blinds rolled down. We stayed up talking till three in the morning. We played truth and dare with our own made-up rules. We talked about our favorite bands, songs and movies. We poked fun at one another and laughed.

Rae was the first to nod off. She was lying on one side of the couch with her feet reaching her sister's belly. Sophie's feet were near to touching Rae's shoulder. Sophie was the tallest of the sisters. She looked most like her brother Johnnie. I only met him briefly at the festival earlier that day. There were pictures all over Alex's house of her family. Johnnie looked a bit like Matt Dillon. Alex always called him a punk, but I knew it was her way of telling him she loved him.

We all fell asleep. I felt Alex tap my shoulder. "Em, your neck is crooked, and you must be cold. Hop onto the loveseat next to me."

I could only open one eye. I struggled to open the other. Alex pulled me up by my forearm out of the sunken beanbag chair. I noticed Rae on the floor and Sophie draped in blankets with the entire couch to herself. I stood up, shuffled and fell into the loveseat. Alex fluffed the quilt over both of us.

Some hours later, my eyes opened before the three of them. Alex was sleeping curled up like a ball in her blue sweats and long-sleeve flannel beside me. She didn't have messy hair. It was still shiny, straight brown hair, long eyelashes and an olive complexion. She was the most European-looking of the sisters. Rae was snoring and still on the floor. She had dirty blonde wavy hair and a much fairer complexion. She was the shortest of the sisters. She had puffy lips, which she hated then; but later grew to love. As we grew up, we all realized that men loved luscious lips, and women would ask Rae where she got her lips done. Sophie looked like she hadn't moved a bit. I stared at the ceiling for a few minutes. It was quiet and the basement was dark, but little bits of sunlight burst through the small opening of the closed blinds.

Pushing aside my untamed curly hair, I looked at these three girls who had only been a part of my life for the first few weeks of summer, and yet they felt like my family. Obviously, not the family I was born into; instead, a family that the universe decided for me. I was so comfortable, so myself.

In this quiet moment, I could picture a path in front of me that was much easier to walk upon than it was to walk

through the halls with my few high school friends.
With an unidentified beam, I decided to roll on my right
side to get up off the loveseat. I was tired and feeling very
unmotivated. Rae looked up from the floor and said,
"Wow, my back is a little messed up." She pulled the
blanket off of her sister and onto her. Soph screeched and
we were all awake. I didn't want to leave. Alex took me
home just before four in the afternoon. My parents were
out buying shrubbery for the front garden. I spoke to Viv
that morning and told her I'd be home much earlier, but it
didn't matter as I suspected they would be out when I
arrived home. Soon after arriving back home, I left Mom
a note on the kitchen table when I got home.

Mom, taking a nap in my room, zzz.

I was feeling the down of the high. My Saturday was over,
and my overnight was over. The discomfort of the beanbag
chair left me with less than three hours of sleep, so I
decided to go up and lay in my bed. I reached over to my
bedside table and hit my answering machine's red, blinking
button. There were four messages which was not the norm.
As if in slow motion, I leaned up on my elbow and pressed
the arrow, "Em, I'm back, and I'm coming over in five."
The second, "Em, I came over, and guess what? You
weren't home! Nobody was home! Where are you? Call
me." The third, "Did you move?" The last message, "I'm
not sure if I should be worried or just so mad at you. What
the fuck, Em?" All the messages were from Mara. I felt a
little wrong to worry or annoy her, but she seemed to be
behaving more like my mother and less like my friend. I
was too tired to pay it mind. I rolled over and as soon as my
eyes shut, I fell asleep.
I briskly sat up when my door flung open, and there she

was. "Mara, what's up? I'm sleeping," I said as I yawned and stretched. "Emily, I got back yesterday before noon. It's now Sunday, almost seven at night! You never even returned my calls. Are you sick or something?" I swung both feet over and they hit the carpet with a thump. I was still in sleep mode and wished Mara was not standing over me like a third-grade detective.

"Mara, I'm sorry. I wasn't home, I went out yesterday and slept over at friends, and I didn't get much sleep, so I came home and crashed out. Cool your pits, anyway!" She was still questioning and seemed ticked off, "Who... what friends? It just seemed like you blew me off. I told you I'd be home on Saturday and I thought you'd be around, and then you never answered my calls." I had to defend myself, "Mars, you were in Maine for weeks, and every time I called you, I talked to Aunt Mil's longer than I talked to you. Sorry but I had plans, and you're acting like I'm supposed to drop everything because you came back from LBH. Now you bust into my room, wake my sorry ass up, and yell at me like Viv. Holy Cow, Mars! And by the way, did Viv send you up?"

Mara sat down on my bed, "Yeah. Your Mom said, go up. I think she's sleeping." We both burst into roaring laughter. She took a breath, "I missed ya, Em. Maine was fun, but it was definitely a week longer than I would have liked. I was worried because nobody was home all day and into the night yesterday."

I hugged her, "I missed you too. Want to stay for dinner? Was Viv cooking something down there?" Mars popped up, "Yes, and it smelled delicious." We headed downstairs to eat.

I opened my bedroom door and saw Vivian fluffing pillows in the guest room and preparing for her sister's visit. "Good morning, Mom." She was in a good mood. "Hey, Em, they should be here by 1 or 2. Do you think we should eat early? You will tell Mara to come by and eat with us, yes?" I hadn't thought about it, "Well, she was just here for dinner last night, but I guess I'll see what she's doing." I wasn't fully awake. I ran my right hand through my hair and scratched my head.

"I kind of want to take Jack to see Jade and Jenna maybe later." She was okay with that and said, "Oh, how Jack loves those girls!" I helped her smooth out the queen-size comforter. "Mom, Lisa told me a funny story last time I sat for them." Vivien was still fixing the corners of the comforter. I just kept talking, "So, Jade scratched up her knee and Lisa sat her on the bathroom sink. She started cleaning the cuts on her knee and Jade started crying about how they stung. So, Lisa tried to make her feel better and told Jade she wished it were she who got hurt and not her (Jade)." My Mom sat on the edge of the newly made bed, listening. I continued, "So when Lisa told her that, Jade said, 'Mom, let's not wish it happened to me, and let's not wish it happened to you. Let's wish it happened to Daddy." My Mom and I laughed about it. Jade didn't love her dad any less than her mom, but for Jade, her dad was strong and a scratch wouldn't hurt him as much.

I ran back to my room to answer my phone. "Hey Mars, what's happening?" She wanted to know if I wanted to go to the park because she had stolen two cigarettes a week prior in LBH. I knew I had time before the company came, so I told her to come. We rode to the park and found our spots under the tree and on the stump. We lit cigarettes. I felt dizzy for a minute. Mara didn't notice I was light-headed. She asked me if I had spoken to Lucy about Adam Byron again, and I told her I didn't. She immediately asked about my two weeks without her and my new friends, "Hey, so when do I meet Alex, Sophia, and Rae? I want to cruise in a Camaro too." I thought it was weird

Mara said that. I wanted to protect my new friendship with Alex and her sisters and not let Mars in. I felt nothing specific against Mars; she was still my best friend but I felt awkward. "I don't know. She works at the Luncheonette, so I guess you will meet her there. Her sister is Sophie, not Sophia like my aunt." Mars suddenly remembered, "Oh is your cousin coming today or tomorrow?" I gently tapped the head of the lit cigarette on the flat tree stump surface beside me. "They are… coming today, so I gotta get home and help Vivien soon." Mara rubbed her sneaker over the cigarette and jumped up. "Okay, I'll come with you. Let's go back to your house and get Lucy too." Then she immediately started talking about how she was so in love with Adam Bryon, and I didn't want to hear it. I didn't want her to come back to my house, and I definitely didn't want to call for Lucy.

I wanted to have my little cousin to myself and take him to see the girls. As we made our way out the gate, I said, "Mars, I was planning on maybe taking Jack to see the girls, and well, I really can't hang out for the rest of the day." I could always tell when my best friend was mad because her eyebrows would mush into her forehead. "So, I can't go with you and Jack to Lisa's?" I shrugged, "It's not that you can't, but I haven't seen my cousin for a while and just wanted to spend some alone time with him. Can we hang out tomorrow for a bit?" She didn't understand, "K Em, I get it and all, but it's just that I was in Maine so long, and it's like you're different and like you don't want me around."

I felt terrible because in a way, I did feel that way and didn't know why. I was trying to make her feel better and I was sorry I hurt her feelings, "Tomorrow is going to be better weather anyway… so come over tomorrow, and we will take Jack in the pool." She hopped on her bicycle and looked over her shoulder, "Tomorrow I have my soccer game that you said you were coming to, but I guess not, huh?" I had forgotten, "Mars, I didn't realize Aunt Sophia was coming, and Vivien expects me to spend time with them. I'm sorry!" I didn't hear what she mumbled. She turned right to go the long way to her house. I called out, "Mars, please don't be mad!"

I walked home holding my handlebar. Uncle John's truck wasn't in my driveway yet, but I knew they were on their way. I couldn't wait to see them and, I didn't want to think about Mara being mad.

Jack's blonde hair had grown long since our last visit with him and my aunt and uncle. He spoke tons more, and his blue eyes became a shade lighter. We all adored him. Shortly after their arrival, we played hide and seek with Jade and Jenna and in the early evening, we swam in the pool while my mother and her sister talked nonstop under the overhang of our backyard deck. My Uncle John and Franco hit a few balls at the range and we convened for dinner. They were planning to stay for three nights, but my Uncle John was called back home to Mystic, Connecticut a day earlier to bid on a massive project for the architecture firm he was soon to be made a partner of. Aunt Sophia and Jack decided to stay with us for a week longer than initially anticipated. I was happy they did and Vivien was even happier.

The last week in July was super-busy. I hadn't heard from Mara, and she hadn't heard from me since I hurt her feelings. The day before I began my editing camp, I brought Jack to the Luncheonette and Alex gave him free lemonade and slices of salami. Jack loved salami.

I didn't see much of Alex after that visit for the next week, but we spoke every night.

I set my alarm for 7:30 am that week. Vivien dropped me off at 8:50 am every morning and picked me up at 5pm.

Most of our day was spent inside a frigid television studio. The second day, I was sure to remember my sweatshirt. There was a control room, a studio with cameras and enormous lenses on tripods that were on wheels. We practiced fluid movements as camera operators and each of my peers took turns on all the equipment in the control room. I learned about switchers and Chyron. There were huge lights mounted on a heavy metal ceiling grid. The CD/audio players in the studio made my MusiCenter looked like a Fischer-Price phonograph. I loved everything about the environment. Multiple decks were used for Beta and three-quarter inch tape, and a controller between the decks for editing. We had one hour for lunch and during our break, we discussed ideas for scripts we would produce by the last day of camp. I was exhausted by the end of the day. I ate dinner at 6pm, showered and played games with Jack until bedtime.

I went to my room every night by 9pm to call Alex and was asleep a half hour later every night that week.

Reb and Daniel were our counselors. Daniel was in his fourth year of college, and Reb was in her third. Dan taught us about the studio equipment and Reb helped us in the control room. They were both Mass Communication majors and hoped to find employment at any of the major networks. Daniel looked like Kevin Costner, and I thought he was handsome. Reb was equally as pretty and had a cool vibe. We had a lot in common. She played guitar and always wore a visor or baseball cap like me. I felt an immediate attachment to her as we had so much in common.

She called me her mini-me, and I was flattered she did. Vivien was late for pickup on the second to last day of camp. I didn't mind because I got to hang out and talk with Reb. I told her I would really miss her but she promised to be the lead instructor for the following year and made me promise to enroll. I told her I wouldn't miss it! I brought my guitar on the last day of camp and Reb and I strummed and sang Stevie Nick's hit, Edge of Seventeen. I left with a VHS video of our jam that day and showed it to almost everybody I knew. Alex didn't know I even played guitar until I showed her the tape. Vivien was so proud and impressed with all I had learned and after Franco saw it, he said, "Good job Emily. I am happy to see the tuition fees weren't wasted." The following year, the program was discontinued and I never saw Reb again. For a long time, that bothered me. I also missed the television studio. It was a costly program; however, my parents allowed me to follow my passions. Those opportunities helped me mature a tad quicker as a young adult than most of my high school friends. Michael and Alex's presence in my life, did too. I know Reb's impression solidified my excitement to work in television someday.

I felt lonely the night after my last day. Alex was at a family party. Uncle John returned and had a quick dinner with us before I watched him drive away with Aunt Sophia and little Jack. It had been six days since I had spoken to Mara, the longest we ever went without talking.

I saw Scotty and Dean talking across the street and strolled out my front door. "Hey guys," I said as I approached them. Dean was bouncing a black handball in the street. Scotty acknowledged my presence, "Hey Emily, where have you been?" I mentioned my camp but they were uninterested, so I didn't provide details. Just then, Mara and Lucy turned the corner onto our block. I assumed they were coming from the park. I felt awkward but acted as I usually would have and started walking toward the girls. "Hey guys," I sounded upbeat. Lucy looked at Mara and at that point, I was sure Mara had told Lucy about our fight. They ignored me and Lucy said to Scotty, "Yesterday was so funny, huh?" Scotty and Dean laughed. I felt left out. "What happened yesterday?" Mara immediately answered, "Nothing, it was a *had-to-be-there* moment. You wouldn't get it." I was appalled and said, "Try me!" Mara said, "Nah, just forget it!"

Scotty made up some excuse to go inside and Dean followed him. The girls said nothing for longer than a minute. The minute felt like an hour and while we were all waiting for someone to say something first, I said, "Do you guys want to take a swim or something?" Lucy looked at Mara again. I looked at Mara too. "Seriously you are still mad, Mars?" She tapped down her kickstand. "Yeah Em, I am. I really am. Ever since I've been back from Maine, you've been weird and it's not just me, right Lucy? Tell her!" I stared down at Lucy. "What did I do to you, Lucy?" She stepped back and said, "You didn't do anything but it's just that you're never around, so it seems you don't want to hang out with us, since you have your new friends." I felt like the entire neighborhood was talking about me behind my back. I was defensive, "I've been at a camp for nine hours a day, and I had family visiting. I mean, really guys?" Mara blurted out all her thoughts, "Ya know, it's true! You have time for Alex and your new group, and even Lucy thought it was so mean you didn't let me go with you and Jack to Lisa's house." I was being attacked and ganged up on. "Mara, you got so offended because I wanted to see Jack the first night he came. I specifically asked you about the next day, and then you were mad I couldn't come to your soccer game, but you spent quality time in Maine without me, with your cousins and *your* family." Mara looked at Lucy again before answering, "Whatever, Em, maybe I need to buy a Camaro to be your friend." I was fuming, "That's so unfair, Mara!" I protested, "How come it's okay for you can hang out with other friends and talk nonstop about Adam Byron and his heavy metal friends? You went to the movies with all of them, but I am supposed to sit at home while you're at LBH. This is so stupid, Mars. We can have other friends and still be friends." She slid her foot to the side of her kickstand and swiped it up. "Best friends or just friends? Whatever!"

She pedaled away and Lucy just stood there. I was angry and said, "I'm done and I'm going in, Lucy." As I walked away, Lucy said, "Sorry, Emily, I'm not the one who said anything. All I said to Mara was that I agreed you haven't been around. I turned back and replied, "Well, this is why! There is so much drama and arguing over Ringolevio and it's annoying and really immature. Whatever, see ya around."

I never knew the Ringolevio game we played that very first evening of summer would have been our last.

Chapter Seven

Brian shut down the Luncheonette for two weeks in August every year. Alex had fourteen days off in a row. We hit the beach every day the weather cooperated. Sadly, summer was almost over.

On a warm, rainy Thursday in August, we took a ride to Aunt Annie's. We had lunch outside on her small porch. The rain stopped while we enjoyed fresh, homemade spaghetti pizza. It was as good as Vivien's cooking. I asked Aunt Annie for the recipe and hoped Viv would make it for me. Annie put out cold cuts and small pastries. She talked so much about her late husband, who died from a fluke heart attack when he was only thirty-four. She seemed much younger than she was. It was the third time we had visited her that summer. She always hugged me, once when we arrived and again when we said our goodbyes.

Annie was a gymnast in her younger days. There were black and white pictures of her wearing metals that hung over her long-sleeved leotard on the walls of her small beach house. She never had children and never remarried, so Annie lived there alone. She loved Alex and welcomed me when I joined in on their visits. I used to listen to her stories about her meets, and she was as interested in listening to stories Alex and I told her about our summer excursions. She seemed happy and Alex told me her husband left her with plenty of money so she wouldn't ever have to work again.

After lunch we were beach-bound as usual after our visit. Alex pulled the blanket out of the hatch and we trekked to our familiar spot away from the water's edge. I took a sip of my Coca-Cola and Alex looked at me with a huge grin. "Why are you staring me down like that?" Alex was beaming. "Well, I got some news you may be happy about!" She had my attention, "Okay, spill the beans then." Alex put her hand on my shoulder, "Okay so, I was talking to Tom next door and…Wait, do you even know Tom?" I didn't, "Tom, who?" Alex took her hand off my shoulder and grabbed my bottle of Coke. She took a swig and placed it back in my lap, "Okay, so Tom owns the travel agency next door to Brian's." I replied, "Oh, I know him! I just never really paid attention to that place. Is he the guy with the short blonde hair?"

Alex nodded, "Yep, that's Tom. His father retired and practically gave him the business. So, we talked about it when I was grabbing hero bread out back. Anyway, he was throwing out some garbage." I was still paying attention but wanted her to get to the point quicker, "Okay, and what's the good news?" Alex said, "Hold your horses and listen to my story. So, he told me about how two girls quit and it was his busy time. Okay, so Em, you have a job if you want it!" I was in shock, "Huh? Me? Tom is going to hire me to work in the travel agency?" Alex was so excited, "Yep, and you need to stop in either later today or tomorrow and talk to him." I was elated.

I would finally be able to earn my own money. I would be working around the block, and right next door would be the Luncheonette and Alex. I rose to my knees and gave her the tightest hug. "Thank you for telling him about me. I can't wait to tell my parents, and wow, did he say how many hours? Did he say how much? Does he know school starts soon?" Alex started giggling, "Oh, hold your twenty questions for Tom but do me a favor?" she asked, "Try to play it a little cooler. You want him to think you're eager to work, not desperate, okay?" I was still thrilled, "Yeah, I'll be cool with Tom, but Alex, I am so psyched! Thank you! You are truly my best friend. I want to go talk to Tom now if we can?" She put her hand in the air and we high-fived. "Em, I know some of my friends think you are just a kid, but I don't care what they say. You are my best friend too."

Her words meant the world to me.

Alex and I left the beach and sang to Almost Paradise, by Mike Reno and Ann Wilson louder than ever. We pulled up in the strip parking lot and I was a little nervous. "Alex, should I be dressed differently? Is this like a job interview?" Alex shrugged, "Emily, you look great. It's fine, c'mon."

We opened the door to Majestic Travel and Tom looked up from his desk. Alex introduced us and excused herself, "Tom, I'm going to get a newspaper. Emily, I'll meet you at Mack's?" I couldn't believe she was bailing on me but she winked as she left. Tom was friendly and asked me to sit beside his desk. He told me he needed me to answer phones and fill out information sheets. He said he always had filing and asked me if I had typing skills. We negotiated my wage, start date and hours within ten minutes.

Tom stood up and reached out his hand. We shook, and he said, "See you at nine on Saturday, Emily. It was nice to meet you." I was excited and started walking to Mack's, "Em, I'm here." I abruptly turned towards her voice and saw Alex sitting in her car. I skipped over and got in. "I thought you were at Mack's?" Alex wanted details. "I didn't need to buy a paper, silly. I just said that so you could talk to Tom. And… well, how did it go?" I deliberately threw my head back against the car seat and exhaled, "Well, I'm starting this Saturday, and he's paying me $4.65 an hour. I can't believe this, Alex! Wait till I tell my parents. This is so cool!" Alex smiled, "That's awesome, Em. And that's more than minimum wage. I'm truly happy for you." I told Alex practically every word of our conversation as she drove slowly around the block toward my house.

My folks were in the kitchen just finishing dinner. I stormed in and Alex was right behind me. I immediately blurted out, "I got a job!" My parents waited for more explanation. I told them about my talk with Tom, and he mentioned he would like to meet one or both of my parents at some point. He wanted to make sure they were okay with me taking a job. Both were! My Dad thanked Alex for getting me *out of his wallet* and Vivien was shocked I volunteered to start in two short days on Labor Day Weekend. "No problem, Mr. Netti," Alex said. "It's time she stops freeloading, huh?" I sneered at her but jokingly, and Franco tapped his hand on her back. I didn't care about it being a holiday weekend. Brian was re-opening that same Saturday, which meant Alex's vacation was over too. I didn't hesitate when Alex sat beside my father, "Well, Mom, it's my last night of summer and I want to sleep over at Alex's cause we are all going out to Rock-a-Fellas tonight." Vivien didn't like that and questioned, "Alex is she old enough to go there?" Alex replied confidently, "Oh yes, Mrs. Netti, I take my sisters there too." Vivien asked, "But they serve alcohol, so I don't understand?" Alex explained, "They let you in if you are sixteen, and they give you a bracelet if you are nineteen. We just dance like fools." Vivien added, "She's not sixteen." I saved Alex from answering, "Mom, I told you Leo owns it and knows Alex's Dad from the butcher shop.

He knows Sophie and I are almost old enough and plus, we're with Alex. Even Rae is going. I promise it's just to go and dance and have fun." Franco slid his chair out and stood up. He handed me twenty bucks and said, "Hey, have fun and be careful. Treat Alex to some food and soda; that's the last twenty bucks you will get from me." He walked away singing his own made-up jingle, "Baby's got a job and is not freeloading anymore." Alex cracked up and Vivien just shook her head. "Mom, can I go and have our last summer sleepover?" Alex looked at Vivien,

"I'll take care of her, Mrs. Netti, I promise." Vivien gave Alex a nod of approval and said, "Yes, go get your stuff. You can go." It was the most incredible end to summer. We danced to the seventies disco. Alex's college friends were there, and Sophie and Rae were there. Johnny stopped by for an hour or so too. It was the fourth time I met him, but the first night he stuck around for more than a few minutes. He talked to me at the bar, but the music was so loud it was hard to carry on a conversation. He asked Alex to order him a beer. He wasn't of drinking age either, but he handed Alex ten bucks and she ordered him a beer.

Some parts of him reminded me of a younger Franco. He took a few gulps, placed it down and grabbed Rae's arm. I watched him pull her through the crowd and head to the dance floor. Alex, Sophie and I followed them. We stood on the threshold of the dance floor. They started dancing together and they were outstanding. Johnny danced like Travolta in Saturday Night Fever. I couldn't believe it. People began making a circle around them, clapping and cheering them on.

The music was even louder on the dance floor. I tugged Alex's shirt and leaned in to scream into her ear, "I didn't know Rae could dance like that, and Johnny is awesome too! Wow, Alex! She leaned into my ear, "I know, right? They are so good. They used to take ballroom lessons together when they were little and Johnny always spins her around at family weddings and... I guess tonight too." Alex didn't see much of Johnny even though they lived in the same house. He was usually with his friends and he had three paper routes in different towns that he and his friend, Anthony, worked before and after school. He was a hustler and always had a lot of cash on hand. I always thought he looked at me disapprovingly and I wasn't sure why, but he was sweet to me that night for a few brief moments before

he grabbed his sister and took off to the dance floor.
Two of their cousins I had met at the festival earlier that
summer showed up. They were dressed up to the nines, in
sequence tops and skirts with long black high-heeled boots.
Alex's three friends from college were there, but they
didn't pay much mind to me or Sophie and Rae.
Alex managed to split her time between all of us. She was
the common denominator and once we were all out on the
dance floor, it didn't matter much who was spending more
time with who.
When Alex danced with Melissa and Joanne, Rae and
Sophie and I took a few sips of Alex's, Tom Collins.
Neither of us liked it very much and we knew Alex would
be fuming if she saw us. Sophie was about to give her
phone number to an eighteen-year-old, at which point,
Alex bee-lined over and broke up that conversation. Alex
grabbed Sophie and said, "Sophie, that guy looks like a
dirtbag and is way too old for you! What were you
thinking?"
I think that's when Rae pointed out Sophie that had too
many sips of Alex's, Tom Collins, and Alex was not
happy. It was the end of the summer celebration to
remember. We left Rock-A-Fellas and ended up at the
local diner eating eggs and toast at two-thirty in the
morning.
Sophie was funnier than ever and Rae and I laughed at
everything she said. Alex sat at the other side of the table
with the more mature and less fun, Melissa, Joanne, and
her boyfriend. Tired and full, Alex drove us home with the
radio low, and Sophie half passed out in the car. Rae
helped her to the basement and we all slept hard and long.
The next day the four of us packed up our bags, stopped at
Arturo's for sandwiches and arrived at the town beach just
before one in the afternoon. It was a delightful eighty-three
degrees with a slight breeze. I took out my writing journal

and a pen. I jotted down a poem that came to mind as I sat there staring down at my feet buried in the sand.

Alex came back from the snack bar without Sophie and Rae. "Where are your sisters?" I asked. "They ran into some school friends, and they're chatting it up. What are you writing?" I handed her my notebook. She immediately returned it and said, "Read it to me, Em." I read my poem to Alex.

I say goodbye to summer, east of the
moon. A comfort in sunsets, gone way
too soon.
Eyes have been
discovered.
No intentions were
revealed.
A soulful calmness and a future
appealed. The newness comes fall.
What is to come?
An awe-wonder something, under a soon winter
moon. Farewell to sand soothing my soul.
And welcome fresh air and blustery snow. ~Kim Mazzei

When I was finished, she said, "That's really beautiful, Em. You just wrote that from outta nowhere?" I nodded and closed my book. "Yeah, sometimes I just think of stuff and if I have my journal, I write it down." Alex thought my poem was good.

"Emily, you should write more poems or even a book. You should become a writer." Alex was not short of compliments; it always made me feel so good. "Thanks, Alex. I don't know about becoming a writer. I think I want to edit music videos for MTV. I do like to write, though. Vivien tells me I should become a writer too."

Sophie and Rae returned, and we spent the rest of the afternoon jumping through waves. We ate our sandwiches and enjoyed juicy watermelon. I let Rae and Sophie bury me in the sand from the neck down and we took silly pictures with my camera. An entire roll of twenty-four. I couldn't wait to develop them and asked Alex to take them to the Fotomat by her house as soon as possible. She promised she would, and I hugged her when she dropped me off at home. "Okay, I'll call you before I go to sleep. I can't believe I'm starting my job tomorrow morning." I blew a kiss to Sophie and Rae in the back and winked at Alex. They all wished me luck and I went inside.

I realized I was so sunburned after my shower. I put on loose-fitting pajamas and went downstairs. I sat on the hassock in front of Vivien. "Mom, can you put this on my shoulders?" Vivien took the lotion from my hands, "Oh my, Emily, you have quite a sunburn. Does it hurt?" I admitted, "It does, Mom, and I am so tired." Vivien understood, "You must be," she said as she gently applied lotion to my back and shoulders. "I hope you drank enough water and now you should get some rest." She flipped the cap to close the lotion and handed it to me.

Franco let out a loud snoring sound on the couch, and both Vivien and I were startled. We both scoffed, "Goodnight, Mom. Thanks for letting me go last night. It was so much fun." She responded, "Okay, tell me all about it tomorrow. Get some rest, and do you want me to drive you around the block in the morning?"

I stopped by the edge of the steps and peeked back in, leaning my head against the molding. "No, Mom, I'm just gonna walk. I'm leaving at seven forty-five and having breakfast with Mara at Brian's before I start work at nine." Vivien smiled, "Oh, I'm glad you two made up." I replied, "We really didn't, but she said we could discuss it over breakfast. So stupid how Mara holds a grudge for so long. Goodnight, Mom." She reminded me that Michael and Audrey were coming back the next day and said we would all have dinner together. I said, "okay," and I climbed the stairs. I settled in bed and grabbed my phone and called Alex. She answered on one ring. I said, "Hey, I'm so tired. I had so much fun last night and today!" Alex agreed, "Rae and Sophie fell asleep in the car on the way home and we are all so sunburned." I told her I was too. We were about to hang up when Alex asked, "Em, do you think everybody sees the beauty in sunsets the way we do?" I smiled and glanced up at my ceiling. I replied, "Alex, it's not just the sunsets; it's who you're watching them with. I hope everyone sees a sunset with someone who *sees* a sunset." I heard her smile. "Em, you're *not* a punk." I laughed out loud, "Nope, Johnny is a *punk*." She answered, "Yes, my John-John is a *punk*."

I pictured her expression. "Hey, kid, you wrote a beautiful poem about a beautiful summer." There was a moment of silence on the line before I said, "Alex, every summer has a story and this summer… was the story of us."

She replied, "Em, that's another great line. Go write that down in your journal. Get some sleep kiddo, and I'll see you tomorrow. Enjoy breakfast with Mara in the morning. I'll be there by noon. Stop in after your first day on the job." I answered, "I planned on it. Goodnight, Alex." I hung up the phone and felt like a grownup.

The summer of 1984 went faster than the blink of an eye. September was fast-paced and ever-changing. When I came home from my first day of work from Majestic Travel, Michael was sitting at the kitchen table with his head in his hands. Vivien was seated across from him, and Franco poured himself a scotch on the rocks. I saw tears in his eyes. I was concerned and walked right over to my brother and put my hand on his back. He hugged me tenderly and whispered, "Hey, Em." He returned home from South Carolina and told my parents how he and Audrey broke up. She was planning to move to South Carolina because her

father knew someone who offered her a job. Michael was upset that Audrey didn't even discuss it with him. She set up her whole life and just told him as a matter of fact, on the way home in the car. Michael said the thirteen-hour drive home was horrible.

I thought Vivien was secretly happy the love affair between them was over, although she never said it. She consoled my brother most lovingly.

Franco told Michael there were other fish in the sea and not to sweat it. I was shocked and devastated months after, and Michael wasn't himself for a long time. He was either miserable and quiet or just plain nasty. I didn't even realize how much I liked Audrey until she stopped coming around. I saw her once more, twelve years later, at an October-Fest in the village of a neighboring town. She was still living in South Carolina but visiting her mom in New York. Her husband gently rocked a stroller a few feet away, talking sports with my then-boyfriend, Jesse. She asked about Michael and my parents. She hugged me and said I had grown into a beautiful woman. She told me Jesse was perfect for me and I should marry him as soon as possible. Jesse pretended not to hear. He said little and waited for our conversation to end.

It was a total fluke that we ran into each other. It was not a fluke; her eleven-month-old son was named Michael.

I started my junior year of high school on Alex's 19th Birthday, September 5th. Mara and I walked to the Luncheonette after school. Brian had a small Carvel cake for her, and we sang Happy Birthday. I didn't stay too long. Vivien was taking Mara and me to pick up school supplies. Before I saw Mom's car pull up outside, I handed Alex a bag and told her it was her birthday gift. I told her to open it after work at home and she said she would. I told her I wished I could see her face when she opened it, but I preferred her to have her gift on her real birthday. I didn't want to wait until Friday night when it was assumed I'd see her next.

I wrapped one big box. I bought her one funny card and another serious Blue Mountain Arts card about friendship. Inside the box were three separately wrapped gifts. One was a mixed cassette with all our favorite songs from the Summer of '84. I made it myself with perfect two-second pauses between each song.

I wrote on the label in black marker, "Our Fav Tunes – AE - Summer '84." I also made a photo collage book. I cut out words and sayings from Viv's old issues of Redbook Magazine and carefully placed them around zany pictures we took throughout the summer. I bought her a Swatch Quartz Watch and wrapped it specially, with a bow that I made from colored ribbon. It had a metallic face and cost me an entire paycheck plus some.

That evening, she called me from her room, "Em, you put so much creativity into my birthday. Your gifts are so special. I am listening to the cassette, and I love it! I am so happy and I can't wait to listen to it together," I replied. "Maybe Friday, we can take a ride?" Alex was distracted, "Hold on, Em," she said. I heard Sophie's voice in the background, and Alex returned a few moments later. "Em, I have to meet up with Melissa, Joanne, and this guy Christian after classes on Friday. We have a group project to get underway, and Friday was just the day that everyone could get together." I was disappointed, "Oh, I just thought we would celebrate your birthday? Will you be working with them the whole night?" Alex heard the disappointment in my voice, "Well, we are meeting at the library at about

4pm, and to be honest, they all offered to take me out afterward for my birthday. How 'bout I pick you up Saturday afternoon, and we hit the mall and grab a bite?"

I was disappointed and upset. I expected to be and wanted to be a priority in Alex's life. She seemed entitled to have a separate life with her boyfriend, work friends, school friends, and sisters that didn't include me. When I had occasional plans to see Mara or other friends, she would seem annoyed by that. When Alex and I had disagreements, it was usually over plans that didn't include the other.

I was tired and not used to the early mornings that came along with the grueling school schedule.

"Okay, Saturday it is. Maybe I'll call Mara or go to that party on Friday." She said nothing, and I gave her the typical blow-off, "I'm really tired and think I'm going to try to sleep now." She got the point, "Talk to you tomorrow, Em." she said, "Thank you for my gifts, love them and love you. Goodnight, my friend."

My room was quiet and dark. I had no intention of attending the heavy metal keg party at some kid Lenny's house. I preferred a night out with Alex, Sophie, and Rae. I leaned over and clicked my night light off.

I thought about the first day of school. It went as well as it could have. I loved my schedule and lucked out with the teachers I wanted. Mara was in two of my classes.

English and Geometry. It was a challenging year, and I was a conscientious student. I met Alex at her campus library to prep for the SATs while she had many exams to study for. She was graduating college that year, and her workload was highly demanding.

My job at Majestic was working out great. I worked three days weekly, and Tom was flexible with my hours. I could pop into Brian's to say hi to Alex, and she popped into

Majestic to do the same.

1984 gave me many firsts, and many lasts. It was my first sunset on a rooftop. It was my last summer of Ringolevio with the neighborhood crew. Lucy was with her boyfriend constantly. Scotty and Dean frequently rented rink time for ice hockey practice. Howie's parents sold their house, and they were set to move in January. Davie played acoustic guitar in local pubs everywhere. He made a few bucks, and he had a local following. He was talented. I always regretted quitting guitar when I heard Dave play.

We were all coming of age and socializing more off the premises of our neighborhood.

Mara and I spent the rest of that summer squabbling over almost everything. We did several more of our usual runs to and from the park and Lanes. It was becoming less enjoyable to hang out both because we were outgrowing Jungle King and outgrowing each other. Mara seemed upset that I became close with Alex and her sisters while she was in Maine and as that summer continued,

Mara probably felt someone had taken her place in my life, and there was some truth to that. I tried to involve her in some of our excursions. She even joined us a handful of times at the movies and the mall, but she didn't seem to blend into the group with ease. It was hard not to notice that Alex and I had an undeniable connection, and Mara and I were simply growing in different directions. It didn't help when Adam Byron asked Mara out in the second week of school, and they were inseparable after that. Joanne, who was dating Adam's twin brother, told me during lunch that Mara was having sex with Adam. I acted as if I already knew. I never asked Mara about it. It was her business to tell or not tell me, and she decided not to. I didn't like Adam and Joe Byron's crowd. They listened to Iron Maiden and went to keg parties on weekends at the houses that did not have parents at home. I wasn't a fan of heavy metal, beer or high school parties.

So, while Mara and the neighborhood kids disappeared into their own lives, I continued hopping into the Camaro, sometimes with Rae and Sophie and sometimes without.

Alex picked me up every Tuesday afternoon and taught me how to drive. Usually, I drove in vast open beach parking lots before we rested or walked by the water's edge, even in the winter. Alex made me swear to her, to never let anyone know she let me drive her car. Sophie and Rae never drove her Camaro and neither did Johnny.

We were always going somewhere and the plans happened impulsively. Vivien had difficulty letting me grow into my own, and the curfews caused fights. I didn't blatantly disrespect my curfew; I just argued and thought it was unfair. Alex didn't have a curfew, and even my friends of the same age seemed to be allowed to stay out later than Vivien proposed. It was frustrating for both of us.

Vivien never said it, but I suspected she didn't love the idea of me hanging around Alex as much as I did. It was how I thought she felt about Audrey. She never said she was relieved when Audrey and Michael broke up, but I knew she was. She liked Alex but always made it a point to explain how she was older than me and how I shouldn't expect to have the same liberties. Perhaps she had other reasons, too.

Chapter Eight

I registered for two classes at the local State University the summer after my junior year. It made my senior year a breeze. I fulfilled my high school math and science requirements and earned a few credits to apply to college. I took AP Literature, Human Geography, and two electives, Creative Writing and Italian.

My eleven-thirty dismissal and my Volkswagen Beetle were the ultimate liberations. Vivien was starting to loosen the collar once I started driving, and she was proud, it seemed. I was growing into a responsible young adult. I was still expected to check in via phone and I did, but I was rarely home. I worked for Tom at the travel agency until he relocated the business two weeks before my high school graduation. I had saved up a few thousand dollars and I was thrilled to have zero commitments other than trying to spend as much time at the beach as possible before my college life began. My GPA was strong, and my SAT score secured a ten-thousand-dollar scholarship to Palm Beach University. Franco was thrilled. After opening my acceptance letter in early January, I hadn't thought much about how leaving would feel seven-plus months later. I was having loads of fun managing a full social calendar.

I was dating Charlie Jensen on and off that entire year. Charlie attended Alex's University. He was a college freshman when Alex was a senior. I met Charlie on their campus in the school library. He dropped a book as he walked by our table. The book slipped out of his hands and hit the floor with an echoing bang that made all eyes gape at him. He was so embarrassed and had red, rosy cheeks. He picked up the book, took a slight bow and pulled out the chair at our table.

Alex and I put our heads back into our textbooks but when I glanced up, I couldn't help to notice Charlie noticing me. We spent another half hour or so before Alex quietly nodded and I knew that meant it was time to pack it up and head out. As we pushed open the heavy glass door to exit, Charlie closed his textbook and followed behind.

He was crazy about me when that book slammed on the library floor, so he told me on our second date. After our casual hello and goodbye outside the library parking lot, he searched to find Alex every day for over a week, and one day he finally did catch up with her. She called me to say, "Em, Clumsy Chuck is stalking me on campus! He wants to date you and wants your number. He ran up behind me like some psycho and scared the shit out of me!" I was a tad excited to hear the news. Charlie was in college and he was adorable. My first boyfriend, in eighth grade, hardly resembled a relationship. In ninth grade, I was Evan's girlfriend for about two months before I broke up with him because he was always sweating profusely. In eleventh grade, I dated Phillip Russo for a short stint but when he figured out, I was not interested in losing my virginity to him, he dumped me.

Charlie seemed like an exciting prospect. "He asked you to give him my number. Did you?" She sounded mortified, "Em, I wouldn't just give your number to some stranger. I mean, we don't even know him. What? We met him for five seconds after what sounded like an explosion in the library."

I laughed out loud, "Oh, Alex, you always bring the drama. He was cute, wasn't he? I'm considering letting him take me out on a date. Who knows, it could be fun. Worst case scenario, I get a free meal and politely decline a second date or tell him to lose my number." Alex giggled at my response, "Well, what if we set something up to meet him with Derrick one night at Larkfield's or Times?"

That sounded great, and I agreed, "Okay, matchmaker, set that up and you can decide if you approve of Charlie." Alex said, "Emily, I'm certain I won't ever think anybody is good enough for you, but okay. We may have some laughs, and Derrick can size him up. Anyway, what are you doing? Want to take a ride? Can you come pick me up because I lent Johnny my car and I have cabin fever?" I was shocked, "You are letting Johnny drive the Camaro?" She answered, "First time for everything, I suppose." I picked her up an hour later and off we went to surprise Aunt Annie.

Charlie and I instantly connected on our first date, finding a shared passion in classic cars. His love for his 1957 Chevy, a gift from his grandpa mirrored my affection for my yellow bug, a car he thought perfectly matched my personality. We had a lot in common. He had a younger sister and their relationship was consistent with that of Michael and me. We both loved classic cars. He loved my yellow bug and seemed to like me quite a bit.

His grandpa gave him his vintage Chevy. I asked him on our first date if he had to 'wax on and wax off' to get it. I knew he had never seen Karate Kid because he didn't get it. I think he thought I was saying something sexual and the whole thing was awkward. Nonetheless, we both had cool rides. Franco loved Charlie's car. Vivien seemed thrilled whenever Charlie came to pick me up and would often invite him to stay for dinner. Usually, we wouldn't. A lot was going on. After work and school, our social lives were our primary focus. I didn't see much of Charlie during the week, although sometimes I would meet him at a local pub for wings and a quick game of pool. Charlie and I would often double-date with Alex and Derrick for dinner and a movie on weekends. The four of us spent a lot of time together.

Derrick worked at his uncle's gas station around the block from the university. Sophie thought Derrick looked like the boy we followed and named Marcello years earlier at the Italian festival. She would ask, "Alex, if you don't marry Derrick, can I?" And Alex always rolled her eyes, knowing that was just Sophie… being Sophie.

As blizzard conditions loomed, I made plans to stay at Alex's on that first Friday evening in February. The anticipation of a cozy night in, stocked up on chips & dip, hot chocolate, and other essentials filled me with a sense of comfort and security.

We were all set in the cozy basement adorned with blankets, pillows and a few movies we rented from Blockbuster. We created a warm and nostalgic atmosphere.

Alex's parents were in Pennsylvania visiting relatives who had come from Italy. Johnny kept to himself in his room. We could always tell when he was up, his footsteps echoing above us every two hours as he made his way to the kitchen and hovered over the opened fridge.

While Rae and I played a game of seven-card rummy, I mentioned that Charlie invited me to go skiing for a long weekend in Vermont. Sophie immediately commented, "Oh my God, Emily, he is so sweet, cute and crazy about you. I heard him tell Johnny at Mack's that his girlfriend is gorgeous and he just went on and on about you." Alex made a face at Sophie and then she asked, "Vivien is letting you go with your boyfriend to Vermont for Valentine's weekend?" I didn't appreciate her tone and became defensive, "Alex, I am not a little kid anymore! And yeah, Vivien is fine with it. We are going with his parents and his sister anyway." Alex said nothing more, and neither did I. She was overprotective and that's how she was with Sophie and Rae too. I knew that's just how Alex was, even though she and Derrick went on overnights.

Sophie popped in Ferris Bueller's Day Off and we snacked on chips and laughed. Next, we watched Risky Business and Sophie could not shut up about how cute Tom Cruise was. I was the last to fall asleep during our third movie rental, Rocky IV.

The weather outside was bitter cold, the kind that seeps into your bones. The snow had fallen overnight, leaving a white blanket of wind drifts measuring three and four feet. By early morning Johnny and two of his friends had the driveway and walkway cleared, the cold visible in the frosty air.

Sophie nudged my shoulder, "Hey, Em I'm going up. I smell breakfast and going to go get me some." I unwrapped myself from the plaid blanket and followed upstairs after Sophie.

Alex and Rae were a culinary duo and made enough breakfast for us and twenty more guests who weren't coming. Johnny, and his two buddies, fueled up with a hearty breakfast of scrambled eggs and bacon before heading out with their snow shovels to make a buck or two. Sophie was the music enthusiast and immediately blasted her favorite new Squeeze album and we danced around while cleaning the kitchen. We sat around a bit. Rae and I played more card games. I tried to teach her how to play chess, but she wasn't catching on. The time spent at their house always felt like home. The kitchen smelled similar to Vivien's. It didn't matter that Rae couldn't quite grasp the intricacies of my chess lesson. What mattered was the bond we shared, the feeling of family that permeated the air. We accepted one another, quirks and all, even when we got on each other's nerves. I never had companions like them in high school. As the plow trucks cleared the roads, I reluctantly drove home in the cold, though the warmth of our friendship lingered in my heart.

The snow had melted and high school graduation was less than six weeks away. I could not wait to be finished with every bit of it. Many of my classmates would stand around their lockers hugging, even crying all day about high school coming to an end. However, I wasn't sad at all.

I didn't feel I fit into mainstream high school. I felt different and I wasn't sure why. There were so many functions and parties for seniors. It seemed overwhelming. There were school parties and then there were private parties. I was mostly invited through a friend of a friend. Mara attended all the senior functions and I saw her when I attended a few, but we had fallen short of our real friendship years past. Alex became my best friend, but she was not always part of my world and was extremely wrapped up in her own.

Charlie was nice to me. Even though we broke up several months before my senior prom, he agreed to be my date. He fit the part. He was appropriate, fun and cute. He looked great in a tux and was in college, making him the perfect date for such an occasion. Once I arrived and settled in, I was grateful he was conversing with a friend of mine. I was then able to veer off on my own.

Truthfully, I only went to my prom so I didn't regret not going. Decades later, a beautiful young girl I named Sami asked me about my prom when she tried on dresses for her own. I was happy her mom had a few stories to recollect. While all the seniors were going to the beach after the party and celebrate all weekend on the Jersey Shore, I opted out of the planned agenda. It was so easy for me to do so. I was still not like the other colors. I could not wait to get home!

Charlie pulled over on a side street close to my house. I knew he had to leave early in the morning for a business trip. In the summer, he worked, for Kraft Foods and traveled to various store openings, usually in New Jersey or Connecticut. He would be gone three or four days, and I wasn't counting. We were broken up after all and it wasn't my vision to spend the upcoming summer together.

I still wasn't shocked when he leaned over, grabbed my cheeks, and placed his lips on mine. It wasn't the first time he chose that dark street to enjoy a goodbye that he would not dare take pleasure in on my driveway. I kissed Charlie back for a minute. I felt his blonde, trimmed mustache under my nose. Charlie was a decent kisser when he wanted to be. He would be too rough at times, and I would have to slow him down just as I did that evening. I pulled back and thanked him, "I know you have to wake up in four hours. Sorry to keep you out so late at a high school senior prom no less. He smiled, "It was fun, Em. Plus, I couldn't let your other boyfriend Justin, take you."

Justin was a boy who drew pictures and gave many of them to me. I was always friendly, and I complimented his work. He was a fantastic artist, but I didn't want to go out with Justin. The whole senior class was aware of his slight obsession with me, but I knew Justin was as harmless as he was persistent.

Charlie loosened his bow tie and placed it in his cup holder, "I like spending time with you," he paused. "I'm not sure why we even broke up. We're great together, Emily." I was too tired to have the same old repetitive conversation with him. "Charlie, thank you for being a perfect date and escort," I said. He took my left hand and held it in both of his, "Emily, I was thinking… don't leave for Florida. Go to college here and give me a few years to finish my stuff. I love you. I told you this. I know you think I'm just saying this because I told you I want to make love to you, but I'm not just saying it. I don't want a long-distance relationship, and I don't want to lose you. Please reconsider and go to a local college, Emily, please."

I felt terrible that I didn't feel the same about him, and I couldn't tell him that again so instead, I answered, "Charlie, I worked my ass off for this scholarship. I'm sorry but I have to go and I want to go." He was sad and then his sadness turned into anger, "You wanna know something, Emily? I waited for you. I never cheated. You and all your... your virgin crap! Why, what for? You are waiting? For who?" I sat there in shock and silence. "When two people care about each other, it's a natural occurrence, Emily. I always went along with any plan of yours. By the way, I can't stand Derrick! He's an asshole, and I tried to hang out with him, with them. Do you want to know why? Because your head is so far up Alex's ass, and she's dumb enough to date that idiot." I was mortified! "Charlie, bring me home now! I'm sorry you spent countless hours with Alex and Derrick pretending you were having fun. And I am sorry. No, I'm not sorry and I'm not ready to have sex with you!" He pulled up in my driveway and I couldn't open the door fast enough. I was already keying in my front door as Charlie stood by my walkway with his hands in the air calling my name. I pretended not to hear him. I slammed the door and darted upstairs carrying my heels in hand. My feet throbbed. I slowly opened my parents' bedroom door.

They were sound asleep. I walked to Vivien's side of the bed and gently rocked her shoulder, "Mom, I'm home." She mumbled something I couldn't understand and said, "Okay Em, you looked so beautiful. Tell me everything tomorrow." I kissed her forehead and whispered, "I will. Goodnight, Mom."

My high school graduation came. Franco and Vivien were proud of the yellow-gold honor cord draped over my gown. I was among the small group of students who graduated with the highest academic honors.

The pool was open, and there was usual company in and out on weekends all summer. However, that weekend Franco and Vivien weren't hosting. They had gone to Atlantic City for the weekend. The boardwalk and casino, their favorite playground.

Michael was on his own and living in an apartment about twenty minutes away. He was dating on and off but primarily working hard for a law firm that swooped him up upon graduation with impressive LSATs. He passed the bar exam and was headed for riches. He wanted to make partner by the time he turned thirty and he did.

That summer he came over weekly and the four of us ate Vivien's infamous Sunday dinner. He never brought a date but always dressed as if he had. He talked about his cases and his rousing nightlife, often meshed with business associates and the latest blonde of the month.

I never asked him how much money he made but he drove a brand-new Audi and dressed in name brands. He often lent me money and when I tried to pay him back, he waved his hand in the air the way Franco did and that meant I could keep it.

We had a decent sibling relationship but didn't spend much time together outside of when he came to visit my folks to get a home cooked meal.

He did take me out every year around Christmas time. He would pick me up and we'd go for dinner and to the mall. He would always treat me and appreciated that I helped pick perfect gifts for Franco and Viv. He used to take them home, wrap them, and on the label would write, from Michael and Em. That was super nice of him I thought to give me credit when I didn't contribute financially.

It was a near-perfect July afternoon and I planned to sit poolside. It was great when my parents left for an overnight stay, and I could enjoy the home amenities even though I hated being alone all night.

I heard the gate swing open and sat up on my lounge chair. Alex skipped into the backyard with a knapsack, brown paper bag, and a towel draped over her shoulders. "Em, I had like zero gas and this morning Rae aggravated the shit out of me. Wait until I tell you about that! Johnny and my mom had a brawl over him trying to move out and you have no idea how I'm so done with Brian too. And does Viv have any of her homemade iced tea? I'm parched!" Alex took a breath. I stood up, "Sure we do, let's get some shall we?" She looked puzzled and replied, "Some… what?" I began walking up the three steps to the door that led into the kitchen, "You're parched, remember? So, let's go get some of Viv's iced tea." Alex nodded in agreement and started behind me, "Did you even hear anything else I said?" I grabbed two plastic cups from the cabinet, "Indeed, I heard everything." I poured us an iced tea with fresh squeezed lemons, "Why is Rae bugging you? And is Brian asking you to switch hours again?"

She opened the brown bag and took out a bucket of chicken, "Here put this in the fridge for later." I was happy, "Mmm, fried chicken from Zonno's, my fav. Thanks Alex!" I put the bucket in the fridge and left the pieces of cornbread and napkins on the counter.

Alex already grabbed her cup and walked out back. I was close behind, placed my cup on the table, and positioned myself in a semi-upright position on my lounge chair. Alex put her knapsack on the pavers and slung her towel over the chair. She walked around and tucked all four corners under the plastic straps.

"Em, I'm sorry about last week. I hate when we have

arguments. I'm going to miss you, and I'm feeling really sad about it. I mean, I don't know how you even feel, and you aren't saying anything. So tight-lipped and you are leaving in a month. Oh my God, Em."

Alex plunged down sitting, facing my lounge. I swung my leg over and sat up to face her. "Alex…" she interrupted. "Em, take your shades off so I can see your eyes." I smiled and shook my head as I removed the sunglasses she had bought me for graduation.

"Alex, I'm scared and excited and I just want to enjoy this summer home before I live in Florida and go to college. I don't know what you want me to say. Of course, I will miss you so much, and Soph and Rae too." Alex took her sunglasses from her knapsack and buckled it closed, "Em, don't even bring her name up. Rae is on my last nerve today."

We had a similar conversation about Florida a week prior that caused a huge fight. And when I said to her, *I got a scholarship! What the hell am I going to do here?* She replied with fierce conviction, "There are colleges here, Em. You can be my partner when I open my restaurant." I quickly replied, "If we're partners, then it's not *your* restaurant. It would be *our* restaurant." Alex was silent after I said that.

Nobody wanted me to go away to school, it seemed. I looked down at the brick beneath my feet, feeling the weight of her silent disapproval. "Alex, are you suggesting that I shouldn't go to Florida?" I asked, my voice betraying my inner turmoil. She didn't answer. A few minutes of silence passed as we both settled comfortably in our lounges.

"The sun on my face feels good," she said. We closed our eyes and listened to Cyndi Lauper's, True Colors blaring through the backyard speakers. "I love this song," I said with my eyes shut tightly. After a few minutes, I started speaking, still with my eyes closed, "You know, the night after prom… Charlie asked me to stay and like well, marry him. And I said no. I'm going. And we had like a big fight about it. Well, anyway."

Alex sat up, "What? Did he have a ring? When were you going to mention that idiot proposed to you?" I opened my eyes. "Alex, it wasn't a real proposal. It was more like, stay and let's keep dating, and maybe eventually we can get married. I am way too young to even think about getting married, that's for sure!"

She was clearly upset again, "Emily, you didn't even tell me that happened." I defended myself, "Oh Alex, it didn't mean anything then and still doesn't. Have I seen him since? No because I am not in love with Charlie and it's over anyway."

Alex shook her head and turned to me again, "I'm telling you, I'm really down about you leaving soon and you bring up Charlie. This is what really bugs me, Em."

I was relieved we both heard the phone ringing from the kitchen, and I jumped up, "Be right back," and ran in to answer it. Vivien told me they had arrived safely at their hotel and checked in. I hurried her off the phone and darted back outside. Alex was sitting on the entrance steps of the pool half submerged.

"Parents arrived," I announced and walked toward her. I stepped down to the first step then over her leg and onto the third step. I stood there for perhaps a minute or less. I felt her eyes on me. I leaned forward and pushed off the step, gently diving under three feet of water.

I tucked my legs together with knees fully bent and drawn to the chest, I flipped around under the water.

When I broke through the water's surface, my head was arched back and my hair was slicked back. Alex shocked me with a two-handed splash right to my face. "You are a beautiful, pain in the ass, best friend. What am I going to do without you?" she said.

I threatened to splash back, but I decided not to. I looked at Alex hoping the tear in my eye wouldn't slip out. "You will come visit, Alex. And in Florida, we shall carry on our BFF status. Winter recess will be great for you to come and we can go to the beach." I didn't wait for a reaction or reply. I dove underneath the surface and swam the entire pool length before coming up for air. I was glad we didn't talk about Florida for the rest of the day.

She told me Rae had stolen clothes from her closet without asking. They had a screaming match over it. Sophie always asked before she borrowed Alex's stuff, but Rae never did. It didn't matter much because they were sisters. They had arguments and always made up shortly after. My job was to listen to her vent about things and I enjoyed doing so.

After the fried chicken and an empty pitcher of iced tea, we headed out to see a movie Rob Lowe starred in, About Last Night. We both loved the movie. When Alex dropped me off, I asked her to sleep over.

I wouldn't admit it but even at eighteen, I didn't love sleeping alone in my huge house, feeling the weight of its emptiness. Alex had a dentist appointment in her neighborhood the following morning, so she opted out. "I can't stay Em, but I'll pick you up after the dentist, and we will go to Tower Records."

The next day Alex and I bought the About Last Night Movie Soundtrack, and I played the entire CD every night for weeks through my earphones. I liked every song, but just as I fell asleep, I would listen to Bob Seger, Living Inside My Heart on repeat until I fell into my dreams.

I hung out with Mara one night that summer and it was weird. She only called me to ask to hang out because Adam was away on vacation. I knew that, but I agreed anyway. I got there after dinner at about six-thirty and stayed till ten. Mr. Conti wasn't feeling well and was asleep the entire time. I wished I had gotten to see him. Mara and I made popcorn and watched a Blockbuster VHS rental she found in her brother's room called, Fatal Attraction. The movie was entertaining and suspenseful, but Mara and I hardly talked, and it felt like I was watching a movie alone. I left that night and felt nothing.

Regarding Mara and my other friends, I knew I was okay with leaving soon for college. Nothing was the same. In fact, everything was different. Mara was so into Adam and had an entire group of friends I hardly knew or wanted to. The neighborhood was so different. Howie moved, Lucy moved in with her Jewish boyfriend and didn't speak to her Catholic parents anymore. Scotty spent over half the year in Canada at an ice hockey camp. All they did was train. I saw him on television years later playing forward for the Edmonton Oilers. I thought it was special, I grew up with someone semi-famous. Davie moved to San Diego with his sister and was doing well playing guitar out at local pubs. I spoke to him via phone a week before I left for PBU, and he said he was pocketing about six hundred weekly plus cash tips doing something he loved. I was so happy for him and told him he better not forget me when he became rich and famous. He said he never would.

As I was getting ready for my first semester, I found myself at home, packing with Vivien. Together we embarked on a few shopping sprees, filling a black trunk with supplies I would need. The anticipation of the new chapter in my life was palpable and the opportunities that awaited me filled me with a sense of eagerness.

Vivien bought all the things she knew I would need and want including new bedding, toiletries and posters, lamps, and a small fridge for my room. When we weren't packing, I was with Alex at the mall, beach, movies or out to eat. Our visits with Annie were a regular occurrence and often we found ourselves engrossed in conversations at our favorite beach. However, the highlight of that summer was Vivien's epic fiftieth birthday bash for Franco. I never saw my father so happy and carefree.

It was a night to remember with everyone including Michael and his lawyer buddies, in high spirits.

Alex came with her sisters. Brian and his wife and most of his staff came. Louie misunderstood a fiftieth party for a fifty's party. He wore blue jeans and a black belt. A white t-shirt with Camel cigarettes rolled up in his sleeve. His hair was greased back like Travolta in Grease. Louie took the foolish banter from Brian and Franco like a man, and our guests laughed at him. It was all in good fun. The men played bocce ball and the pool was open. Mara, Mr. Conti, and the neighborhood friends came too. I met some of my mom and dad's cousins and friends for the first time. It was the biggest and best party Vivien and Franco had ever hosted. That day, eighty people took a group picture on our backyard lawn and I assumed all the family and friends that attended that day would be in our lives forever, but that changed through the next decades. My parents' friendships were shifting too. I never knew why. However, tremendous life changes were about to take shape for all of us.

Chapter Nine

It was less than a week before I was set to leave. I stretched and opened my eyes. From my bed, I stared at the packed boxes and felt nervous. Even though I knew I would be home for the holidays, it didn't seem real that I was moving to Florida for the next four years. I decided not to think about that; instead, I turned up my radio and headed for the shower. I was looking forward to the evening. Brian and Mack planned a first-time-ever strip store block party and there was much to do. The party was a celebration to commemorate the end of summer.

I pulled a black mesh tank top over my head and sang with Irene Cara to the Fame Soundtrack. I didn't hear Vivien knock and was shocked to see her standing in my room. I wasn't sure how long she had been standing there but I'm sure she heard my rendition of, "*I'm gonna live forever, I'm gonna learn how to fly... high*!" I saw her feet as I was bent over towel drying my hair. "Hey, Viv," I said. I flipped my head, shook my hair, and threw the towel on the floor. Vivien shrugged.

"What?" I asked. "Em, please turn that down. I can't hear myself think. And please don't leave the wet towel on the floor." I reached over to the knob on my stereo and turned it to the left.

"Ah, better," she said. "Are you going to Brian's to help set up for tonight?" I sat on my bed and pulled an ankle sock over my foot. "Yep, I'm heading over there now." She sat on my desk chair and looked at the boxes, "I can't believe how fast this summer went, and I can't believe my little girl is going off to college." I sat with the other sock in hand

and looked at my mom. "I know. I can't believe I am going either, Mom. But today I don't want to think about any of that. Today is going to be great and look at this weather!" Vivien stood up and tucked the chair under the desk.
"Okay, well, your dad and I will look at cars, but we will stop by eventually, perhaps after dinner."
I positioned a baseball cap over my wet head and pulled my ponytail out. "Mom, plenty of food will be there, so don't bother cooking later. Just come and eat and be merry. By the way, Michael said he might come but don't tell him I told you. Please, Mom, don't ruin it because I will never tell you anything again." I tripped over some dirty clothes to answer my ringing phone. Vivien picked up my wet towel, tossed it at me, and left my room. It landed on top of a pile of clothes. I left it there.
"Hey Alex, I am leaving my house in ten. Where you at?" Alex said the Luncheonette had a busy morning, but things were calming down. She told me Brian, Mack, and the other guys were setting up.
"I'll be there soon to help. We are going to have a great time. See you in a bit." She sounded pumped up about it too, "I think the whole town is coming by tonight. Okay, get your butt over here!"
When I arrived, a few guys were roping off the vast parking lot, signaling we were close to the beginning of an exciting summer evening. Danny owned the Laundromat, and his son was setting up a tremendous blowup slide for the younger kids in the corner of the lot. Brian's nephew, Matt, was a young DJ. He was setting up turntables and two gigantic speakers, adding to the buzz in the air. The corner between Mack's card store and Swirls, frozen yogurt shop that opened earlier in the summer, was being transformed into a music haven with stacks of vinyl in several milk crates.

Donny and his wife, Eleanor had rented the space after Carvel closed and turned it into a frozen yogurt shop. They seemed like a nice couple.

With Nick and Louie's help, Alex and I set up ten tables outside so people had ample room to offer their food or drink contributions. After setup, Alex and I had an hour to cruise back to my house, freshen up and get back. I was already dressed when Alex came out of the bathroom wrapped in a towel. I tried not to notice how pretty she was, but I did notice.

We returned to the strip forty-five minutes later and were happy the night was about to begin. By seven in the evening, hundreds of people gathered in and out of Brian's. Matt's music roared outside, and people were dancing in the open parking lot. Some guys were throwing around a football. Little kids were enjoying the bouncy house and it was still light out.

Most had a red plastic cup filled by one of the five keg stations outside the storefronts. My old boss, Tom and his wife were there. It was nearly nine in the evening, and everyone was enjoying the party. Vivien and Franco were inside Brian's, talking with acquaintances. Michael came later in the evening and brought a date. I noticed she was gorgeous like all his others. I was talking to Matt and a bunch of people near the DJ booth when I saw them enter the Luncheonette. I excused myself and darted to catch up to my brother.

My folks were sitting with Brian and Louie. I gently pushed past people standing in the hallway to the booths and arrived in time to hear Michael introduce her. "Vivien, Dad, this is Charlotte." My Dad stood up and Vivien replied casually, "Hi, Charlotte, it's so good to meet you." I grabbed Michael's waist from behind him. "Hey Mike, fashionably late as usual." Michael turned to face me looked at Charlotte, and said, "This is my kid sister.

117

Em, meet Charlotte. Charlotte, this is Emily." At first impression, I liked her. She seemed genuine even though she was stunning. She didn't hang all over Michael like most of his other girlfriends. Until Charlotte came around, I still missed Audrey the most.

I stuck around for a polite three minutes. Truthfully, I was waiting for the right time to escape. Michael was telling Brian about a case and Vivien was delighted by Michael's story. I quietly tapped Charlotte on the shoulder, "Hey, it was nice to meet you, but I'm going to disappear into the fun zone." She quietly replied, "I don't blame you Emily, I'll see you again." I winked at her, stepped backward until I was in the back of the Luncheonette and decided it was an excellent time to use the bathroom. The ladies' room had two stalls, and both were occupied, so I waited. The white door flung open and much to my surprise there stood Alex. She had a great big smile and I felt happy to see her, "Oh my God, where have you been?" she asked.

Some girl we didn't know left the other stall and sprinted out of the bathroom without washing her hands. Alex and I just looked at each other disgusted by that. I had so much to tell her and didn't hesitate to ramble on, "Michael is here with some gorgeous girl. Her name is Charlotte.

I escaped the family and was just about to look for you. Matt is playing great music, Mara left with Adam, and they are *whatever*." Alex grabbed the paper towels to dry her hands and said, "Em, I cannot believe how many people are here, right?" I agreed, "Totally more than I expected. It's been a great night, but I met some weird people tonight, Alex." She grabbed my hand, "Me too, wanna go see the stars?" I knew exactly what she meant.

We slipped out the back door and Alex jumped onto the breadbox. I followed and was the first to hoist myself up. "Grab my hand, Em," Alex said. I wrapped my hand around her wrist, and she wrapped her hand around mine.

I tugged her upward as she jumped up from the breadbox. Alex's hand slipped out of mine and I fell back. "Ugh, Alex, I hit my head," I whimpered. Alex was concerned, "Are you okay, Em? Oh my God!" She knelt over me took her hand and placed it under my head. "Em, I feel a bump. We better get down and get ice on that." She was nervous, but I wasn't. I was calm and looked up at the stars. "Alex, I'm okay. Promise. Let's just lay here and look at the stars." Alex faced me still with her hand cupping the back of my head. "Are you sure? Because it feels like a bump, Em?" I knew I was okay, and I started laughing uncontrollably. I couldn't even speak. She wasn't laughing. She was staring at me. "Em, you are a nut. You are just a crazy nut."

I caught my breath, and there came a gradual silence. Suddenly I felt my heart racing. She moved closer to me. "Em, I'm just… Em?" I looked at her inquisitively, "What, Alex? You are just what?" She glanced at the sky, and I took my hand to her cheek and eased her face towards mine. "Alex? Tell me what is happening right now?" She moved closer than usual. I put my arms around her, and she cried. I didn't let go. She said nothing. She moved away, but I gently yanked her back. I loosened my grip to look into her eyes. She leaned forward and her mouth met mine. We were frozen together, and I tasted her tear. I felt her lips. They were soft and unlike Charlie's. They were as soft as mine. I felt a motionless caress as her lips folded perfectly over mine. I wanted to gently slip my tongue into her mouth, but I didn't.

I was in shock, and I could not move a muscle. I did the complete opposite of what would have presumably happened naturally. Instead, I instinctually pulled away. I heard some pristine inaudible voice that ordered me to stop. I didn't want the kiss to continue, nor did I want the kiss that barely started to end.

Our lips unlocked, and I felt awkward.

Alex jumped up abruptly. "Holy shit, I think the cops are here. She crouched down and crawled to spy over the three-foot brick wall encompassing the roof. She observed the parking lot in the front of the strip. I followed her, but she whispered, "Em, stay there. We gotta get down." I saw red flashing lights from my space on the rooftop and heard some commotion down below. Alex crawled back and we hopped down to the breadbox and casually slipped inside the Luncheonette back door. We walked through the front door to see what was happening. The cops asked Matt to stop playing the music because some of the surrounding houses had called to complain about the noise.

Brian was friends with most of the cops from the town precinct. He often gave them free coffee and sandwiches. Brian assured them the party was winding down and Matt was packing up his DJ system. There were still over fifty of us sitting on the curb of the parking lot and hanging around and inside the Luncheonette.

By midnight Brian locked up, and the crowd was dwindling. Before heading to his car at the far end of the parking lot, he instructed Nick to stack the empty kegs on the breadbox. Alex shot me a look and I knew that meant thank goodness we had vacated the roof. Everyone pitched in to help clean up the tables and the food, but it was mainly Brian's staff, me and Alex who did most of the work.

Mac locked his place up much earlier; however, Donny still served free frozen yogurt to anyone who wanted. It was an ideal night; tons of bright night stars and cool enough to wear a long-sleeved cotton t-shirt. Some stayed sitting on lawn chairs until the wee hours, staring at the sky and sipping coffee or what was left of their beer.

Sophie strolled over to where I was sitting with Rae and

Alex. "Sis, I'm tired. Can we go home?"
Alex looked at me and back to Sophie. "Yeah, can you guys go find Matt too. Brian asked me to drop him off." Sophie and Rae skipped away to return minutes later with Matt.
I hoped Alex would have said something about the roof and the kiss. She didn't, and neither did I. We sat silently, occasionally glancing at one another but our eyes never met. It was late, and I assumed the conversation would come in days to follow. Eventually we did talk about the roof and the kiss. That conversation took place more than ten- thousand plus, days later.

I stood in my empty bedroom. I glanced at my belongings scattered about the floor. There would just not be enough space to bring everything on my excursion. I looked around once more trying hard to remember everything. It was time to leave and embark upon liberty and freedom. I took a deep breath and wandered nostalgically out of the doorway and down the stair. I raced back up and down the hall towards my bedroom. On the back of my doorknob hung a black rope like necklace with a small crystal at its end. I slid the necklace over my head, lifted my hair off my neck and hurried back downstairs.
Franco was carting out a few boxes. Michael had been helping him load the van since morning. I stood by the glass door looking out to the front lawn. I noticed the untidiness of our Maple and just a few fallen tree leaves. I was both relieved and saddened; I would not be able to help Franco rake the yard as fall began.
Dad and Michael were still on the driveway. They were busy shifting things around in the van, somewhat proud of their ability to make everything fit. In the kitchen, Vivien wrote instructions on a small writing pad for Michael about watering the plants. She posted the note to the fridge with

one of our family vacation magnets and secured the windows. She always took care of the tasks before leaving for an extended period.

"Do you have everything, honey?" I smiled, "According to Michael and Dad, I have enough stuff to last me through four years plus grad school." Mom and I laughed. "Emmy, boys will be boys. Your father thinks a carry-on with clean underwear and one outfit besides the one he's wearing is enough for a week's vacation."

Michael entered pushing the front door open, and wearily sat at the kitchen table. He led out a loud breath, "Think you have enough shit, sis?" I rolled my eyes and smirked. He continued, "Guess this means I'm rid of you till May, huh?"

Mom answered, "Oh Michael, it's barely September… Emmy will be home for Thanksgiving and Christmas… maybe the upcoming Jewish holidays." I interrupted, "Mom, I didn't even leave yet. When I get my schedule and settle in, you will be the first to know when I am coming home. We're not Jewish, so I'm thinking I'm not coming home for those Viv." Mike laughed.

"Let's get the show on the road, girls," called a voice from outside. Michael got up from the kitchen table and walked towards me. "Have a blast, Em" he said, "…invite me down for a weekend to meet all the good-looking sorority girls, okay?" I didn't answer but gave him a familiar sneer. Michael kissed my forehead and proceeded to the fridge for a cold drink. "Thanks for helping Dad this morning," I uttered, "I left my dorm room phone number on the fridge; call me when Mom and Dad start getting on your nerves." He nodded, took a gulp and said, "See ya Emmy. Have a good time. You'll be alright if you can lighten up a bit." I replied, "Don't be a nerd!"

I grabbed one of the many gifts given to me by Alex, a black-leather Kenneth Cole knap and my Sony Discman. I strolled outside to find my father impatiently waiting on the driveway. My mom followed close behind.

Michael waved good-bye from the front door.

I was cropped up against some pillows in a small area on the back seat of the van. I woke from a long nap, stretched, and leaned forward. "Where are we?" I yawned. Dad answered, "Approaching Raleigh, South Carolina and I don't know about you and mom but I'm ready for a good dinner, a glass of wine and a good night's sleep." "Sounds good to me," Vivien agreed.

They paid close attention for the next lodging sign. Franco pulled off the road and into a parking lot of a Holiday Inn. After dinner, the sound of live music lured me into the bar area.

Vivien and Franco decided to retreat to their room for some television and much needed rest. The bar was hopping, and I took a seat. I ordered a Tom Collins and figured on hanging out for a little while.

"Here on business or pleasure?" a voice behind me asked. I turned around, "Me?" A well-groomed man in a suit responded, "I'm sorry didn't mean to startle you. Would you mind if I sat down," he pointed to the stool to my right. I answered, "No, not at all." He introduced himself, Kevin Pace.

He was a twenty-something-year-old insurance broker in town to meet a perspective client. I then told him a bit about me, "My mother and father are driving me to Florida, WPB University." Kevin listened intently and flattered me, "I love your Long Island accent. Is that where you're from?" I was proud of my New York heritage and confessed his assumption was correct. We talked into the night. It was approaching two-thirty in the morning and the band had stopped playing an hour earlier. I was exhausted though I did zero of the driving.

I glanced at my watch, and Kevin immediately stood up,

offered his hand; I thought to shake. But he kissed my hand ever so gently and said, "Our conversation will definitely be the highlight of my trip and I wish you well in college, Emily Netti. You are very beautiful." He handed me his business card and told me to look him up if ever in the neighborhood. I was pleased with the encounter. I thanked Kevin and left the bar to head back to my room. Promenading down the long corridor, I carried myself with a mature demeanor and confidence.

For the first time ever, I felt like a full-fledged grown-up. I felt that conversation with Kevin, had prepped me for a whole new kind of independence. I was more than ready for new people, new places, and a whole new kind of feeling. I passed my parents' room and continued on to mine. I took my key from my pocket and opened the door. I flung off my shoes, lunged onto the bed, and giggled out loud. "Thank you, Mr. Kevin cutie Pace," I said out loud. I felt beautiful.

I woke to Vivien's thump on the door. "Emily, are you up?" I fought to get out of bed after only five hours of sleep. "Yeah, hold on, I'm coming," I opened the door. There was Viv's, showered and looking rested. "Dad and I are going to get a cup of coffee and we'll meet you in the restaurant by the lobby in a half hour." I agreed, shut the door and headed for the shower.

At breakfast I told my parents I sat at the bar and listened to a band for a while. I didn't mention Kevin or the other guy, Tom Collins. Breakfast was over quick, and we had a long drive ahead.

I went with Mom and her bag of quarters to call Michael while Franco took care of the check. We met outside ready for the road. I was close with my parents. I was glad they were driving me to school. It was nice to spend quality time with them without the distractions at home.

During our long road trip, I confessed my fear and spoke about college and what I thought could become my future. I talked about how much I would miss them, my friends, especially Alex, and maybe even Michael. I sat on the edge of the back middle seat and leaned forward, "I mean, I've never really been away from home for a long time." Franco reassured me, "Emmy, you're going to be fine. You're going to love it. I'll be surprised if after the first few weeks, Mom and I will even be able to persuade you to come home for a weekend." I sighed, "It's just that I'm a world traveler for short periods." I sat back. I started to get a lump in my throat just thinking about it. It hadn't hit me until that moment. I was leaving my home and I didn't feel ready. Franco glanced into the rearview mirror and noticed I was holding back tears. "If you don't like it after the first semester, you'll come home. That's all," he added. I didn't reply and I stared out the window.

Viv knew I was getting upset and changed the subject, "Did I tell you Angela's son, Paul is getting married?" I was semi-interested in the information, "No, to who?" She replied, "A nice girl from Chicago. They met in college." I asked Viv if she thought I would be invited to that wedding, and we chatted for almost an hour about that and other subjects.

Franco put his two cents in when we touched upon his favorite topics: business, jobs, politics, and money. Some of Franco's garble bored me to tears, but I loved chatting with my mom. We talked about everything and nothing. We were friends, the closest in the world. The conversation ceased and I settled back, fixed my pillow and placed my earphones in my ears. I fell asleep to Don Henley, Wasted Time.

We drove up a long road and came to a full stop at the security house. There were palm trees and the complex looked like a vacation. The officer approached the car.

"How can I help you, sir?" Vivien handed Franco the requested paperwork. Franco handed it to the man. The officer took a quick look and handed Franco one set of keys and a card. "This is your daughter's temporary ID card, my friend. She will need to take a photo up at the clubhouse," the security guard pointed up the hill. "She will receive a permanent via mail within a week or so." Franco nodded. He gave Franco directions and opened the gate to let us through. "Thank you, so very much," Franco said and drove through the opened gate.

"I dread unpacking," I said as I peered out the window. I was excited though I had queasy feeling in my belly. "This place is going to be very cool. You think?" I asked Vivien for reassurance. She was impressed, maybe even envious, "Yeah, I think it's lovely. I never would imagine going to college when I was eighteen and in a place like this. Wow, I am happy you are going to get this beautiful experience." I stepped out of the car and my parents followed as I keyed into the apartment. It was beautiful. The scholarship awarded also upgraded me from the regular dorm rooms to the further off campus higher end living quarters. It was still close enough to walk to most of my classes. In the event of rain, the school provided a free shuttle that ran throughout the day and into the evenings.

A few hours later, Franco carried in the last box. He looked exhausted and was relieved to finally be in the air-conditioned apartment. Mom made my bed with the new sheets and comforter set. I was nearly settled in my new digs. I had completed emptying the box of my mom's old glassware into the cabinet to the left of the sink when I saw Vivien standing over Franco. She bent down and shook his shoulder. "Hon, we should get going." Franco opened his eyes and sat up.

Viv stood up straight, took a deep breath and looked around, "Well Em, do you think you need anything out of the cooler?" I answered, "Nope, I'm good until morning, but you guys will come by like nine, right?" Franco rose from the sofa and softly, mumbled, "Yes, we will go for breakfast and then you and mom can go food shopping and I'll nap." He pointed to the sofa, "Comfortable!" he said. Viv took a sip of water, "I can't believe it kid but I think you're pretty settled for now." I felt tired, "Yeah, I feel settled enough I guess and whatever, we will finish tomorrow. I'm so tired, Mom." She kissed my forehead, "Goodnight, my sweet. Dream in color and see you in the morning." I walked a few feet out onto the walkway. Franco opened the door for his wife, and she climbed in. He ensured she was all tucked into her seat before he shut the car door.

I watched the van back up and pull away. The bright, red brake lights dimmed as the van made a right and out of my distance. I wasn't sad because I knew they would be back after a good night sleep.

Once inside, I sat on a cardboard box and dialed Alex. She didn't answer, and I didn't leave a message after the beep.

Chapter Ten

I woke up with a sharp pain inside my abdomen. It was noisy, and it was early. I peered out my window. The early morning light of the sunrise was soft and diffused. Mounds of bright white snow piled in the corners of the empty parking lot. I dreaded the unwelcome company that would show up, whether or not I was up for it.

Evie was quietly replacing formula and diapers on the bottom of the stainless-steel bassinet.

I struggled to sit up, and she was immediately attentive. "Gud Mawning, Miss. Emmy," she said in the sweetest Jamaican voice. "Good morning, Evie." I reciprocated her smile as best I could.

"Waah Gwaan? You need Evie to get you a lil something, Ms. Emmy?" I answered, "Oh, Evie, what will I do without you when they kick me outta here?" She quickly replied, "Guh cotch yuh batty and luv dat baby girl, so sweet." I laughed too hard; it hurt. I grabbed my belly with both my hands and crouched over. "Mi deh yah, Evie here, my lady." She put her hands on both of mine. I grabbed hers and squeezed them. Her hands were soft and brown and warm. "Evie, I need Sami as soon as possible, but I don't need all the company soon to come."

She looked into my eyes and asked, "Will deh come with two long hands?" I was confused, "Oh Evie, you were my guardian angel and pulled me through labor and delivery, but I don't know what the hell you are saying, girl?" Evie suppressed her chortle and spoke in her best American, "Ms. Emmy, I said you when you arrive home, you will move your butt and take care of your little girl, and then I asked if your family soon to come will arrive with nothing?"

I said, "Oh Evie, no... they will come with plenty of gifts and excitement over Sami. I should be grateful, and I am.

I just want some time to reflect on my beautiful second miracle. I just want a minute with her. Plenty of time for family to visit with her when we settle in at home."
Evie clenched my hands, still clutching my belly with both of hers. "I shall bring her to you now, then, Ms. Emily. Time to eat again anyway." I dipped my head onto her shoulder. She smelled like Vivian's line-dried clothes and her heart was worn outside.
The sun had risen bright and would melt some snow by midday. I felt like my insides had been ripped apart until Evie placed Sami in my arms. "Yah, gyal deh yah. I understood and replied, "Yes, Evie, this is my girl." I swaddled her close to my chest and watched Sami drink from my breast. I promised her I would be a good Mom, maybe even a great one. I was hopeful and awestruck and genuinely felt blessed for the second time in my life.

Jude walked into the room first. All I noticed was his curious spirit and his big green eyes, searching to take a first glance at his baby sister. He came to a standstill, and he stared. I spoke to him in a whisper, "Come, my love. Jude, come meet your baby sister, Sami." He ambled, and Jesse came from behind and hoisted him up onto the hospital bed. His sweet voice and first words to her, "So you're my baby in my mommy's tummy." He looked up at me, and his smile was gigantic. The biggest I'd have ever seen in all of his three and half years. I tried to ignore the sharp pain in my abdomen and the burning feeling inside my vagina.
"Jude, come honey. Sit here on Mommy's lap, and you can hold Sami." He nudged himself closer into the fold of my arm. I draped my hand around his shoulder.
I gently placed Sami into his arms, and I knew at that moment I had made for him a friend.
My two healthy, beautiful and perfect beings were in my

arms. Jesse grabbed the camera, "Jude, look at me, buddy." With buoyant smiles, I propped Sami up towards the lens. I grabbed Jude even closer and set my face in between theirs.

It was a moment of pure joy, and all physical pain subsided. The flash made Sami flinch, and Jude giggled. That would become one of the many happy snapshots hanging on our wall for the next decade.

For the next several weeks, I concentrated on Sami without forgetting to entertain Jude. I was absolutely exhausted. Jesse's life hadn't changed so much after our children's birth. I recognized a dramatic shift in my wants and needs, and he seemed the same. He enjoyed playing pool and managed to get out to see the boys for a few beers after work from time to time.

He managed security for a large chain of corporations and was assigned to various buildings in Manhattan. He mostly commuted, but his hours widely ranged between days and nights, and he often picked up overtime shifts when his staff needed time off. Although he was partial to his non-structured schedule, I never much enjoyed it. I would often attend family events by myself, and I didn't find the fun in preparing my small army of two for an outing that required two bags filled with diapers, bottles, and an array of wardrobes for lousy food at a Knights of Columbus celebration. I loved my time at home with Jude and Sami. It was peaceful. It was hard work, but I was in love with them from the second they were born.

When I wasn't hustling around to family affairs, I tried to manage some of my career but I spent most of my time taking lint out of the dryer and tackling chores. It was as boring as it was overwhelming.

It was a typical evening and four-month-old Sami slept. I stared at her in her swing. My instinct was to move her to her crib and grab a few hours of sleep in my bed until her next bottle. Jude was asleep on the couch. I stared at his long, wavy dark hair. The Toy Story DVD returned to its repeated opening menu. I was utterly transfixed. I felt my body sink into the recliner. Hours later, I was startled by the tap on my shoulder. Jesse whispered, "Hey, I'm home. I'll feed Sami, and I'll put Jude in his bed. Go get into bed." My vision was blurry. Jesse kissed the top of my head. "What time is it?" I asked. I glanced down at Sami in her swing seat, which had long since stopped swaying. Jesse spoke softly, "One-thirty, Hon. I'll come to bed in a bit." I nodded, muddled down the hall, crawled under the covers, and slept.

A few hours later, I looked to my side and wondered if I had dreamt Jesse came home and fed Sami, and I didn't remember putting Jude to bed? I leaped up in a panic and ran to Jude's bedroom.

He was on his side, snuggled in his bed and Sami was in her crib with a full belly and a clean diaper. I made my way downstairs.

Jesse was on the computer. He would either be there or on the couch. I repeatedly confronted Jesse about why he rarely came to bed, but when the conversation fell upon deaf ears, I concerned myself with the children and I started not to care what was so engaging for Jesse. My disapproval stayed quiet. I never wanted to sound like one of those nagging wives, not cool enough to understand that he needed time to unwind after a long day at work. I should have spoken up sooner.

In the five years of courting, I had so many reasons to be so confident we would be that couple who made it and not stuck in a miserable union; ours would be epic. After a few short years, it became abundantly clear that we were just regular and boring and bickering, and intimacy, connection, and sex that made the world tip to its side would never happen. We had only been married for a few years and already lacked passion.

We were fleeting and advancing in our routines, hardly noticing when the other was there or not. Our social life was primarily based on family. By the time Sami was born, I definitely knew we had never built a relationship uniquely our own and separate from our busy lives and our extended family obligations.

In the following years, Jesse could escape the fortitude of requests to meet some of my needs, although I was busy meeting his and the children's. I spent more time with my mother than I did with my husband. Viv thought that was normal but I didn't.

Vivien adored newborn Sami as much as her first grandchild, Jude. Michael's twin girls, Maya and Meghan, arrived between my two. Charlotte gave birth to Jake two years and five months after Sami was born, and the last of Vivien's fabulous five were here. They became her most precious loves and were seriously spoiled by their doting grandparents.

The visible lift of any regret I thought my mother may have felt through some of her *forty-something* years remarkably seemed to disappear. Vivien became an even better cook, and I didn't think that was possible. She would prepare five particular favorites for each of her grandchildren when they visited.

We would gather frequently, and tradition would persist like an easy summer day. Franco, Michael & Jesse would meet up, and it would be eleven of us often. Year after year, the food and wine were plentiful. The conversations were thunderous and often politically charged in nature. We would sit for long hours until the moon was overhead.

Charlotte and I would meet three or four times weekly with our infants and toddlers. We would discuss how tired we were and which kid pooped, sneezed, or cried all night. I would hold baby Jake, a carbon copy of Jude; often people would assume they were brothers. Eventually, as teens and into adulthood, they were even closer than brothers despite their almost six-year age difference.

Charlotte's decision to leave her job and embrace the role of a stay-at-home mom was a stark contrast to Michael's career-driven life. While it seemed like a dream, there was a piece missing from Charlotte's puzzle. The twins were a handful, and her husband's absence was a constant reminder of the void in her life.

Michael's life took a different trajectory about two months before Charlotte's pregnancy announcement. His career as partner in the firm accelerated, with wine-and-dine client meetings becoming his norm. His workdays stretched to fifteen hours, six days a week. The financial rewards were substantial, and Michael didn't shy away from enjoying the fruits of his labor.

In Cove Canyon, luxury was not a rarity. The grandeur of their home was evident from the moment you stepped into their enormous foyer; your eyes drawn to the Italian chandelier hanging twenty feet above. Marble tiles, imported furnishings and authentic artwork adorned the walls, each piece carefully chosen from the exhibits Michael and Charlotte frequented earlier in their marriage. I didn't realize how wealthy Michael was until I visited his home. He was not pretentious and out of the confines of his rich dwelling; he was simply just my brother.

Michael and Charlotte hired a live-in au pair, although Charlotte was very present in her mom role. They had a swanky lifestyle, yet both managed to not flaunt it. Jesse and I lived a much simpler life in comparison.

I thought Jesse and I were like the majority of couples I noticed around me. I didn't put too much thought into it back then. I was busy learning and transitioning into motherhood. I started to fall in love with my stay-at-home mommy role, and I ate, slept, and breathed them. I missed working but could reconcile that my career would resume as soon as kindergarten started. We weren't wealthy, but we had enough and always did enjoy the riches of my family gatherings. Michael never came empty-handed, and Franco was never short on paying for good spirits. Jesse seemed comfortable and complacent. If I seemed quietly content, he did too.

There were good times, and there were days when I felt that was how I envisioned a marriage should be, busy juggling babies who grew into toddlers almost overnight. When we argued, it was about the lack of presence, even when he was home for short stints. We had little in common and agreed on close to nothing.

He seemed to revel in the glory of fatherhood. The kids became trophies. I must have known on some level that I was compromising to an extent, even at the beginning of our relationship. That's what I thought being a grown-up was all about; sacrifice and compromise.

I liked his willingness to follow through on any decision I made for us and with daily enthusiasm. Being around such a carefree spirit who worried about almost nothing was easy initially. As I would learn in the decade-plus of our union, his inability to grow was quite the burden for me, and I felt like I was raising him and two kids. I took care of the household and the checkbook. I was the vessel's captain, and he was a responsible first mate. We were always with family. Franco showed him the ropes, and Jesse was quite charming and a quick-learn. I had to fight to believe there was still a connection and that the marriage would succeed.

"Hey, Doll, there is a girls' night out with the first-grade moms. It came home with the school packet today. You should go, and I'll babysit," Jesse said with reassuring approval. With a cutting-edge to my tone, I asked, "You will babysit, Jess?" His defense came quickly, "I mean, c'mon doll, you should go. I'll ensure I am home from work in time, and you should get out and have some fun." I squinted and rolled my eyes. I answered him, "Jesse, there is nothing about that for me; that is fun. And the thought of you just telling me you'll babysit. I mean, really, Jess?" He defended his previous comment, "Oh my God, Em! I didn't mean babysit. I just want you to know you are free to go out with the girls and have a good time, and I'll make sure I'm home so you can."

I was sarcastic in my response: "So, you will make arrangements to babysit, or do you mean you will make arrangements to father and clear your schedule so I can go out with first-grade moms I hardly know, and according to you... that should be a great night out for me?"

He grabbed my arm. "Honey, calm down. You need a break, and yes, you need to get out. Sign the paper and here," he said, taking two folded twenty-dollar bills from his front pants pocket.

"Just send this in tomorrow's envelope; it's forty bucks. Go have some fun with the girls and talk about how the kids don't nap anymore, and you can even vent about how much your husband is an ass for calling himself a babysitter."

He touched my cheek, and he smiled. I smiled back and grabbed the forty bucks from his hand. A peck on the lips and off I went.

Jesse had a charming essence. I certainly wasn't the first or last to fall for him. He said all the right stuff when it really counted. He justified every reason why I should step out of my comfort zone, do something different, and start getting to know the moms of the PTA.

"Okay, Jess," I said, "I will sign up and go to the first grade Ladies PTA Night Out." He grabbed me, leaned in, and kissed me hard. At that moment, I am not sure I was expecting sensuality, but most of our kisses weren't a sign of any. At that moment, he tilted his head down while simultaneously grabbing my cheek and said, "Doll, I promise the kids and I will wreck the house, but just a little, and oh, they may not have veggies and only pizza with pepperoni, and they will go to sleep two hours past their bedtime; and not like a bad babysitter but like a cool dad! Is that better?" I looked at my husband, "Yes, I guess pizza is fine, but Jude hates pepperoni, and why wreck the house? Can you just be a great babysitter and not a cool dad?" He laughed, and I laughed. I discovered there were times Jesse gave me silly perspectives and lightened my heavy thinking.

For a few years, I regularly made an effort to be dressed when Jesse came home from work, although my bra had been off all day. Some days, I didn't leave the house, but I always rose from what I was consumed with to greet him at the door when he walked in. These actions seldom came naturally, but I would make an effort because I read books and listened to advice from the love gurus I would hear on television.

For a few years following wedded bliss, I was satisfied. He would assume the role that I had been taught to expect. I married what was expected and even better than my close circle had decided on for a spouse. It seemed to be enough.

It was a reverie of folding my husband's underwear and ensuring my kids had the correct number of fruits and veggies on a given day. I would sit on my porch while the kids were napping, and Jesse was driving home and think, *Yeah, I can do this. What complaints can I possibly have?* My silent sub-conscience-self asked and my conscience-self answered. Some of those questions were not answered truthfully.

I was so caught up with what would come next. I never realized where I was. I was busy prepping for the next cross-out and checkmark on my list. I was excited on the days I took the kids for a picture sitting or to their first bouncy house birthday party with a preschool friend. I enjoyed a Saturday afternoon outing to see Vivian and Franco and the many vacations the eleven of us took together. It all seemed so Utopia.

During the week, I kept house and busy working while the kids napped and still waited for what would come next. By dinnertime, every ounce of energy was used up. Jesse was the hero on weekday evenings. Sami would stop whatever she was doing and dart into his arms. "Hi, Sugar-pie," he would say. Sami's sweet reply, "Hi Daddy," and she tilted her head to its side and lay it on his shoulder. Those moments made my heart melt.

I would kiss him hello, and he would retreat to the bedroom to slip off his suit pants and tie. At dinner, I would listen to Jesse talk about his day. I would pay attention, but it was like many of our superficial conversations. Dinner wasn't an optimal time to discuss anything that sparked my interest. Jude and Sami's interruptions didn't help, and our connection slowly disappeared. I often wondered if he would ever ask me about my day and was relieved at times he didn't. There was definitely something lacking in my day-to-day enthusiasm.

As the years passed, it became easier to live on the surface. Jesse was the master of it, and I negotiated with myself about fulfillment; What I could have and did have, to make up for what we didn't.

The boat ride home from Fire Island was stunning. I had a VIP seat as the sun began to hide beyond The Great South Bay's horizon.

Jude was sprawled out on the vinyl seat bench on the top deck of Franco's Sea-Ray. Jesse was sleeping a few feet away. Sami was strapped into her pink and white stroller. She was wide awake, tapping the sea fish mobile attached to her stroller. Sami cooed and giggled when the dolphin would spin around and brush her arm. She loved the dolphin, which chirped when she got hold of it. I adored witnessing her amuse herself.

Franco's lips gripped the stub of a Cuban cigar as he steered the vessel westbound. Vivien held baby Jake's head in place as it slung over her shoulder. Michael and Charlotte took the twins to see their first Broadway show, and Jake was ours for the day and Vivien would keep him overnight. I reached for my camera to snap a picture of his angelic face resting on his grandma's shoulder.

The boat's engines drowned out the radio, but I recognized bits and pieces of a familiar Nat King Cole melody. Vivian and Franco loved Nat King Cole, and I grew up appreciating the Rat Pack and the music that depicted the era when my parents first met.

I peered out the back of the boat, noticed white foam left a trail of uniform effervescence, and I snapped the shutter down. It was later than usual when Franco finally docked. We didn't stay long. Jude asked to stay overnight with his cousin and Vivien would not dare tell him no. Jesse drove as I looked quietly out the window feeling the windburn on my cheeks. Sami was asleep in her car seat. I closed my eyes, listening to Jesse sing the wrong words to one of my favorite songs, and finally, we were home.

I had a few things to tidy up. There were bottles to sanitize and bags to be emptied. After placing Sami in her crib, Jesse was already settled on the couch. I sat down with a hot coffee and inserted the compact flash card into the printer slot. I stared at the spinning rainbow until the pictures popped up. One of them was an incredible image of the brilliant foam spraying right up against the lens. A world-renowned photographer could not have planned a droplet ever so unfocused to bring such beauty to a picture. I gazed at it in wonder. I chose that and eight others to bring into Photoshop. I began to upload to Facebook and thought of a tagline. I started typing, *Helluva... day at sea, sir - with the gang*. I pressed down on the delete key repeatedly. *Fun in the sun with the fam*! I glanced at the pictures again and highlighted the text. I pressed delete. Typing resumed, *Great South Bay - Happy Summer*! I hit the blue post button with certitude, picked up my coffee, and headed downstairs.

Jesse was fast asleep on the couch. I turned off a few lights and hit the delayed-start button on the dishwasher. I heated up a bottle and headed up to Sami's room. The nightlight dimmed her plush green carpet. The pastels of pink, green, and blue blended with the bumpers in her crib, Sami was leaning upon them with her legs extended and diaper in the air. She was an easy child and happy to play in her crib for hours before crying for me to come to get her.

She heard the floor squeak as I snuck into her doorway. She stood up and extended her arms beyond the crib gate. "Hi, Sami," I softly spoke. She waved in a sophisticated manner, "Mommy," she said with her binky almost falling out of her grin. I reached for her, and she lifted her tiny body and folded into mine. She grabbed her bottle which was tucked under my arm. I sat in the glider and held her. I could have handed her a bottle in her crib, and she would have remained content to let me leave her for a while. But I wanted to hold her like *yesterday* when she was an infant. I felt she was growing up even faster than Jude did. She gazed into my eyes while letting the bottle soothe her. I

stroked her forehead and touched her silky unruffled curls.
She enjoyed the bottle, simpering and swallowing warm
milk. With a gentle kiss and all tucked in, I walked down
the hall and felt the cozy shag carpet under my bare feet. I
climbed into bed, found the remote, and much to my
delight, fell asleep to one of my all-time-favorites on HBO;
Under the Tuscan Sun.

I blinked an eye, and Jude was a fourth grader. He was a
strong, thin boy. His pants always hung on his hips. He was
fair-skinned with jet-black hair. It was long and wavy only
in the summer. Unembroidered, he would come to me
every fall, "Mom, it's time for me to take a haircut." That
always made me smile, and I never corrected him. "Okay,
Jude, I will set an appointment for Saturday and you
will… *take* a haircut." Then he would nod and continue
eating his ham and cheese. Jude was bright, creative, and
beautiful on the inside and out.
I watched Sami struggle to keep up with her brother,
climbing on the jungle gym Grammy and Poppy bought
for a birthday past. They reminded me of Michael and I,
and that brought me joy. The backyard had corners of
shrubbery, and the flats I planted were in full bloom. The
new black mulch and fine-edged line of the grass were
neat and well-kept.
Jude wore khaki shorts in the summer like his father.
Complimented by an aqua Ralph Lauren tank top, which
brought out his green eyes.
His feet were covered with worn and comfortable brown
leather deck shoes. Sami pulled the strap of her one-piece
romper over her shoulder and hurried, barefoot, to catch up
with Jude flying across the monkey bars like a circus
trapeze artist. Cats in the Cradle poured from the speakers
mounted on the underside of the lower roof. I listened to
the lyrics and could not believe Jude was nine and Sami

had just finished kindergarten. Time hurried.

Jesse surprised us and came home early that day. "Hey Jess," I said. He immediately interjected, "Yes, I am home and happy to be!" I was happy to see him, too, "So, Lincoln freed the slaves?" I asked. "Yes! Yes! Lincoln did! I will change my clothes, and I'll be back." That evening was spent in the yard. We toasted S'mores after dinner, and the kids ran around. I listened to Jesse's detailed description of his golf outing and appointment securing another building to guard before opening on Wall Street. I stood up. "Hey, Jess? I would like to go check emails. Is that okay? Can you be on duty?"

Jesse purposefully extended a casual, nonchalant invitation for a bike ride and ice cream, the kids jumped wildly like it was the best idea they had ever heard, and as I heard giggles and glee running out the front door, the house grew quiet. For the first time in weeks, I wasn't serving and assisting; It was just me logging into my Mac with no worries. I replenished the soft glow of solitude.

My hand hovered over the mouse. I pulled my hand down and clicked the mail icon in the dock. My eyes immediately focused on it.

From: "Alessandra" <Alesa29@aol.com>
Date: June 29, 2006, at 2:40:22 AM EDT
To: Em3018@optonline.net
Subject: Hi Stranger:)
Em, like my restaurant... I know you're on Facebook, girl? Are you? You must like my page. I hope this is still your email. I ran into Josephine Sareto, at Larsen's in the village. She lost a ton of weight but still, that face, OMG. I can't help it! God forgive me. She said you and her haven't been in touch for years... I didn't know that. Well, how would I? We haven't been in touch for years. I haven't aged, have you? Thought I should reach

out. Anyway, come down to Hoxie Ales (in Beltmore) and tell the bartender you are Em… free drinks and chances are I will be there with bad hair. xo, Alex

I paused and rubbernecked the computer screen. I hit reply and eagerly started to type.

From: Em3018@optonline.net,
Date: June 29, 2006, at 10:08:13 AM EDT
To: "Alessandra" <Alesa29@aol.com>
Subject: Re: Hi Stranger:)
OMG, Alex! I cannot believe you own a restaurant but then… Yes! I can! And no, I haven't heard from Josie in years. God forgive me too because I laughed out loud for real… while reading your email.
I will stop in for free drinks soon, um… I've asked you to have a drink in every email for over twenty-something years. In case you didn't notice… I gave up on ever expecting to get a reply. I am really happy you reached out – cool! Wow, Alex… not shocked you OWN a restaurant and still have BAD hair. Proud of you… seriously proud and no aging here either (I wish)!

I hit send and was instantly swept away by a wave of nostalgia and shock. What just happened? It felt like a moment suspended in time.
I was in my bedroom when I heard the front door fly open. They all walked in with a usual loud entrance. The kids were hyped. They all came boisterously into my room. "Hi, my Mommy," Sami said and kissed my head. Jude added in a quiet whisper, "Mommy, I am going to read Goodnight Moon to Sami. Good night and he leaned in to hug me." I lifted my head from the pillow and hugged Jude, "You are the best big brother in the universe. Goodnight, guys. I love you even more. I love you most!" Jesse went to get them

both settled. The kids paraded out and Jesse stopped by the doorway. "Hey, Em… I'll be in a minute, k?" I grunted, "k, I am tired." I saw the time on the cable box 10:22. I closed my eyes.

I heard my bedroom door open. He entered. He undressed in the dark shadows. I struggled to read the green numbers on the cable box, 1:38. He didn't notice I was coherent enough to note the time. He quietly slipped under the covers. I felt his arms reach around me. I heard him make a series of low, feeble sounds. Jesse tried to make love to me that night. I pretended to be sound asleep and he turned to his side. His snoring kept me awake. I stared at the ceiling and quietly thought, *I can't believe Alex bought a restaurant.*

Chapter Eleven

It was an early summer evening, filled with anticipation. I had just come from an appointment with Justine Katz, a blogger with a huge following. She was a friend I had freelanced with at a post house, years prior. She was producing a promo for her blog and called me to come aboard. My writing and editing skills were a bit rusty, but I was thrilled to get the call. It was a chance to step out of the role of the badly dressed mom I had gradually become and into a more professional one. I called Jesse from the car and he answered. "Hey, how did it go?" he asked. I answered, "I think it went well. I am unsure if she knows what she wants me to do for her, but maybe our paths will cross eventually. She's a brilliant woman and I really admire her. Plus…" Jesse interrupted, "Does she have kids?" I wondered why he asked such a bizarre question. "Why? What does that have to do with her blog?" He sounded blasé, "I was just asking, is all." I decided to move on with what I thought was a more important conversation. "So… how are the kids, and how are your folks?"

Jesse had taken the kids to visit his parents, who were going to visit his Aunt Evelyn. His aunt had never been the warmest person and I couldn't shake the feeling that she didn't particularly care for me. It had been a while since I had seen her, ever since she moved upstate, a two-hour drive from us. Despite our differences, she had always been kind to the kids and they were excited about their visit with her and their grandparents. It was the first time Jesse had taken them anywhere without me, and the thought was unsettling. At the same time, I couldn't deny the relief of having a mini-break from the three of them.

Charlotte and I planned to enjoy a rare moment of peace and freedom and booked a massage, facial, and lunch for Saturday. Their au pair would take the kids to the park, and Michael would watch baseball and let Charlotte have her *me-time*.

Friday night, I made a conscious decision to stay home, take a bath and start a good book. It was a rare moment of solitude, away from the constant responsibility of the kids. Until then, I had never had that much time apart from the kids. I chose to embrace it, rather than dwell on the pang of missing them and worrying about them being out of my sight.

I arrived home late that afternoon and I knew Jesse and the kids had arrived safely. I emailed my friend Laura and thanked her for setting up the appointment for the meeting with Justine. I hadn't figured out a plan for that evening and I didn't know what to do with myself. I changed into a baggy sweatshirt and flannel pants. I sat down in the silence but was not enjoying the tranquility of the moment. My phone rang, and I picked it up after seeing the caller ID. "Hey Charlotte, what's doing?" She sounded bubbly, "I can't wait for our spa day, Em!" I could not have agreed more. "I am looking forward to it too!" She asked, "So, did you have that appointment today, and are Jesse and the kids at wicked Evelyn's?" She snorted after asking. I told her my appointment went well and it was nice to get dressed for business instead of wearing a t-shirt that Jude wiped Cheese Doodle remnants on. I asked, "Remember Jesse's cousin, Barry?" She grunted, "Vaguely, why?" I answered, "He has a six-year-old son. When I spoke to Jude, he sounded happy Travis was there, and you know Sami is completely adoring of any kid around her age or younger." She was interested in my story. I always appreciated Charlotte's excellent listening skills.

She told me that she and Michael had a minor disagreement but were still planning on having a few people over. She invited me, but I declined, opting for a relaxing evening in. "Ya know, Charlotte, I think I'm going to unwind tonight; maybe order some Chinese takeout and watch a rated R movie or something equally as thrilling." She understood my need for some alone time, and we confirmed noon the next day at Socrates Spa. I searched Netflix and watched many trailers before I turned off the tv and opened my laptop.

I began searching for past emails to and from, Alex and me. I found one that was more than a half-decade old, which brought back a flood or memories.

From: Em3018@optonline.net,
Date: February 12, 2001, at 3:18:13 AM EDT
To: "Alessandra" <Alesa29@aol.com>
Subject: FYI
Hey, do you know I am a mom again? Here is a pic of Sami Gerise (she's almost 6 months). Jude is 3$^{1/2}$, and he's really great with his baby sister. She's perfect and I am truly grateful to be their mom. Jesse is an equally great father and husband. Guess life is good. How are you?
Married? Single? Career? How are your parents and sisters? Hey... I could use an 18-hour night's sleep but I'll settle for a glass of wine with my long-lost best friend. I'll buy...Wanna meet up?

Alex replied to that email four months later.

From: "Alessandra" <Alesa29@aol.com>

Date: June 13, 2001, at 2:13:08 PM EDT
To: Em3018@optonline.net
Subject: Congrats!
**They are absolutely beautiful! Sorry to not have
responded sooner. I hardly go on this email anymore
but a lot going on for me as usual. I am out of town next
week but I'll be in touch upon returning. Enjoy your
beautiful babies. Get sleep too! Xo**

When I read that email years earlier, I remembered I
wondered where out-of-town Alex was going? I wondered
about her future plans and the company she kept. It had
been many years, and our lives had taken such different
paths. It seemed she had little interest in rekindling our
friendship or was the least bit interested in meeting up for a
drink or dinner. Our friendship, once so unique and special,
was never quite the same after I left for college. We
exchanged the occasional hello and always remembered
each other's birthdays. I shared a few snapshots of Jude and
Sami over the years, and she would respond with updates
of Johnny's three girls.

All of her nieces were beautiful and looked more like Alex
than Johnny or his wife. In one of Alex's emails, she wrote,
"…they are my everything! They are adorable and all three
of them look like me. When I get stopped and people tell
me they're beauties, I just say thanks. Hah, so I get to act
like a mommy and then I bring them home. HAH!"

The absence of Alex and Mara was always felt in my life.
I met many friends along the way, but none could fill the
void left by my childhood bestie Mara, and certainly there
was no one who could replace Alex. Their absence was a
constant reminder of the unique bond we shared, and I
often found myself longing for their presence.

I sat back in my desk chair and stared down my black cotton nightshirt. I was amazed at how much my belly had shrunk yet I still felt flab in places I had never recognized before giving birth to two children, which made me think of my younger years and my tighter abs. I thought of the neighborhood kids and wondered what might have become of them. I thought about Mara and how I wanted to try to contact her. I thought about Alex and how our occasional emails never became a get-together.

My mind wandered further back to the first few months of my college day when Alex seemed so distant. I was consumed by homesickness, and every time I tried to reach out to her, I was met with her answering machine. I hated leaving messages and I always hung up before the beep. I wondered if she even knew how much I called.

I called Alex the day I met, my roommate, Bonnie. It was my third day living there and much to my surprise, Alex picked up.

The dialogue took work. It didn't flow naturally and I found myself trying to be casual, "I unpacked everything, Alex. The apartments are as beautiful as they looked in the pictures." She was quiet that day on the other end of the line. I kept saying, "I hope you can come down and visit and maybe with your sisters too." Alex said very little and although I was so bothered by her lack of enthusiasm, I opted out of asking why and continued, "My roommate is supposed to get here sometime today. She sounds very bouncy over the phone. I hope she is not going to be too much to live with. Her name is Bonnie." I was startled when I suddenly heard the door open, I jumped off my bed, "Hold on, Alex." I tossed the cradle down on my bed.

I curiously peaked into the living room. The sun was setting, casting a warm glow over the room. Bonnie was struggling with three bags over her shoulders, a big cardboard box and a plastic bag wrapped around her wrist. I immediately noticed there was nobody close behind. I ran to help, "You're going to stop circulation girlfriend." I took hold of the plastic bag wrapped around her wrist and placed it on the couch. "So, you are Emily and not some weirdo in my apartment?!" She said with a snicker and dropped the box to the floor. "Yes, I am Emily! Hey so my friend from home is on the phone. Let me hang up; be right back!" I ran back to my room. I picked up the receiver, "Hey Alex, she's here. My roommate just got here so I guess I should go." She replied, "Yeah you better, wouldn't want bouncy Bonnie to lose circulation. Talk to ya, Em."

Bonnie stood by my bedroom door. Hey I got a car. Want to go get something to eat?" I replied, "Yeah, I do." I uncapped the handset and asked, "Alex are you there?" She replied, "Yup, Em, I'm here but you are obviously going to eat now. Go have fun." She sounded mad. I said, "Ok Alex. Talk to you soon." I heard a click before I said, 'bye.' We rarely spoke after that. Alex was still busy juggling her further education and work and I was meeting new friends and trying to manage my studies.

When I was done reminiscing, I pushed myself out of the recliner and shuffled down the hallway. The soft carpet under my feet and the familiar scent of my home enveloped me. I stood in my closet, the cool air from the air conditioner brushing against my skin, I debated what to wear. I ran my fingers across the hung clothes, feeling the different textures and fabric I had to choose from. The velvet clothes hangers I ordered from Amazon some months prior kept my closet neat and organized. I stopped on the Calvin Klein, casual woven short sleeve sweater. I pulled my black linen slacks down and my black wedge sandal with small silver rhinestones. I looked at my reflection in my full-length bedroom mirror. I looked good; Casual and smart, without trying too hard. I took a deep breath, grabbed my bag, car key and pressed the garage button to exit the house. As I drove, my mind was filled with memories of my high school days and the years that followed. I pressed scan and sang softly along to the radio, trying to calm my nerves. I flipped down my visor and pulled the mirror open. I applied lip-gloss and pressed the ignition button to turn the car off. I reached for my black denim jacket and walked towards the door. Before I pulled it open, I counted twenty-plus years that had passed and my heart started to beat a little faster.

I wondered why after many years, it was that day I was about to walk into a restaurant she told me she bought, via email, almost a year before that day. She was my best friend during my high school years and the one I lost touch with upon my freshman year in college.

With palms a little damp, determination in check and with a hint of nervousness, that was almost overwhelming, I hoped she was there. *Would she be happy to see me?* Not knowing the answers, I pulled the door open.

Hoxie Ales was darker inside than I thought it would be. I don't know what I pictured but I didn't picture that. I suppose I pictured a higher-end dining establishment and less like the Luncheonette or a pub.

As Sophie was seating a family of four in a corner booth, I couldn't help but notice how little she had aged. The wooden bar and the familiar chitchat among what seemed the regular clients added to the nostalgic atmosphere. But what caught me off guard was Rae's sudden recognition. She stood frozen for a moment, then rushed towards me with open arms, a look of disbelief on her face.

"Oh my God, Emily. You look beautiful. Oh my God!"

I hugged her and saw Sophie walking briskly towards the back of the restaurant. I was sure she had noticed me but perhaps she wasn't certain who I was. I pulled away from our embrace and grabbed Rae's hands, "We are all grown-up. You are too… still so beautiful!" Rae grinned, "Does Alex know, like… you were coming? Wow, Em," and she grabbed my hand and started leading the way.

"Well, she invited me," I paused, "about ten or eleven months ago, so yeah, she probably expects me tonight." Rae turned around laughing, "Em, you still got your witty sense of humor, huh?" Her smile led the way. I followed her to an open door in the back of the restaurant.

Alex was standing in the corner of a tiny room on the phone. I felt a familiar serenity and a beaming smile swept my face. Her eyes grew big and she reciprocated the smile and the feeling. I waited for her phone call to end. Rae said, "Em, we are super busy tonight but I'll be back in a few." She disappeared down the corridor. I stepped closer into the tiny room I assumed Alex used as an office. There was a small high-top dinette and one barstool. A clipboard on the tabletop and boxes stacked up in the other corner. She never took her eyes off me.

"Okay, Aaron, sounds good… okay yes, sounds perfect… okay. Let's touch base next week then, k bye Aaron." She simultaneously placed the receiver on the wall cradle and I felt a tap from behind.

I turned, and Sophie exclaimed, "I didn't believe Rae! How are you… here? Emily Netti?" She had a friendly yet inquisitive expression. "Yes, it's me, just with a few more pounds and a few more wrinkles." I hugged Sophie and there the three of us stood in wonderment at this impromptu reunion. Alex started to move towards me and Sophie moved swiftly out of her way.

"Em, Wow." I wrapped my arms around her as I did moments earlier with Sophie and Rae. Sophie snuck around us as there wasn't much room. "Okay, Em see you in a bit; we got customers.

Please stay until we close, and we will do a shot. Lord knows after today I need Patron." As soon as she left, I said, "Soph hasn't changed a bit, huh?"

I could not believe I was standing in Alex's presence. It felt surreal, and I knew she felt the same. "Em, want to sit at the bar? Are you hungry?" I answered, "I guess. Sure, I mean, I'm not starving. Well, is this a bad time for you? This place seems really busy." Alex shrugged, "Follow me." She walked and said, "It's always busy, and my mom isn't here tonight. Johnny needed her to babysit John-John." I asked, "I thought your brother had three girls?" She grabbed my hand, "...and oops, then came John-John. He's a little terror, but I love that kid!"

I followed her to the bar. We sat in the corner, and a young girl came right over. "Maggie," Alex requested, "Two of your best Cosmo's, please." Maggie winked and went to shake us up a cocktail. "As in, Cosmopolitan?" I asked. Alex pulled her bar stool closer to the bar, "Do you not like Cosmo's?" She casually asked. I answered her, "I never had a Cosmo, but I'll try anything once or twice if I like it." Then, I laughed at my own joke.

She looked so surprised, "Seriously, Em? You seriously made it passed forty and never had a Cosmo? Well, what do you want? I'll drink both Cosmo's, for Pete's sake. Maggie's are the best in town." I laughed and said, "No, this is as good a time as any to try a Cosmo, Alex. I think this drink together is long overdue!" Maggie set down two martini glasses and poured from the pewter cocktail shaker. There were bits of ice shavings and she filled our glasses to the rim." Alex lifted the drink with finesse, and I was cautious, trying to not spill it like a child. We carefully tapped our glasses, "Welcome to Hoxie's, my long-lost Emily."

I took a sip. "Do you like it?" I nodded, smiled, and raised my eyebrows. "Love!" I said, "It is a perfect drink to mark this momentous occasion. Yes, very good." I watched Alex sip and gently place her glass in front of her.

"One day Em, you are going to tell me why tonight, after decades, you walked into Hoxie's but right now, I have to take care of something. Can you give me five?" I answered, "Of course, go! I shouldn't have barged in on a busy Friday night anyway." Alex touched my forearm, "Stay, please if you can. I'll bounce back in a few. Meanwhile, order an app or anything you want." She excused herself from the bar stool. It reminded me of our visits in the Luncheonette. The only difference was she owned the place.

In between her brief absences, I thought about how time says goodbye so quickly. When she returned, we effortlessly reconnected, as if the years apart had never existed.

Once the corner booth on the other side of the bar opened up, we moved ourselves and our second round of Cosmo's over to it. That table was private and we were able to talk more.

I didn't feel the lapse of two decades. Alex didn't seem to feel it either. She told me that she recently sold Hoxie's and it was the last two months she would be operating before the transition. She told me she made enough money to invest in a new restaurant further out East. I was not surprised and was so proud and happy for her. She was following her dream. The same one she spoke of, on the roof of the Luncheonette, our favorite spot for deep conversations, decades earlier.

Sophie and Rae sat with us by evening end for a bit. Rae slid close to me in the booth. The smell of her shirt reminded me of my youth. We had spinach dip and other appetizers. Sophie brought over four shots of tequila with lime wedges and salt. The four of us held them high in the center of the table, and Sophie exclaimed, "To Emily... back in our lives." I loved Sophie's toast and we laughed like teenagers. We shared the spirits. We talked about the old times, like naming the cute boys at the feast Marcello, and Ernesto and we touched upon some new ones. Hoxie Ales felt like home.

Alex walked me to my car, "Em, that was a lightning-fast four hours." I felt the same. "Yes, it was. I agree. Alex, it's been way too long."

Her expression may have been tinged with sadness, yet she managed to smile. "I feel like we hardly talked about your life! So, how's married life and... ya know, being a mom?" I knew the answer was too complicated, so I just said, "The kids are a blessing but I can't say it's easy." She waited and was expecting me to say more. Perhaps she expected a different reply altogether. I wasn't sure how to answer. I was trying to avoid the truth. She asked the same question with a new set of words.

"Are you happy, Em?" I breathed through my nose and exhaled, "Hey Alex, I don't want to stand here in this parking lot and tell you this, but I don't believe my marriage will succeed. But I just did say that, didn't I?" She was definitely caught off guard. She nodded, looked at me for a few silent seconds and then asked, "Em, are you around on Sunday?" I usually could not have replied as I did however, Jesse would still be away, "I am free all day!" Alex took her phone out of her back pocket. "What is your cell number?" She carefully dialed in the digits as I called them out. My phone vibrated in my bag. I reached in and hit decline. "Okay, we are officially back in touch! Em, life is way too short. I don't know what took you so long." She stepped forward and hugged me.

I opened my car door and settled in. I started the ignition and lowered the driver-side window. "Alex... um... my kids and Jesse happen to be away this weekend visiting his parents but will be back Sunday night, so earlier would be best for me."

She put her hands on the bottom of the open window holding tightly onto the door and leaned back. "Hey then, I'll pick you up before noon. I would like to take a ride and we will have time to talk. There is something I want to show you too."

I put the car in reverse and started backing out slowly. "I'll see you then; I will text my address. You do text, right?" She giggled and that sound brought me back to my teenage years. She said, "Em, of course, I text! I'm not that old!" Alex waved and didn't re-enter the restaurant until my car made the left out of the lot.

Early Sunday morning, I called Jesse. He picked up with a hint of frustration. "Emily, Sami is being a handful. Can I call you back after church? I pleaded, "Can't we just talk for a minute?" He was half listening and ordering Sami to stop whining. "Jesse, put her on the phone!" I heard the phone rustle, and then Sami's voice, "Hi, Mom," she said, sounding a bit disgruntled. "Hey, sweetheart, I miss you!" Her voice immediately softened, "I miss you too, Mommy." I smiled on my end, and I could feel the impact of my smile on Sami's end.

"Hey Sami, is Dad making you wear a dress to church, and that's why you are giving him a hard time?" She said, "Uh huh." I figured. "Hey Sami, when you put Dad back on the phone… um, go and put on your new romper from Justice or your favorite blue dress. Daddy will see how pretty you look and what a big girl you are for getting yourself dressed and choosing your own special outfit for church. I will try to keep him on the phone, but you must be quick." She seemed delighted with the idea and that I was on her side. I added, "Don't forget to brush your hair and teeth. I will see you tonight and maybe we can have a sleepover in your room." Sami was delighted, "Oh, Mommy, can we watch the Barbie DVD movie?" I agreed, although I hardly enjoyed it the first twelve times, I saw it. I knew it was her favorite and said, "Of course we can and then you can tell me all about your trip." She replied, "Goody, Mommy!" I requested, "Sami, put Daddy back on and give Meems and Grandpa a hug from me."

She did, and Jesse immediately asked, "How did you do that?" I answered, "Jess, choose your battles. Give her a choice of two outfits that are appropriate for church. This way, she will feel like it was her decision whichever she chooses. Let her wear what she wants. It will make it easier for you. I mean, she really doesn't have to wear a dress to church." Jesse disagreed, "Emily, I don't know why you let her get away with everything. She's a little girl and should wear a dress to mass." Naturally, he would contest me. "Oh, Jesse, she's six years old. Her romper is entirely appropriate, and neither of you will be miserable." He sighed. I asked how Jude was and if he wanted to speak to me. Jesse told me he was playing outside with Travis. "Okay Jess, you sound busy, so I'll let you go. What time do you think you will be getting on the road?" Still distracted, he responded. "I don't know; I'll let you know later. We will probably grab a bite in the early afternoon, and well, I just don't know if I will ever get out of the house with Sami behaving this way." I felt minimal sympathy, "Okay Jess, sorry… but welcome to my world: Everyday! If you would react differently, Sami would too, and she wouldn't carry on." He was curt, "Yeah, Em, I got it. I'll call you when we are leaving later."

Moments later, Alex arrived at my door. I waved her in. She crossed the threshold of the door and looked around. "I love your porch, Emily. You have a beautiful home." I invited her inside. She studied the pictures on the wall but saved her comments.

"Can I offer you a drink or anything?" She chuckled, "Em, it's a little early." I smiled, "I meant, like water?" She giggled, "I was only kidding. Hey, I want to take a ride. Are you up… for a ride? How long before, uh, the fam returns?" I stood up and grabbed my sweatshirt off the back of the chair. "They won't be back till late this evening and yes, let's go." Alex said, "Alright then, what are we waiting for?"

Her Highlander was immaculate and unlike my sports utility. There weren't toys or DVDs or a booster seat with cookie crumbs. "Nice ride, Alex! I like trucks. I will never buy a car again." She agreed, "Me neither. This is my second Toyota and I just love it. I looked at others but I love this car, so yep, it's my second. Not quite a Camaro, though, eh?" She made a turn and headed eastbound. "No! It's not a Camaro! So, my friend; where are we going?" I asked. She removed her sunglasses from the overhead compartment and slid them over her eyes. "Well, I would rather not say. I just want you to see something, and we will be there in about an hour." I nodded in acceptance of the mysterious road trip. Reminded me of the days she took me to meet Aunt Annie eras earlier. We didn't struggle to talk during the ride. We had many years to catch up on and it was with ease; conversation flowed like a river. There were brief moments when Alex would turn up the radio volume and conversations would cease during a song. We still had the same great taste in music. The ride seemed shorter than I would have liked, and we pulled up onto a gravel driveway and parked in front of a white Victorian home with light blue trim and wooden shutters. It was a sight to behold, the beauty of the Victorian home captivated me. Alex stepped outside, "So, are you coming?" I climbed out of the car, "Alex, who lives here?" Her eyes were full of mischief. "Nobody lives here, Em. C'mon. It's not like we are going to get arrested, although that sounds fun."

I followed her up three steps and watched her insert a key into both the top and bottom locks of the door. The metal clinked against the wood, echoing in the spacious entrance. There was a podium upon entering and an eight-foot entranceway into a massive space. I looked up at the high ceilings, feeling the vastness of the room and noticed the long bar with a gray-cement countertop, its smooth surface inviting to the touch. Tables were strategically placed and chairs were stacked along the wall's edge.

"Alex, what is this? Where are we?" She cast her bag on top of the bar. "Emily, we are here… at the BlueIris Grille." I looked at her inquisitively. She added, "And I own it!" I loved it, "Alex, it's beautiful. I think I pictured *this* when I walked into Hoxie's?" She twirled around three hundred and sixty degrees. "I bought Hoxie's as is. I knew I eventually wanted to open and design my own place. The contractors just finished the bar last week. I hoped to open sooner but so much more must be done." I thought the place was so cool, "How exciting, Alex!" She flipped on a set of six light switches and explained, "It was a quaint bed and breakfast. The couple who sold it wanted to begin their retirement, so opportunity knocked and here I am. I know! I am crazy!"

At first, I was so envious. "Oh my God, Alex! Um, no, you aren't crazy. This is unreal! This is unbelievable! It's beautiful! How did you do this? I can't believe it!" She frowned, "I took out an enormous loan, Em, and I am terrified." I couldn't help but admire her courage in taking such a big step. She asked me if it reminded me of anything. I told her the color scheme reminded me of the Luncheonette and she beamed. We walked around and she showed me everything. She was proud of the kitchen with its shiny oversized appliances and endless counter space. A narrow stairway led upstairs with only a desk and file cabinet in one corner of an enormous empty loft. "Alex, will you have more seating up here? Wow, there's a lot of room up here!" I walked briskly around, feeling the infinite freedom. My voice echoed in the emptiness. Alex burst into fast forward. "Well, I will do it up when funds become available. I'm thinking a mini-apartment, slash office." I was shocked, "Are you moving here above the restaurant?" She answered, "No, I don't want to live above the restaurant, but it would be nice to make it comfortable enough to crash after a long night. She put on reading glasses and shuffled some papers.

"There is a bathroom and shower behind that door and she pointed to the other side of the empty room." I walked towards it. "Ugh, Em, it's gross… don't even look at it. Use the one downstairs if you need to." I stopped dead in my tracks and I faced Alex. "Just looking, don't need to pee at this particular moment." She gasped, "Thanks for the down-low on your bodily functions." I stared at a picture that hung behind her.

"Alex? Marilyn?" I pointed, "…from… Brian's? I remember that picture. Wow, Alex! It's classic!" Alex slid her reading glasses off. She looked up at the framed picture behind her, deep in thought. Still staring at the picture, she said, "Em, those days were such good times!" I didn't let her finish, "Was it a can of soup or art? So funny, so many laughs." I said, "I remember those days, Alex. That was one of the best summers of my life." She continued to gaze, "Em, you are the only person that would know about that picture.

When Brian closed the Luncheonette… Well, I asked for that. I've definitely missed you. You are part of all the memories, all the innocent, all the…." She looked away from the picture and down to the papers on her desk. She put her glasses back on. I stared at the picture. Vivid memories flooded my mind. The Luncheonette and my younger years and Alex. She returned to her paperwork, and I quietly said aloud, "I remember all of it and have thought of you so many times throughout the years. Whatever kept us apart... well, life is too short and I could use a friend right now.

For whatever it's worth, my heart was beating fast when I opened the door to Hoxie's on Friday and it's surreal to be here with you right now. Alex, I'm asking Jesse for a divorce." Alex looked me square in the face. She heard my every word. She didn't reply.

Chapter Twelve

I boarded the plane with a heavy heart. I held Jake's hand tightly but hoping he would not sense my anxiety. I handed the attendant the boarding passes with Jude and Sami and the bickering twins, close behind. Charlotte struggled to manage the twins arguing about who was going to get the window seat. I felt a mix of emptiness and sadness not wanting to go on this trip but feeling obligated for the sake of the kids, Charlotte and Mike and our parents.

Vivien and I were at odds. She seemed to expect our family traditions to remain unchanged, even though Jesse had moved out just four months prior. I felt she, in turn believed I was the cause of my own situation. The tension between us was a constant reminder of the shifting dynamics in our family.

When we arrived in Aruba, I felt a wave of nostalgia. It was so hard to make sense of all the emotions that came with the tradition of family vacations that had developed through the years of my marriage. A key player was missing. We all felt his absence, yet nobody spoke about it, except Vivien. She brought Jesse's name up more than I would have liked, reminding us of his absence. I felt like I had ruined everything for my parents, children, and Michael's family too.

We settled quickly. It was as familiar as home. Franco upgraded his unit twice to meet the needs of the growing family. His once studio was now an upgraded suite with five bedrooms and four bathrooms. There was ample privacy for all of us. Michael helped purchase the roomier upgrade, and Franco and Viv, spent six weeks on the island yearly during the winter months and their stay became four or five months as years flew by.

Our unit was a beachfront duplex, the salty breeze from the ocean always lingering in the air. My room, with its partial ocean view, was a sanctuary. I would often find myself lost in the rhythmic sound of the waves crashing against the shore, a few minutes of solace before joining the crowd for our morning shenanigans.

Vivien and Franco's master suite was a luxurious retreat, complete with a Jacuzzi. Michael and Charlotte, not to be outdone, claimed the king-size bed with its breathtaking ocean view and private bath. Charlotte, always the protective one, insisted Jake sleep on the bottom bunk in the boys' room. Jude was thrilled to sleep on the top bunk and the three girls, in their usual fashion transformed the open den into a playful mess that filled our traditional weekly visit every year since Jude was born.

As usual, we took an early flight eager to make the most of our time in paradise. Vivien prepared a delicious lunch while Charlotte and I settled and helped the kids suit up. It was before noon with full bellies and sunscreen applied. We all headed out the sliding doors to the beach, the warm sand beneath our feet. Charlotte and I sat at the beach hut, our favorite spot for people-watching. I ordered her a Pina Colada and myself a Mudslide.

"How are you holding up, Em?" I sipped my frosty delight, trying to hide the turmoil within. "I am okay. Why do I not... seem okay?" Charlotte, always perceptive, gave me a sympathetic expression. We toasted and sat in silence. My unspoken words were hanging in the air. I watched the boys build a sand castle with Mike and it felt like a bittersweet reminder of the joy that seemed out of reach. Charlotte stood up from her bar stool, "I'm going to take a walk by the water. Do you want to come?" I stirred my straw inside the clear plastic cup, contemplating her offer. "Nah, I will sit under the palapo for a bit. I think I'll start my book." Charlotte approved, "Who ya got this vaca?" I winked at her. "The Beach House, Jane Green." Before Charlotte walked away, she gave me a thumbs-up and grinned, "It's a good one, Em. Read it a few months ago."

Sami, Mehgan, and Maya Rose ran on the golden sand without hesitation until the crashing waves threatened to reach their toes. Charlotte fully engaged in their game. I watched the four of them inch toward the water. Sami sprinted away when the spinning wave turned up the surf with white foam. A squall of water diffused into the air behind her. Her smile lit me up inside. She waved to me from a distance. I waved back to my mini-me. I always considered Sami a much better version of myself. As she ran from each wave, I retraced moments of my life in her every footprint. Each one representing my own footprints etched in the same sand decades before she existed. Sami looked like I once did with better curls. I was once the same untroubled eight-year-old making brazen forward steps deeper into the sea.

I tried to trust where I was and why I was there. I sat back in the lounge chair. It was peaceful. Vivian and Franco talked to other owners who they became friendly with, since they bought their timeshare when I was still a teen. I waved to Jude when he stood up and pointed to the giant sand castle he made with his uncle and cousin Jake. He looked happy, but I knew he was missing Jesse's presence in his life while building that castle. The trade winds made it comfortable enough to read in the shade before my eyes felt heavy. I dozed off into a hypnotic nap.

I was woken by the shadow I felt on my face. Sami was standing over me. She blocked the intense ray of the setting sun. Her silhouette was as beautiful as the sun's glimmer on the white sand. "Mommy, everyone just went in to get ready for dinner except Uncle Mike." She pointed to Michael sleeping in a fetal position on Jude's wet towel in the sand. I rubbed my eyes and stretched like I had slept for eight hours. "What time is it, Sam?" She draped the blowing towel over me. "Um, I dunno, Mom? Should I go in?" I sat up and pulled the towel to my neck. The wind had kicked up, and I felt a chill. "Yes, Sami, go shower and I'll come inside in a few minutes." She kissed my cheek and sprinted away.

Four steps met the sand's edge up to the sliding doors. I watched Sami slither the door open and step inside. I sat for a few minutes and breathed in the crystal air.

I wasn't used to being there without a husband, and it felt strange and unsettling to be uncoupled. The beach, usually a place of joy and connection, now felt immense and empty. I stared at my brother, out cold on the damp towel. Memories raced. I was still, in fact, grieving my loss. I wasn't sure if I was saddened to be without Jesse or just uncomfortable not being with anybody.

I woke up every day for over a decade and slipped a ring onto my finger. It was a habit and became part of my every day. I stared down at my ring finger. It was as bare as my empty heart. I gathered my belongings and started inside. My foot tapped Michael's back. "I'm heading in; get up nerd," I said. Michael barely opened his eyes, raised his thumb, and I knew he would shortly follow.

After dinner, Michael and Franco volunteered to take the kids to the beach by the bonfire. They would throw around a tennis ball and roast marshmallows with friends who shared the same week or weeks of timeshare owners throughout the years.

Vivien, Charlotte, and I were kid-free for our annual girls' night out. With full bellies after fine dining, Franco held Jake's little hand in his, and they walked back toward our duplex at a six-year-old's pace. Michael kissed Charlotte on the cheek and trotted away. He scooped up Maya and sat her on his shoulders. Sami and Meghan looked up at her, wishing Mike grabbed one of them instead.

My brother was six feet, two inches tall with broad shoulders and developed muscles. His dirty blonde hair, much lighter than mine, was always cut short above his ears. He was always neatly shaven; his Tommy Bahama Men's Tiki and Ralph Lauren shorts exhibited stature, even on vacation. Michael was a great father and uncle. I loved when he was around my children. At that time, Maya was chosen to get Michael's attention and to be hoisted onto his shoulders but he made equal time for all the girls to be his special princess.

Franco showed indistinguishable patience with his youngest grandchild Jake as he did with Jude years earlier. I started to recognize Franco was aging, and it bothered me. As they walked further away, the three of us turned to walk up the hill. We arrived at the entrance of the small, quaint island casino. A few hours later, underneath the dusky sky we walked and laughed about losing money in the rigged slot machines.

Vivian lost two hundred dollars, and we laughed as we promised, we wouldn't tell Franco. Charlotte decided not to mention the exact dollar amount she may have lost. I won a few hundred, and that slightly helped to lift my mood. On our walk home, Vivien mentioned she ran into Erica from Ohio, earlier that day on the beach who thought the three girls were triplets. They could have passed for triplets, only five months apart and wearing matching bikinis. They were all gorgeous.

Vivien retired to bed while Charlotte and I remained outside on the porch overlooking the sand and listening to the sounds of the evening. The distant sound of the beach huts' reggae music created a serene backdrop to our conversation. It was a quiet and tranquil evening. Charlotte asked me if I was okay again, a question that often led to our many profound discussions.

"I know the divorce has a shelf life, Charlotte. I suppose the memories of living with Jesse are slowly losing their sting. On the good days, at least." Charlotte listened intently as I poured my heart out. "I am trying so hard to be fully present in my role of a mom and to rediscover my own joy. But, Charlotte, I'm lost. I was a wife, and now I'm struggling to recognize the woman I've become."

She sat upright and poised. She demanded my complete attention. "Emily, I am watching you emerge as an independent, single mom, and I see you getting more done in a day than most can in a week. Give yourself a break. It's only been a few months. You will get through this!" I nodded in agreement. I appreciated my cheerleading sister-in-law. She told me about some tough talks she had with Michael about always working and never being present. I understood her frustrations. We spoke a half hour more before Meghan came out and sat on Charlotte's lap.

I leaned in, playfully taping my niece's knee. Hey Meg, you look like a sleepy little chicken! Meghan, the lightest of the twins, with her curly blonde hair and dark, expressive eyes, was a sight to behold. She was my heart and I loved her fiercely. I loved both my nieces and nephew, as if they were my own. She rubbed her eyes and started to whine.

"Aunt Em, I wanted to go to sleep, but Sami and Maya are being so annoying." I stood up, reached for Meghan's hand, and commanded, "Come with me; let's go beat them up!" Charlotte giggled. Meghan hopped off her mom's lap and we entered our beachfront.

It didn't take long to settle the kids. Thankfully, the bright sunshine all day made them tired. Jake fell asleep on Jude while watching a movie in the living room. The three girls were sleeping in their room. Michael picked up Jake and placed him in the lower bunk. Franco stayed in the living room and finished watching Cars with Jude.

I climbed into bed, and my mind still raced. My life was not easy and convenient. It was hard work, and there was no sidestepping my responsibilities. A far cry from the freedoms I had raising and maintaining children and a household with a helping husband. There was nobody to pass the buck off to, and I realized I did pass the buck off for many years of our union, especially after the children were born. Jesse did make my burdens easier. He made up for whatever we lacked in passion, taking care of everyday responsibilities without complaint. Suddenly I felt alone and afraid. If I didn't complete daily tasks, they simply would not get done.

Those first years were hard to make up for his absence. I had to change light bulbs, shovel snow, and clean the barbecue. I missed having him take care of the maintenance. I took those amenities for granted, and he took for granted his laundered underwear placed neatly next to an opened Viagra bottle he never told me he had. I couldn't sleep and remembered weeks earlier endlessly searching the garage for a screw gun in an attempt to fix a cabinet hinge. I could still hear Sami's high-pitched memo, "Mom, the cereal cabinet door is about to fall off!" I yelled from my office, "Yeah, I know, sweetheart. I'll deal with it! Just open it gently for now, okay?"

It took three more weeks, but I eventually found the screw gun. I set a ladder, climbed upon it and tightened the screw into the hinge. It was finally fixed, and I felt like a brain surgeon. *I got this*! *I'm going to be okay. I would stop procrastinating. I would clean out a drain or paint Sami's room*, as she had been begging me to do all year.

It took time, but I eventually learned a great deal about how capable I was. It was an invaluable lesson for Sami as she observed and often helped with such tasks. I learned how to take the garbage out joyfully and feel confident in my abilities to keep up our home.

Weeks later, the hinge I thought I had fixed eventually loosened again. *Damn it*! I thought. It was stripped and would never fasten tightly. The entire hinge needed to be remounted and required a new assembly.

That was not one of the good days. In fact, there were lots of mornings that started with milk that had gone bad or the mildew that had set into the clothes I forgot to switch into the dryer, the garbage disposal clogged and other things unhinged, especially my mental state. Though Mike and Franco had the talent and the funds to do whatever they wanted in their homes, I never had the money to call in specialists and things went undone. I hadn't the time and was not inclined to become Bob the Builder, so I ignored the problems for as long as possible. Jesse had nothing to give and the kids and I had the bare minimum.

Many months later, on a cold, snowy morning, Vivien came by to sit with the kids because I had to leave early for work. She must have noticed the cabinet was loose and mentioned it to Franco because that evening, he came by to take a look. He disappeared and returned with a few tools and a bag from the hardware store. Twenty minutes later, it was fixed. *Check mark*! I never had to look at that again.

I thanked God for my parents. I always knew through all the struggles and disappointments my divorce caused, my parents were standing by, making sure I would make it through; and I did make it through because they were… standing by.

I was home from Aruba with a glowing tan. I felt great physically, but mentally I was about to break. I sat on the ledge of an enormous window wall with my feet crossed at my ankle, looking over a man-made lake. I would have preferred to lounge on the ledge, but I was sure that wasn't appropriate in family court. I glanced out and noticed the lake's army green color. The word *muck* came to my mind. Surrounded by an over-crowded parking lot that represented some of the muck in the building.

The dark gray blanket of clouds hovered over the blowing American flag as if the system I was unwillingly sucked into was something to be proud of. The system sucked; I thought perpetuated by monies and lawyers who were the only ones who could victor.

At that moment, it occurred to me that Jesse wasn't ever a problem solver. He needed someone else to decide for him. That was my job during our marriage. That day I suppose, was the honorable judges' job.

Jesse's lawyer sat about thirty feet away with his briefcase, and I waited for the briefcase attached to my representation to arrive. I was dressed like I was headed to Sunday Mass and kept all the emotion locked inside the deepest part of myself. I glanced up and noticed him walking up the corridor. I chuckled to think he seemed to have realized the way he was dressed on our previous matrimonial court dates was antiquated, and now in full view was his best suit and tie.

"Hi, Emily," he said in his deep and assured voice. I looked up from my place on the window ledge. With my best poker face, I only nodded. Instead of cordially walking by, his smug-self stopped and backed up, his eyes lingering on me for a moment longer than necessary.

"Sami's run looks fun, huh?" My puzzled face did not stay concealed. "We are about to walk into a courtroom and you want to have idle chatter about Sami's Student Council walk for Breast Cancer? You must be kidding, Jess?" His words were sharp, his tone impatient. He walked away, his steps echoing in the corridor, leaving me with a sense of relief. His suit pants were on the short side. I shook my head and re-opened my laptop, the tension in the air lingering.

He was a chameleon of sorts. I am still unsure which personality demonstrated throughout the years of our marriage was his most true self. I was far less anxious, and it was less unpleasant than our first court date and the ones that followed almost a year prior in the same attempt to get unmarried. I felt more accepting of the process and my lack of any control to make it go my way or any faster. It was in my lawyer's hands and in God's after that. Divorce is a multi-billion-dollar business, and I knew why.

After several hours and more of the same legal jargon that completely wasted our time and emptied our bank accounts, I was able to get out of there. Jesse saw me walking out of the building and offered a quick handshake and goodbye to his lawyer. He hurried to catch up, and I pleaded, "Jesse, please!" I stopped dead in my tracks and looked straight ahead. He stepped forward, then back and spoke, "Em, I told you this was going to be a financial nightmare! How much do you think I have to give?" I turned only my head towards him. "Jesse, you have made a mess of things. I have to go to work now. I am not engaging in the same conversation with you. Broken promises, Jesse." I darted forward, and Jesse kept talking, "Em, I didn't work my whole life to give you all my money. I need a house! Is it fair that you have a house? Your life hasn't changed. My life did! The kids' lives did..." I never turned around. I kept walking to the far end of the parking lot. He didn't follow me. His voice trailed off. My state of mind was varying degrees of heartbreak and anger. I thought, *He doesn't get to do this*! *When things were bad, he wasn't present! He was all in for the good times. I was present and trying to fix it, and he simply wasn't. Trials and tribulations and the roller coaster… When the dip came, I asked him to show me how we would make it back up, but he had nothing but a blank stare and wanted to watch a baseball game or porn after I went to sleep.*

As I drove home, the weight of my self-doubt and blame began to crush me. It was a moment of reckoning, a time to stop the self-inflicted torment. I needed to open my eyes to the truth of the day we decided to part ways. He suggested a vacation, but I knew deep down what we needed was therapy, not another escape.

Despite my anger, I still cared about him and understood that his actions resulted from his own pain. He was missing the stability of our family life, no longer living with his wife and children. However, he moved on quickly, fully engaged in a new relationship weeks after our separation. Two years later, he was still seeing that woman, along with a few one-nighters in between. I knew very little about Jesse's life; however, a friend of mine was still his Facebook friend and at times, I was privy to posts and pictures of Jesse in bars surrounded by many friends and blondes. I wondered if he was happier being single or would not have preferred divorce. I am sure he saw my Facebook too and I didn't care one bit. I never un-friended his cousins and other connected people. I did unfriend his siblings because they only heard Jesse's side and I thought they hated me. Many people on Facebook are only spying. I was rarely at peace and had barely a minute to breathe. I had so much discontent that we didn't make it. I had to overcome so much guilt and regret. I was coming to terms with a broken family dynamic and a financial nightmare. Jesse wasn't coming around to spend as much time with the kids as I thought he would have. I was even more disappointed with his decision to pay for less than I needed to keep them in the lifestyle they were accustomed to. He didn't handle the divorce any differently than he did the marriage, except for a new side of anger, I had witnessed in small increments. We weren't even close to a settlement. The financial pressure felt suffocating.

I hung up my court clothes and immediately sat before my Mac. Jude and Sami were with Vivien and Franco at the local Arena Circus.

My cell phone vibrated on my desk, and I saw Alex's picture on my screen. I swiped to answer. "Hey, Alex," I said. I heard some muffling, and then a voice emerged. "Hey Em, Where the hell have you been? What's happening?" I put her on speaker and spoke from my desk. "I had court again today, and ugh, whatever. Another waste of time and money." Alex blurted out, "What the hell is going on? Why is your divorce taking so long? Seems to me Jesse is just prolonging the inevitable." I didn't have anything new to report. Each court date amounted to nothing but another invoice from our law firms. "Nothing much, Alex. I don't think it is Jesse prolonging it. It's the greedy lawyers and all the nonsense. I really don't want to talk about it." She understood I was utterly frustrated. "Hey, want to meet up at Respa's for happy hour? Sophie and some of her friends will be there." I told her that sounded great, and we planned to meet at five o'clock.

Before I took a shower, I checked Facebook. I saw a message and clicked on the notification. I hadn't heard from Mara Conti in years. I read her message.

Hi Emily, I just joined Facebook. I can't believe I saw your

name pop up, and so how the hell are you? I am living in New Hampshire but coming to New York next week. I would love to get together. Is your profile picture of your kids? They're beautiful! I have one myself and she's everything. Please message back asap.

I typed.

Welcome to Facebook Mars! Yes, they are my kids, and I would love to hear about your kid? Name and age, please? And yes, for sure-to getting together next week. LMK when you are coming around and what can work for you. Better to text or call me... 516-333-1410. I hate Facebook but can't seem to quit it... lol.

I waited a few minutes while catching up on some emails, but Mara never replied. I shut down the computer and decided to get ready to meet the girls at happy hour.

I was a half hour late and didn't reply while driving to the numerous *where are you* texts from Alex and the one from Rae. I walked in, and Alex had already ordered me a glass of cabernet.

"Sorry, I am late! I hugged and cheek-kissed everyone. Sophie introduced me to a few friends I hadn't met, and I said hi to the handful of others I had met. Alex handed me my glass of wine. "Thanks... and cheers." We both took a sip of our drinks and exhaled loudly.

Alex closed the BlueIris, two long weekends per year. Once in the summer and once at the end of January. On those weekends, it was customary to start the weekend with happy hour at Respa's.

"So, tough day again?" She said, "Yeah, court sucks, and as I stated before, I really don't want to talk about it." Alex didn't reply. I wanted to tell her I heard from Mara, but Sophie's friend had her ear for a while. Rae and I ordered another round of drinks and Friday night had begun.

The bar was loud, and the music was lower than expected. I was silently wondering how many court dates I would have to endure. I was amid grievance, confusion, regret, and blame. Nothing was changing in my life, and yet everything had changed.

I stared past Sophie into the distance. She was married but wasn't able to have children. She and her husband, Landon, gave up after spending thousands on fertility. Rae was just single. Nobody ever questioned why. Personally, I never thought she was gay or unattractive. I thought Rae was just asexual. She was also the kindest person since day one when I met her cramped in the back seat of the Camaro. I never heard her complain that day or any day after that. Just as Rae returned from the ladies' room, Alex managed to extricate herself from Sophie's friends. I couldn't contain my excitement as I blurted out, "Guess who I heard from on Facebook today?" Both of them looked at me, waiting for me to reveal the identity of the mysterious messenger.

Without hesitation, I exclaimed, "Mara! Can you believe it?" Alex raised her eyebrows. "Really? Wow! Just out of the blue?" I explained, "So… she said she's new to Facebook and found me. She said she is coming back to New York next week and wants to try to grab lunch." Rae interjected, "I think I remember her a little, but did she hang out with us?" Alex answered Rae, "She was Em's friend and not really in our club. She didn't like me because I stole her…," she pointed to me, "away from bike riding." Then she asked me, "Are you going to have lunch or *no way*?"

I thought the 'stole me away' comment was a bit immature, but I ignored it. I answered, "Hell yeah, I def will try to meet up with Mars. The last time I saw her was at her wedding, like um, what?" I paused to think, "I guess fourteen years ago." Alex looked puzzled, "Wow, you never told me you went to her wedding?" I shrugged, "I think I saw her once after her wedding. I think we had dinner with some girl from high school, and I can't remember her name?" Alex was snippy, "Okay, so why couldn't you tell me you went to her wedding?" I sensed dismay. "Alex, I don't know. Mars hasn't been a huge topic in our discussions. We did lose a few years in between. I guess there are many things I didn't mention that happened in twenty-something years." Alex was pissed and said, "I'm sure there is Emily. And really, we're not twelve! You can stop calling her *Mars*." She walked away. Rae and I were left standing there looking at each other. "Why does she act like that?" I asked. Rae shrugged her shoulders and had no comment. I ordered a third glass of wine, feeling increasingly uncomfortable. I wasn't having a good time and Alex was distant the rest of the evening.

I arrived home and washed up. I called Vivien as it was approaching nearly nine and the circus ended at seven. She answered on the first ring," Yes, we are late because your father is a sucker, and we went for ice-cream." I chuckled, "Of course you did, being that you probably didn't buy them any popcorn or pretzels at the circus." Vivien knew I was being facetious. "No pretzels but popcorn, yes, and chicken tenders and two hotdogs for Jude." Vivien laughed. "We are home now, and Charlotte is here to pick up Meghan. She will drop off your kids in about an hour." I said, "Okay, I just crawled into bed with a book, but I will be up. How was it?" Vivien said Sami loved the monkeys, and now she wants to become a veterinarian." I was impressed. "Well Mom, be sure to tell Dad to put away some funds because vet school is expensive.

Hey, and tell Charlotte if I don't see her on the driveway, I'll talk to her tomorrow. Thanks for taking them." We said goodnight and hung up the phone.

I poured myself some more wine I had left over from two days prior. I placed it on my nightstand and stared at the front cover of a new paperback. I was too tired and buzzed to read. I thought, *who are you kidding?*

I sat in silence and began to think again. I wasn't changing. I wasn't comfortable with how I was conducting my life. The divorce was taking a toll. I wanted to run from what I had created and start anew, but there was no way out.

A few years after the onset of our separation, Jesse maintained and rebuilt his relationship with the kids. He was almost absent and only there for his every-other-weekend obligation and once weekly dinner for the first few years of the divorce and left all the hardships of raising the kids to me. When they became easier and old enough to hang out with, he re-emerged into this super fun dad, bonding and planning adventures with them and his girlfriend on his weekends.

He started coming around more often, and our kids were responding to him. I was happy that was happening. But at that time, my discontent for him was at an all-time high. Some days I was failing and felt like he was the come-from-behind win parent, while I was an absolute mess. I went into self-destructive mode, especially after a court date. I felt like an epic failure. The anxiety was met with wine, and the wine caused more anxiety. I was a disaster. I called Alex, "What did I do? I am falling apart! I just can't." Alex replied, "Okay, there ya go again, Em. Yes, you are a train wreck. You are out of control after a court date, and you have two kids. I am unsure why you married him but you do have two amazing kids." Another comment that was true but a confusing comment coming from one who claimed to be one of my people. "Hell, I only got Johnny's kids, and as much as they love me and I love them, they aren't my own and I don't make decisions with or for them. I celebrate them, yes," I interrupted, "You spoil them, is what you do." Alex gleamed through the phone, "Yes, I do! I do spoil them, don't I? Are you still drinking wine? I immediately said, "Yes, and why do you have that tone? Are you my friend, or are you... my mother? And what the fuck was the cold shoulder when I told you earlier about Mars? I mean Mara because I'm not twelve anymore and should not refer to her as that?" She was cold, "Emily, get your shit together and stop with the wine. Whatever, Em, I'm tired, you're drunk and I'm going to bed." I said, "Good! Okay, Alex. Great talk! Goodnight. I pressed end and sat there shaking my head. We were fighting like two twelve-year-olds; Just like we always did. Her excuse was always to blame it on me, way back when and now she would blame it on the wine.

A few minutes later, Jude and Sami walked by my room. "Hey guys, heard you had fun." They both sat on my bed, and I listened to how Poppa Franco bought them cotton candy and glow lights. Vivien took them to a photo booth and they showed me silly pictures. After a bit, I reminded them to brush their teeth and not stay up too late. "See you in the morning," I said. "I'll make pancakes." Jude said he would play video games online with his friends and Sami said, "Yay, pancakes! Night, Mom!" She closed my door, and I passed out.

My kids knew the nights I drank too much, and that was one of those nights. As they grew towards adolescence, they knew I was struggling, but they were still too young to process coping mechanisms. As parents, we can only keep our true selves from emerging for a short time. They knew much more about what I wanted to shield them from and tons more than I was willing to admit.

Chapter Thirteen

I met Mars on Main Street for an early dinner a few days after she arrived in New York. She was staying in a nearby town at Lucy's house. I was shocked they kept in touch through the years, and I was saddened that Mara and I hadn't. Mara told me Lucy was married and had five children. She married a born-again Christian and became very religious. I asked Mara how they remained so close and how comfortable staying in her house was. Mara said her father dated Lucy's Mom in the early nineties. I was blown away. *Mr. C and Lucy's mom?* Although their relationship didn't last long, it put Mara and Lucy back in touch after our years when our neighborhood friendships fell short, and they had since kept up with visits and phone calls. Our dinner lasted a few hours. I told her about my divorce and Jude and Sami. We showed each other pictures of our lives. She told me about her eleven-year-old daughter Loreen, and I enjoyed our time together.

I needed to get home and pack for Aruba. I told Mara all about Vivien and Franco and our yearly trips to the island. She said she missed them dearly and made me promise to see them as she visited New York frequently. I told her after our annual vacation, I would arrange a visit with them the next time she was in town. We split the check and made a promise to only let a little time pass before our next plan to hang out again. I told her I missed her and the sentiment was reciprocated ten-fold.

I returned home, and Vivien and Franco were at my kitchen table with the kids and a huge bowl filled with ravioli. "Mom, what are you guys doing here? I told you I made them dinner and they could stay alone for a few hours." Vivien pointed to the bowl, "I made too much ravioli, so I figured we'd bring it by and eat with the kids. Want some?"

I didn't, although Vivien's ravioli was hard to pass up "Well, I just ate, so no… but next time you bring ravioli and meatballs, try to do it on a night when I don't make meatloaf, please." Franco poured a glass of wine, and I grabbed a glass out of my cabinet and poured myself one too. Vivien started to clean up the table, and the kids asked to be excused. "So, tell me, how is Mara?" Vivien was excited we had dinner plans. I showed her a selfie we took and she thought Mara looked great. I thought she did too. Vivien asked me if I was packed and ready for Aruba. I said, "No, not even close, which is why you and Franco can stay, but I need to get into my room and start fighting with my bathing suits." She scraped the ravioli and the few leftover meatballs into Tupperware and secured its lid. I gave them both a hug and told the kids to say goodbye. I started to pack for our trip.

That year was the first time Michael couldn't join us in our fabulous beachfront. Charlotte was furious that he backed out after plans were set and flights were booked. He said he had a meeting with the partners he could not miss. I was bummed about it. Michael was a big help with the kids, and I hoped they wouldn't miss him. Our week was good and even great at times. We all missed Michael much like we missed Jesse a half a decade back, but we frequented the same restaurants and enjoyed the days on the same beach. The kids found friends their age to play catch and build sand castles with.
I observed my parents as aging seniors. I began to realize how much I would miss them when that time came to say goodbye. I was slowly becoming more present in each moment and recognizing time does not slow down for anyone. Years came and went, and traditions continued.

After another year in Aruba, we returned home. That trip

was by far the easiest for me. I was happily single, and life seemed to have some purpose and happiness again.

The divorce was close to being wrapped up, and I had a bit of hope for the first time in a long time. By then, I had learned to be uncoupled. I was happy to have escaped the cold for a week and equally happy to return safely home.

Life had returned to normal and I was busy with work and my children. I spoke with Alex every day and we made an effort to have fun while the kids spent time with Jesse. On Saturday nights, I would sit at the bar and chat with Maggie while Alex worked the restaurant. I always felt I was closely observed. Although Maggie was friendly, I knew her loyalty was to Alex. She pretended to welcome me, but I thought she would prefer me not to be in Alex's life at all.

Alex's mom was there until her usual ten at night, and sometimes we would have a brief exchange. Her broken English was never easy for me, and although Alex and her sisters had an undeniable love/hate relationship with her, I knew she never liked me very much. Nonetheless, I could always count on the best Cosmos in town and whatever food I wanted.

I watched Alex shake hands and double-cheek-kiss the regulars. She was very good at public relations and made BlueIris, a tremendous success. She was very impressive, worked hard, and she rarely complained about having to put in long hours. Alex was doing what she always set out to do.

That night, Maggie was the last one to say goodnight. We locked the back door and shut the dining room lights. Alex grabbed a brown paper bag from under the bar. "Em, lock the front door?" She threw me her keys. She had a bag full of cash and credit card receipts in hand.

"Come on up to the loft for a few?" she asked. I followed

her upstairs to the office. Alex had done what she told me she would and, with Johnny's help and on less of a budget than she anticipated. It was cozy. She emptied only the receipts onto her desk and paper-clipped the pile. Cash stayed in the bag, and she rolled it up and pulled a rubber band around it.

Her desk remained in the office partition where it had been years earlier before Iris opened. Warhol's Marilyn still hung behind it. There were two more file cabinets and an off-white bench seat covered with her assorted blazers. The half wall on the other side of the room had a small black fridge next to a mini stovetop oven with a microwave hanging above. It was a tiny yet very functional kitchenette. Two stools tucked under a six-foot wrap-around countertop. Johnny did all of the work for his sister. Alex told me he did it for free, but she repaid him by spoiling his four children as much as humanly possible. He built another wall with a clear opening doorway that enclosed the living room/bedroom and in its corner, a roomy bathroom with a stall shower. He used a rich crown molding to finish the place.

Alex's beach theme add-ons were a perfect addition. She stayed there every so often. It was a great apartment, and I often wondered why she didn't move in permanently. "Do you mind if I just do this, Em? I hate coming back here on Sundays to do paperwork." I didn't mind at all. I answered, "Do you mind if I watch tv?" She insisted, "Please do. I'll be done in twenty minutes."

Alex finally meandered in and sat on the edge of the old recliner she had taken from you mind her parent's basement. It was worn, and it reminded me of our many adolescent sleepovers. I couldn't recall the numerous times I slept on that recline and the matching loveseat. I noticed more cracks in the brown leather. I felt a rush inside from my toes to the top of my shoulders.

Alex came in and handed me a glass of pinot. "What's left of the Murphy's bottle... we may as well have one for the road." We clinked, "Hey, Alex. Do you remember the summer of nineteen eighty-four?" I knew she did. She threw her legs over the arm of the brown leather. "Em... do you remember?" She called me out, and I felt awkward and regretful that I had asked the question. I didn't plan what I would say or even think about how Alex might reply. I just knew the question felt so long overdue.

I answered, "I remember the music in the Camaro. I remember being fifteen and wanting to be eighteen. I remember the long rides and cool summer nights. I remember the summer days too. I remember the festivals, and I can still smell a Subrosa. I remember lunches with Annie and sharing a soda on the beach. I even remember Marcello and how Sophie was gonna marry him." Alex grinned. I chuckled nervously and continued rambling. "I remember you teaching me to drive and getting Tom to hire me. I remember the sunsets, Alex. I remember everything, and I remember many nights on the roof. And I remember that one night on the roof." She squinted and her eyes looked away. I sat in silence. I just waited for her to say something. "Alex, please say something. Please. It's been over twenty years, and here we are."

Alex was still and silent for a minute that felt like an hour. She swung her legs around in front of her and leaned closer, "What do you want from me, Emily? You got married! You have two kids! I didn't choose that; You did! You showed up at Hoxie's outta the blue years ago. Now you are in the middle of a lengthy divorce! And now... What? Are you looking for answers from me... to your confusing choices?" I was appalled, "I'm not gay, Alex. I'm not!" She stood up and left the room. I stayed put. I couldn't believe I said that. I wanted to rewind the conversation. I didn't move; hoping, praying she would come back.

She finally did with fire. "Let me tell you something, Emily; I am not sure who you are, but I am certain who I am. I didn't ask you if you are…. gay or straight. You walked back into my life, and I welcomed you back as if, so many years haven't passed. Now you sit here with proclamations and your bullshit? You want to talk after not twenty-something Em, twenty-seven, but who's counting, right? What the fuck are you asking, Emily? What can I possibly help you with?"

I started to cry. It wasn't a thunderous or audible cry. It was sad. Heartfelt tears dripped down my cheek. I just could not hold back.

"I don't know, Alex. I am sorry. I am confused, and I…"

She was furious. "You got married, Emily, and Vivien invited me to your wedding!" I was shocked, "She did?" Alex laughed, "Yeah, she did." We both stopped and let out a deep breath. There was an entire maddening minute of silence.

She threw her hands in the air in complete frustration and stood up. I attempted to defend myself, "Alex, you dated Derrick forever and the entire football team." She had an immediate response, "I didn't fuck him, Em, and I didn't marry him or anyone on the football team either." Alex let her guard down, and there was a slight sign of vulnerability. "Emily, I never thought you would re-enter my life, but here you are. It took a long time to get over you and well, all of this and I am, I was; I mean… I am happy now, and it took me a long time to get here. I've worked so hard and I am finally successful, and well, you are challenging me, and I am not sure why I am letting you do that." She sat down next to me. I grabbed her face with both palms of my hands. She didn't resist. My lips met hers. We kissed like we did on the rooftop. But this time, we kissed with experience and neither held back.

I fell hopelessly back in love with her. It felt like nineteen-eighty-something.

Alex and I stayed at Iris that evening. Our love was not just physical, it was a passionate, intense connection that I had never felt before. We talked all night, our words mingling with our shared breath, creating a bond that was as strong as it was fleeting.

The sun rose, and though we didn't witness it through her tiny windows in her loft apartment, I felt like I had finally arrived into the person I was supposed to be and be with. It only took a moment in her arms to know what was lacking in my life and my marriage. Everything I had left years before. It was an unbelievable feeling. I could not describe how I felt but knew I wanted to feel more of it. Our love affair became fast and furious, and we remained a secret for many months. Our secret was okay initially because it was exciting and with all my other responsibilities, it was all I could manage. When I was with Alex, I revisited the happiest parts of my youth. She reminded me of who I thought I would have rather become, who I really felt I was. The many roads presented to me in my youth and the paths not chosen. It also made me question why I was willing to explore this path and… at *forty-something*, a time when most people are settled and sure of themselves.

Chapter Fourteen

I watched Jude and Sami climb the three stairs and get off the bus on time. Sami ran down the sidewalk with a Vera Bradley floral book bag flung from side to side.

"Tell me something beautiful that happened to you today?" Sami eagerly replied, "Mom, drama in the sixth grade!"

"No way?!" I opened my eyes big and reached out my hand to Sami's little fingers up in the air as she told her story with both inflection and flapping hands. Sami described the parameters of being in and *not being in* 'the squad' and the note passed through seven classmates from Tristan to Kenzie about Melissa liking Cole. As Sami rambled, Jude walked up the driveway and stopped to kiss me on the cheek. He opened the storm door and stepped inside. Sami continued, "…And then on the way home from the field trip, Max took out his phone and he didn't get caught, but he wasn't even allowed to have it, Mom and uh, but nobody told on him anyway." It was a great and somewhat confusing after-school, ten-minute exchange. Sami was done and hurried inside. Her book bag, lunchbox and a half-full water bottle scattered on the porch. I slightly shook my head with a smile, took a deep breath, and continued gardening.

On my knees in the garden, I looked into the most transparent blue sky and with gloves and shovel in hand, I silently prayed. "*Please, God, help me to stay present in these moments with Jude and Sami. Help me to learn forgiveness and how to co-parent with the enemy. Help me to feel the joy. And thank you, God, for all I do have.*"

I finished planting the last of the flats, pre-ordered from the St. Christopher's Mother's Day Sale three weeks earlier and headed inside to wash up.

Jude was asleep, napping with his bedside window open. I paid close attention to my high-schooler, sprawled out on his full-size mattress as the breeze softly blew his longer-than-usual jet-black hair. I did not wish that moment away. I smiled, watching him sleep, then proceeded towards the bathroom. I washed my hands with the warm soapy water I often reminded him to use. The water washed my hands of the garden and I silently thought about how much I loved Jude and Sami. There was a place only reserved for them in my giant heart; unconditional over and over-again love that reminded me I enjoyed being their mom. It was hard, but we had come so far. I was proud of us. With clean hands, I left the bathroom to find Sami stretched out on the sofa, watching television with a bag of popcorn in hand.

"It's a beautiful day," I suggested, "Why not go find some friends and make the most of it?" Sami looked up at me, her eyes sparkling. "Mom, will you go with me for a bike ride cause Keira has a softball game and Danielle is busy too." They were the neighborhood girls she spent the most amount of time with.

I opened the freezer door and took out the eggplant parmigiana I had made several weeks prior. That would become our evening dinner. Sami with her head leaning over the window opening in the wall, was looking into the kitchen. "Mom, can we?" My mind was on other things, "Um, can we what?" Sami sprang up from the sofa and exclaimed, "Mom, let's go for a bike ride!" I left the tinfoil-wrapped Pyrex on the granite countertop and answered her, "Absolutely, Sami! Let me leave Jude a note in case he wakes up and we're not here." Sami slipped into her flip-flops and tied her hair back into a ponytail with one of her scrunchies she wore as a bracelet. We left through the garage, venturing further from home than Sami would have dared alone. As we neared home, a familiar voice called out from Noel's driveway. "Sami, want to play?" Sami's bike screeched to a halt.

"Mom, Can I?" I was relieved and eager to return home. "Sure, I'm going to head home." Noel was as delighted as Sami, "K Mom, see you at home then. Thanks for bike riding with me." I pedaled leisurely down the block and reminded Sami to text me when she was on her way home. As I made a sharp left turn, I was enveloped in the familiar, comfort of our neighborhood.

When I walked inside, I began preparing the garlic bread I would heat up with the homemade eggplant thawing on the countertop.

I emptied the snack drawer to reorganize when Jude stumbled down the hall. "Hey, Mom, Where's Sami?" I threw out the expired breakfast bars that didn't go over well with either of the children from early September. "She's at Noel's." He bent down and grabbed a bag of chips. He settled into the sofa with his Beats and his laptop with a look of comfort on his face.

I heard a text notification and glanced at my iPhone.

Em, a food critic from Zagat, was here today for lunch. Tommy made the Sole. It tasted like I caught it myself this morning. Divine, indeed. Yep, Sous Chef Tommy. I'm going to make millions and buy us everything! Now dealing with the dinner crowd. What's happening on your side? TTYL

I immediately replied:

Oh no, not the Sole... Tom's lobster roll and Maggie's Cosmo are the only two respectable items on your menu... hope you know that. Feel like it's my job to make sure you do! Anyway, tell me everything later. I'm good. Sami won first place for her essay. Making dinner... "Sous Chef Me." Hanging with the kids. Miss you, Zagat Fav - Yay! Hope your mom behaved herself.

187

She replied quickly:

Lmao, I knew they were coming, so I made Johnnie ask her to babysit. It went really well. Call me later. I'm staying here tonight, exhausted and need sleep. Xo

I didn't speak with Alex that night or most nights. She was swamped and wasn't able to text until I was asleep. I left her hanging without replies more often than not. I was up before six on weekdays to make lunches and get the kids off to school. Alex could sleep in on most weekday mornings, though she got less sleep than me in general. She was a night owl and stayed up till the wee hours. The restaurant was thriving and the kids occupied most of my time. Alex and I were able to get together less and less. Just as I was about to put my phone down, another alert chimed. My fingerprint opened iMessage. This time, it was from Sami.

Riding home with Noel and Keira.

I replied:

K be careful

After dinner, the three of us settled into our usual routine. Sami was engrossed in the television and Jude was forever on his laptop exploring the latest YouTube trends. I tidied up and cleaned the kitchen and set the dishwasher to start four hours later. As I silently made a mental list of tasks, Jude's chatter about Pokemon characters filled the air, and Sami, in her usual fashion asked if I heard the new Taylor Swift.
I sat down on the recliner and the usual loneliness crept in.

It felt like green slime was being poured from a bucket overhead and down my head to the bottom of my feet. It was just like the game show Sami was watching on Nickelodeon. I remembered The Good Wife was recorded on my DVR. However, it wasn't a program appropriate for Sami, so Nickelodeon it was. I got up and began folding the laundry. I heard another text alert.

Em, Can you get here on Sunday in hostess garb?

I replied:

No, Sunday is Sami's gymnastic meet and I thought you and Rae were coming?

Alex replied:

OMG, Em, I totally forgot, and I'm sorry, but I just received a call from a Nascar representative who wants to meet with me today regarding a private luncheon for big- time sponsors THIS SUNDAY! Em, like Dale Earnhardt peeps!!! And sorry, but I need Rae to dress up, look cute and serve. Can you take my mom... kidding? I know that wasn't funny at all. I'm sorry, Em, but this could be great press. I feel bad, but I will have to root Sami on from Iris.

I replied:

If it's a private meeting - how could it be great press, and Dale Earn is well... RIP. He's dead, really lol ☺

She texted back:

HA HA! If we pull off the private party with the bigwigs, we tell the press we are good at hosting secret affairs for the rich and famous. Honestly, I am sorry to miss the meet.

Videotape it. Ugh... I wanted you here too.

I answered:

And I wanted you and Rae at Sami's meet but it's okay; I know it's great for business. Ugh just bummed, but I understand.

I was disappointed after our text exchange and finished folding laundry. I knew my double life was taking a toll on my psyche. I decided to relax and scroll through my phone. That was a mistake too. My Facebook friends were posting their seemingly perfect lives and I, in stark contrast was feeling miserable. Some days, I found myself regretting all of my life decisions, yearning to turn the tide. Their happy snapshots served as painful reminders of my own past, now distant and unattainable.

I came to a realization that people weren't posting their kids having temper tantrums. They weren't posting the fights with their spouses. They were carefully selecting and sharing only the moments they wanted their audience to see. These were the memories they wanted to account for later on, to be a witness to all that felt good. I, too, had done this during my marriage, without being fully aware. Facebook was a new platform then and we were all learning how to navigate it. As it evolved, it became clear who took it to another level and those who used it moderately to share and find long-lost friends.

I deeply reflected on the choices I made regarding how to manage my life after my separation. Social media had a significant impact on my wellbeing. Looking back, my older self would have advised me to quit social media the day we filed papers.

I couldn't post the moments in my life I shared with Alex. I could only post moments with my kids, which made me look like a single mom trying too hard to show the world I was indeed happily single and doing well. Neither was my reality. I wanted to post the moments with Alex. Those were equally genuine moments of joy.

Prior to finalizing my divorce, I was concerned that the judge who would support catholic school tuition could also be anti-gay. Jesse's behavior was erratic and I couldn't bear the thought of losing custody. This compelled me to remain hidden, making everything more problematic than it needed to be.

Facebook was becoming a nuisance in my life, causing me to compare and contrast. It made me question my half-hidden life. Eventually, I realized that I had lived a superficial life even when I was married, and that this had less to do with my newfound sexuality and more to do with a lack of substance in my life.

I considered the day my divorce would be finalized and imagined announcing it on Facebook, but I never did. I was overwhelmed by countless thoughts running through my mind, feeling like a prisoner of my never-ending divorce. My ex still had a hold on me and I felt stuck in my own life.

I missed my old life when it was just me and my husband before I discovered I was in love with a woman. Falling in love with a woman was complicated and I was struggling to come to terms with my sexuality and our relationship. I spent hours trying to find the answers within myself, wondering if I was lesbian, bisexual, or just a misfit? There were days when I felt completely unbalanced and inauthentic, trying to reconcile my feelings and identity. My family didn't seem to understand growth and evolution, they only saw destruction. Even on my worst days, I knew the pain wouldn't last forever. I felt the storm inside me, tearing me down but I knew it would eventually lead to rebuilding.

Blaming and criticizing myself excessively for everything was awful. I knew I had to reinvent. I made a plan to define my core and get me back, better than ever. That just took a bit longer than I would have liked.

A few months later, I fell into his arms that day at the courthouse after it was done, and for a memorable moment, his embrace felt familiar. Jesse was everything of particular remembrance especially when it was about my children. I silently pondered; If so many needed elements such as trust, weren't missing in my marriage, could I have stayed happy enough married to him?

Before that day of our legal divorce, I had already learned to forgive, both myself and him. Yet a profound sadness, too deep to articulate, lingered. It was a journey of self-realization, a process that required time and understanding. Divorce, I came to understand, is a reality that many confront and while it may be the best course of action, it is undeniably a difficult path to traverse.

Chapter Fifteen

It was a damp morning and the clock had not yet struck seven. Sami asked, "Hey, Mom, you think Daria can come over after school today?" I peered through the rearview mirror and saw Sami staring out her window. "I'm not sure it's a great idea to have a friend over while your brother has the flu." She was disappointed but understood, "Yeah, guess so."

It was Wednesday and I was taking her to her Rosary Council early morning meeting. I was proud of her for joining, and didn't mind taking her a little earlier than usual. I was never much of a morning person, but my kids' schedules forced to become one.

I pulled up in the Westbound drop-off lane. It always reminded me of a line from the movie Mr. Mom, "*South to drop off, moron.*" I didn't share the thought with Sami, but she noticed I sort of chuckled to myself.

Sami powered off her phone and tucked it deep into her Vera knap. She leaned over, and I planted a no-hands kiss on her sweet little lips. "I love you most and even more. Have the best day ever." Sami smiled wide, "Mom, I will. You too, Mommy." She opened the door, cast her bag over her shoulder, and headed down the blacktop to the school entrance. I opened the passenger window and shouted to the back of her, "Hey Sami, if Jude is better, maybe you can have some friends over this weekend." She beamed, "A sleepover, maybe?" My head tilted, and I grinned, "Maybe," I answered with a smile and a wink. She stopped and waved before Nikki Donovan commanded Sami's complete attention. I watched the girls enter the building, talkative and independent.

After six grueling days of testing positive for the flu, Jude was on the mend. Charlotte would surely ask me why I bothered with flu shots since they didn't seem to work.

Regardless of the outcome, I felt that it would have been far worse if Jude had not received the flu shot. The conviction in my decisions for my children, despite my imperfections, instilled in me a sense of responsibility that I believe made me a reliable advocate for them.

Later as I surprisingly watched Sami disembarking from the bus, accompanied by Nikki Donovan close behind, the girls walked the familiar path from the corner toward me. My cell phone vibrated in my hand, and I pressed accept. "Hello?" I heard some ruffling and a voice, "Hi Emily, it's Carol Donovan! Nikki is on Sami's bus. She was supposed to get off with Hannah, but apparently, they got into some kind of argument. Nikki took it upon herself to get off at your stop." I sensed the worry in her voice. "Carol, no worries! Nikki can stay until you can come to pick her up. They can do homework together, and I will make cookies." I heard her sigh of relief. "Thank you, Emily. You're a lifesaver. Guess I'll be there about five-forty-five." Sami and Nikki were now at the foot of my drive. "Ok, Carol, see you then. No biggie at all. They are both walking up my driveway now." She thanked me again, and we disconnected the call. Nikki Donovan hadn't been to our house for a few years.

They were friendly in first grade, always playing together during recess, but seemed to grow apart after second grade. "Hi, ladies," I greeted them both. "Hi, Mrs. Giumaro." I was kind, "Hi Nikki, Welcome!" I wished she had said, *Hi... Mrs. Netti or even Emily would have sounded better.* As I pondered over the idea of reverting to my maiden name, I couldn't help but feel a strong attachment to the Guimaro name. It was my married name, but it was also the name my children carried. I didn't want to sever that connection. A family name is where your roots begin. I resolved that if my kids were Guimaro's, I would remain one too.

Sami looked at me and explained, "Mom, Nikki's mom is working, and she and Hannah…." Since I knew the story, I interrupted my daughter. "It's fine, I spoke to your mom." I looked at Nikki and said, "Your mom will pick you up after work. C'mon in, girls, but let's try to be quiet. Let's go to the kitchen because Jude is resting." Nikki was sweet, "I heard he has the flu. It's a bummer. I got it once, and my sister had it three times." I followed them inside and answered, "Yep, it is a bummer. I will bake some cookies while you do your homework." They were pleased with the idea.

The smell of the cookies and melting chocolate chips filled the kitchen with warmth and comfort. Jude strolled down the hall to fetch himself four or five. "Hey, you are feeling better?" He nodded, "Much, Mom." His color was back, and his response eased my mind. "Good, Jude. You'll take one more day off from school tomorrow and start a new week on Monday." He gave me a thumbs-up with one cookie in his mouth and a few more in hand. He retreated to his room.

Carol was late. Nikki, who had stayed for dinner, was a delightful surprise. I was impressed by how much she had grown up in the years that passed. Her manners were quite enchanting, and my opinion of her was a complete three-sixty. When tucking Sami in later that evening, we talked about Nikki. "Sami, I didn't know you and Nikki were friendly again." She flapped her sheet over her comforter as she did every night. She snuggled in and fixed the pillow behind her. When her pillow was perfectly positioned, she spoke. "I was never, not… friends with Nikki. Just, like… ya know we… like all have different clicks if ya, like know what I mean." I chuckled. "Yes, I do know, exactly what you mean," I replied. "I noticed Nikki matured quite a bit and was very polite. She is welcome back anytime, Sami." She sat up to give me my goodnight kiss. "She is nicer, Mom. Like, I don't know, but like last year... like... she just changed from kinda mean to nice." I was impressed that Nikki changed her ways, and I was even more impressed Sami noticed she did. I liked the way Sami handled social situations, despite her youth. She didn't de-friend Nikki. She put some distance between them in the kindest way. Three years later, Nikki found her way back into friendship with my daughter. It happened organically. Raising children provided most of my greatest lessons.

Before I fell asleep that evening, I thought about how Nikki changed and how I changed. I thought about how Jude and Sami grew leaps and bounds. I thought about how sick Jude was and how taxing that made my week. It reminded me how awful things can be and then become remarkably better. I recognized change was inevitable and change would often come by surprise. In my opinion, change was a good thing disguised as exhausting.

The night was coming to an end. The house was dark and quiet. Sami fell asleep. Jude was in bed, reading The Wringer by Jerry Spinelli. He told me it was gripping, and when Jude loved a book, he read it from cover to cover until he finished. Half dozing, I still heard his voice through a three-inch crack in my open door. "Mom, this book is so great. You should read it." I didn't answer immediately.

After another moment of silence, I heard his quiet voice again, "Goodnight, Mommy." I couldn't see my face in a mirror, but I felt my smile. The room was dark, and I kept my eyes closed. I mumbled, "Goodnight, Jude. I love you most."

I thought about how Jude was still just a boy. He was young and I realized that I was the most important and constant person in his life. I fell asleep feeling content and peaceful, knowing that I wanted to hold onto them for as long as possible, or even forever if they would let me.

The following day Alex called early to tell me she booked a cozy bed and breakfast on the eastern end of Long Island. I had a list of obligations to tackle before the fast-approaching getaway. My heart raced with enthusiasm, and I was busy and diligent to carefully check off all my have-to-do's. A few days later, we began our venture. We watched the sunrise, its warm hues painting the sky and we witnessed another exquisite sunset, the sky ablaze with vibrant colors. We enjoyed the shops, dinners, and intimacy, the sounds, smells and tastes of each experience adding to the richness of our time together. I reveled in two days and nights of abundant freedom and very little responsibility. I was at ease, finally comfortable in my own skin and with someone who felt comfortable in hers. Eventually, and what seemed quite suddenly, our overnights would come to a halting end. We had to retract from each other and become grossly involved with our families, work, and our own realities. The transition was not easy. The emotional toll of balancing a romantic relationship with family and work responsibilities was immense. The kids were consistently dropped back home after dinner. I always tried to be home earlier for a thirty-minute window to regroup. I would reassemble myself from the free, gay woman I had been into the stable mom of two preparing for a week of obligations. Alex had her own commitments regarding her restaurant, but she also had freedoms that I did not. I was rooted at home. I had children. She was the owner of a restaurant. She worked long hours but was able to socialize with customers and leave her sisters to operate Iris so she could run errands or take time to disappear. We spent as much time together as a couple as we could.

Alex also made time for her three nieces and baby John-

John. Her favorite, Jana, would sit on her lap and ask Alex what she brought for her, and Alex would always have something special for her, every visit. Alex loved Johnnie's kids. I think Alex loved Jude and Sami, but I always felt the thought of living with them and helping me raise them was something Alex had absolutely no interest in signing up for. It was clear to me that after Alex stopped by Johnny's house to visit her nieces or even dinner and a visit with my kids, she was relieved to get out of there and back to her own life. She didn't fit into my reality, which was at times, was agonizing.

I felt that Alex was using the restaurant and my divorce as an excuse not to commit entirely. The frustration was mounting inside of me daily. Our relationship was trapped in a cycle of slow-brewing fights, a strategy that made it easier to spend days without seeing each other. Alex's discomfort with being challenged led to constant tension, with me consciously challenging her all the time. The three days of silence were unbearable, feeling like a lifetime. The disconnect was profound and I detested it.

The kids were at Charlotte and Michael's, and I was late for pick-up. On my way, my cell rang, and I hit the Bluetooth accept on my steering wheel, "Hey Charlotte, I am on my way to pick up my offspring. Sorry, I know I'm late." Charlotte laughed at my rhetoric. "Oh, Em, I buzzed you on the home line. I was hoping to catch you before you left. Can they stay?" I was still driving towards Cove Canyon. "Well, I guess… but Jude was supposed to go to Liam's tomorrow and Sami to Danielle's. Remember, I am free-lancing at the Amity Tribune." Charlotte remembered, "I know, which is why, when they asked, I figured it would help you out. Honestly, Em, Jude is a Godsend with Jake, and the triplets haven't killed each other yet."

We started calling the girls triplets years before in Aruba,

and somehow it stuck. I thought about how nice it would be
to have an evening alone. "Well, if you want five instead of
three, and they want to stay, then keep them. I'll call Liam
and Danielle's Mom to reschedule. It will be easier for me
to get outta here in the morning without them anyway."
Charlotte asked, "Want to speak to either of them?" I
replied honestly, "No, I'll call them later before bed. I'm
off to frozen foods and will buzz when I get home."

I found myself immediately eastbound and on my way to
the Iris. The restaurant was slow. Brian and Donny were
perched upon their usual stools at the bar. They were a gay
couple that Mama DePetrao always snickered at. Maggie
loved them. Not only were they regulars who lived within
walking distance, but they were funny and left huge tips.
They knew Alex was gay, and they knew I was her partner.
Apart from them, our relationship existed in a half-hidden
world. Rae was standing, talking to them. I entered and
gave a double-cheek kiss to Rae, and she pointed, "She's
up in the loft." I hugged Rae and headed upstairs. Alex was
at her desk. She heard the stairs creak and was probably
expecting one of her sisters. I reached the top stair and
peeked inside. She was unmoving and stared at me. I
gestured hello with a subtle wave, a familiar comfort
settling between us. "What are you doing here, and where
are the kids?" I set foot closer to her desk. "They are at
Charlotte's, and so I decided to come by." The phone rang,
and Alex glanced at the caller ID. "I have to take this, Em;
get a drink or whatever, and I'll come down in a few
minutes.
As I made my way back downstairs, I could hear the faint
hum of conversation and the clinking of glasses. "By the
way, any customers down there?" Alex asked. "Just Brian
and Donny and two tables about to leave." Forlorn, she
answered, "Yep, slow this week; At least Maggie will be

happy." She picked up the receiver, "Hey Aaron, perfect timing. I have my order ready for you." I motioned to head downstairs and found Rae sitting alone at the bar. She was drinking a Malibu Bay Breeze, and I asked Maggie to bring me the same. Sophie walked in with her bestie, Lisa, and we all sat at the bar.

Hours later, a very sober Alex joined us. The restaurant was locked up, and most of the staff was gone. She seemed annoyed that we were enjoying spirits while she was upstairs. Maggie set down one shot of chilled Patron in front of Alex. She nodded in approval and tipped the shot glass in the air. After she poured it into her mouth, she boisterously exclaimed, "Party's over, kids!" The gang broke up quickly. It was just the two of us. The Iris was empty, and I watched her peruse through the tables, shutting off each set of lights; always keeping on the outside deck and the inside forum where the hostess desk stood. She hadn't been talkative even while Rae, Sophie, and Lisa were there. After their exit, she grew quieter until she mumbled, "Em. I'm tired, and we should go now." I stood there in disbelief and couldn't remain silent. "Alex, I have been waiting for you all night, and that's it? Why can't we stay here together? The kids are at Charlotte's. You have locked up and want to go now?" Alex picked up her bag from the edge of the bar. "Yep, Em, I want to go home. I am tired, and while you were having free Malibu Bay Breeze's, I was upstairs working."
I felt the storm surge raging inside. Fueled by alcohol and triggered by Alex's noiseless nasty pose, I unleashed all my bottled-up emotion, "Alex, time will not wait. If we wait until it seems perfect... we will be waiting forever." She didn't even look at me, "You're drunk, Em and you want to fight! I want to sleep. I have a busy weekend." I was disgusted with her pomposity.

"I too, have a busy weekend with the kids, Alex! I should have gone food shopping and have to work too." She said in a harsh tone, "Em, it's time to go now," she added, holding the door open for me. As I walked out, I felt sadness and anger. I wished she would have shown me some kindness and comforted me, but instead, she seemed indifferent. "Then you shouldn't have come, Em," she quipped.

I longed for her to embrace me and protect me from the outside world, but she didn't. I had always seen through her tough exterior and into her heart, even when she was being cruel. I stepped out through the open door and said, "No, I shouldn't have come!" She then slammed the door and locked both the bottom and top lock. I stood there motionless and she turned to me, her eyes filled with anger and fear.

"Go back to him, Em. Go back to him! Go back to your perfect life, your perfect family, and leave me alone," she shouted at me. Her eyes met mine with fury. I saw her fear more than hurt or hate.

Alex was unsure why I re-entered her life after the onset of my divorce. She questioned my sexuality almost constantly and was looking for answers from me that I never could give. I didn't plan out the timing, it just happened. The universe has its own way of planning and timing. Lashing out at me was the only way to express her twisted emotions. She knew if we were going to be together, she would be forced to come entirely out of the closet and own it. At that time, she wasn't ready to do that anymore than I was. I looked her square in the eyes, "Fuck you, Alex! Fuck you!" I bolted to my car. She didn't notice my tear-filled eyes and firmly stood statuette, peering from outside the front door of the Iris. "Go drive home, you fucking… drunk bitch!" I didn't look back. *Fuck you, Alex*! I couldn't listen to the radio as every lyric reminded me of her or some other sad occurrence in my pathetic life. I drove home in the rain. The droplets on my windshield blurred my vision as confusion swept through every part of me and sent a chill throughout my body. The drinks didn't help anything, and thankfully, I didn't get pulled over.

It was a quiet Saturday morning with the curtains drawn. I heard the wind blowing outside my bedroom window, so I picked up my phone and searched for Justine's number in my contacts. When she answered, I told her I wasn't feeling well due to a late night and asked if I could work on the ad from home and send it in before 3pm. She had no problem with my request and we ended the call.

I thought about calling Alex but decided not to. Despite the ongoing conflicts, we always found our way back to each other after a blowout. When we did reunite, our soulful connection kept us both coming back for more. Since the kids were still at Charlotte and Michael's, I decided to pay a visit to Vivien and Franco. I didn't shower and threw on a pair of shorts and a t-shirt. I slipped my AirPods underneath the rim of my Nike cap and set out on foot to my parent's home less than two miles away. According to my iPhone, I burned two hundred-ten calories. Franco was watering the lawn. "Hello there." He said, "What do we owe the pleasure?"

I popped out my pods, "Dad, you have a sprinkler system!" He released the nozzle. "Yeah, but this is how we did it way back when. It works better," he said with confidence. I kissed his cheek and he smiled. "Just a walk and a quick hello. Viv inside?" He nodded yes and continued watering. Vivien was sitting outside with the newspaper in hand. I plopped down and set my sights on the breathtaking view of the Great South Bay. "Did you walk here again?" I wiped the sweat off my brow. "Yep, I can't run yet. My knee is still acting up, so I walked." She told me I should go see her chiropractor. Vivien believed all ailments could be healed with exercise and a good chiropractor. The older I got, the more I agreed. "Where's Jude and Sami?" she asked. "Still at Mike's. I'll call Charlotte after I get home and shower." I answered.

"So, what is going on with Jesse?" She wanted the scoop about the recent court dates and the progression of the divorce. "Well, it's hard to explain, Mom. It's like we have a court date, and lots of stuff seems to get solved, but six weeks later, there is another court date." She looked puzzled. "Maybe you need a new lawyer?" I let out a deep breath. "I don't think it's my lawyer's fault. I think if two people can't agree, then there is a lengthy process to let a judge decide on every stupid thing. There isn't much I can do to speed up the process."

I am not sure how my mother truly felt about my divorce. Sometimes, I felt like she wished I had stayed in the marriage. It made me feel I had let her down.

"How are the kids doing with all of it?" She asked with concern. "Mom, I guess they are social and eating well. They sleep well. Their grades are excellent and I think they are good." Her expression questioned my answer. I felt she was always overly worried about the welfare of Jude and Sami. I wished she had worried more about me, and I felt terrible. I felt I had my kids' best interest intact and put all my energy into them. When I had no energy to spare, I wanted my mom to have mine. Vivian just wasn't like that.

"I would just feel better about everything that's going on if the divorce was final," she added. "Well, what do you mean when you say everything that's going on?" I asked. "You know, regarding the situation." I felt the arch of my back tightening up. "What situation?" I didn't let her answer. "Viv, you act like you are the one going through the divorce." Vivien charged back, "This is hard on everyone!" I was outraged and the fight began. "Mom, how can you? How can you think of you? This is hard on you, Mom? I am so sorry my divorce is hard on you! Imagine how I feel? After all, it's my divorce." She was bent out of shape. "Oh, Emily, you didn't think of your family. You thought of only yourself. This entire situation with Alex could have waited."

My heart was racing, and it felt like it was breaking into a million pieces. I replied, tearing up like a river, "Vivien, it could have waited? It waited, Mom! It waited. We waited, and we are still waiting! Did you know, Vivien?" She hurriedly stood up and walked away. I followed her. I pressed her and asked again, "Did you know I was in love with her? I knew the answer and so did she. It was the root of my anger towards her. It was the root of her disappointment in me. I felt that expectation got in the way of unconditional love. I felt angry and she did too.
It was awful. "Mom, I gotta go. And Mom… Alex… She is my family too." I rose from the chair and started out the door. Vivien felt terrible, "Em, I didn't mean. Em, I'm sorry." I held all my emotion inside, "Me too," I said. I left the house and cried all the way home. I hated to hurt my mom and she hated to see me hurting.

I wanted to be around Alex twenty-four-seven. Vivien saw it as an obsession, dangerous and unhealthy. I felt like that in nineteen-eighty-four too. I was stuck in my heterosexual surroundings and could only explore this new side of myself occasionally. I wasn't *out* at home. Jude and Sami knew Alex was my best friend, and they told me as adults, they may have known we were in a relationship, unlike others I had with my female friends, long before I told them. I never felt like I had to explain the transition to them. They never made me feel they needed me to.

Had they asked, I would have been truthful. Our threesome was an open forum, and there was no topic we did not touch upon. Sami and I discussed boys and sex and periods. I taught her to shave and brought her to get her first bikini wax. Jude was as open as they come, and we discussed girls and sex and sports. My family was quite the untraditional threesome and much different than the family I had been raised in.

Vivien's concern often made me feel it was all so dysfunctional. I did not feel it ever was. Divorce wasn't easy but it wasn't dysfunctional, all the time. I sometimes wondered why my parents didn't get divorced. I wondered why Mike and Charlotte didn't either. They all seemed much more dysfunctional than my divorce.

My house had very few rules. Vivien survived on structure, and I broke out of routine every chance I got. I was proud of my kids' independence and adaptability.

I knew I helped those traits to develop. I was sure I was the best version of being their mom, as I possibly could be.

Chapter Sixteen

Slipping my first pair of non-prescription reading glasses
out of its flowery case, I opened the matching frames and
pushed them over my ears. As I reached for my book club
novel, a profound silence covered me, whispering secrets
of solitude and reminding me that I was still in the process
of learning how to be alone. My bedroom door was
slightly ajar, a gateway to my world of solitude. It wasn't
until hours later that I heard a peep from Jude or Sami.
While they were in their separate bedrooms, engrossed in
their digital worlds with laptops in hand, earbuds turned
up on YouTube or Snapchat, playing Toontown,
Minecraft or Roblox, I was immersed in the pages of
Nancy Thayer's new paperback, my only companion. I
managed to read twelve chapters.
Sami hadn't even used the bathroom before she Face-
timed her cousin Meghan. Jude strolled loudly out of his
dwelling. "Good Mornin,' Mom." I attempted to peek out
of the small door opening from my place on top of my bed.
"Good morning, bud. How was your sleep?" Bang! The
bathroom door had shut and no answer from Jude.
Moments later, I heard the door erupt open and Jude
meandered towards the kitchen to fetch himself a banana.
Down the hall again, back to his room, he laughed heartily.
"O-M-G, Liam, that was so cool!" I listened to his
bedroom door close and the exclamatory buzzwords that
comprised ninety percent of my kids' vocabulary. "*Wow*!
"*No way*! *Really*!" I wondered how they did so well in
school.
They seemed happy, and I was content lying on top of my
made-up bed. I couldn't concentrate on reading. I was
distracted and listening to the kids. It was a virtual
hangout with their friends via devices. It felt like ten kids
lived here most of the time. I learned not to walk in front

of my kids' laptops or devices without my bra on.
I learned to ask Sami to press mute before I told her
something that wasn't necessarily anyone's business.
Within the walls of my home, privacy had become a
forgotten luxury. Yet a profound sense of isolation clung to
me. It was a blatant contrast from the warmth and
camaraderie I had known in my core-four household. The
once vibrant conversations had dwindled to a whisper,
leaving only an untalkative three behind. Following the
divorce, the shifting household dynamic and the children's
maturation ushered in a transformation, altering everything
I had once known.

That afternoon was delightful. The kids were outside after
pancakes and bacon. I found refuge in cleaning and laundry
I tackled earlier. I slipped on my Calvin Klein leggings,
Nike sneakers, and a three-quarter-sleeved polo. I decided
to try to run. I popped in my pods and opened Spotify. I
added GPS to my App. I was off to a moderate trot before
my knee forced me to walk. As I approached the corner,
Jude was fully engaged in a driveway basketball game.
Hi Mrs. Giumaro, said Rodney. I waved back at Rod. "Hey,
Mom, going for a walk?" Jude asked. I barely stopped,
"Yes, but it will be quick. Where's your sister?" Jude
pointed down the street, "She's at Keira's."
I waved and popped in my right earbud, feeling
determination. "K, Jude. See you in about an hour," I said,
my voice filled with the hope of a productive run and the
promise of a peaceful hour to myself.
When my knee began to hurt again, I walked briskly when
my music lowered to a ping in my ear. It was a text from
Alex.

Not sure why you haven't called me?

I stopped walking and texted my reply:

I'm unsure why you haven't called me either since you're constantly walking out of my life.

She replied immediately:

Please, Em, let's not fight via text.

Please, Alex, let's not fight at all!

She replied immediately:

Okay, deal, let's not. I miss you. Meet me for dinner later at a new place on Conklin... it's called the Library. I've been meaning to check it out, and we can talk.

I answered:

Okay, I will be there at 5pm... good?
I really do need to talk to Alex.

She answered:
I'll be there Em☺

It was a Wednesday evening and Jesse picked up Jude and Sami on time. July was ending, and summer nights were not super-abundant. I'd heard about the Library and, got there before Alex. The humidity was on the rise through the slight breeze and the summer evening heat was more comfortable than the inside air conditioning. I decided to get us a table outside.
It was a rustic feel with both bar food and chef-like dinners. The waitress approached and introduced herself with a warm smile. I told her I would take a Grey Goose Cosmo to

match the laid-back atmosphere. The scent of summer filled the air, mingling with the coconut oil Sami and I had bought earlier at Bath & Body Works, adding to the comforting vibe.

Alex met me with her eyes from inside the restaurant. She strode in confidently, her oversized bag threatening to spill its contents of paperwork. Approaching the table, she gestured, "You couldn't wait for me?" Her gaze shifted to my drink, a playful accusation. I rolled my eyes, "Seriously?" Her silence spoke volumes and I knew that wasn't how I wanted to start our evening.

She raised her hand to catch the attention of our waitress. She ordered a Martini, straight up with three olives. As she settled into her seat, she remarked, "You look good. Did you get your hair cut?" I said, "No, just took a blow dryer and a straight iron to the beast." She laughed, and I laughed too. We always joked about our hair.

The patio was fenced in. My gaze fixed solely on her as if she were the only thing that mattered in the world. At that moment, my mind and body found solace, unwinding and releasing the tension allowing a profound sense of relaxation to wash over me. As my attention sharpened, her face gently faded into a hazy backdrop while the vibrant hues of the flowers adorning her hair took center stage, painting a mesmerizing rainbow of color. We effortlessly resumed our customary exchange about life, seamlessly picking up where we had left off after our hiatus.

I watched her lips move, and I listened. "Em, please tell me how to fire my mother? Eff, Em, I'm going to hell on a bobsled. Who fires their own mother?" My expression shared an agreement of horror, "What did she do now?" Alex gently grabbed my wrist on the table before me before retracting it and moving it to the stem of her martini glass. She took a sip and continued, "Last night..." she swallowed, "I was appalled. My mother didn't remember

long-time customers, John and Fay, that older couple
from Quogue. She wasn't dressed right. She sat the Feretta
reservation at the wrong table. On top of it, my sisters were
arguing all night over what... I have no idea. I need a staff that I
am not related to. But mom is the real issue. She can't be my
hostess anymore. She is not putting out the right vibe for the
Iris. Oh my God, Em, I'm so stressed."

The waitress, Laura, was back. She was a bit chatty and
interrupted our bitchin' session as far as I was concerned.
She overstayed her welcome because Alex prompted the
predictable conversation. She questioned the waitress about
everything. Laura told us how the place had only opened
two months prior. It was doing well and was in a great
location with plenty of parking for its patrons. The private
patio, a hidden gem, was an excellent addition. It was
surrounded by trees and flower boxes, creating a serene
atmosphere. It was nice to peer through the leaves and
catch a glimpse of people strolling along the busy Main
Street.

Alex, always inquisitive, didn't mention she owned Iris.
Though the ambiance, menu and clientele were different at
each restaurant we frequented, Alex's curiosity led her to
question the staff at each.

Finally, Laura left to fetch us another round of drinks even
though she didn't make them like Maggie. At last, time
would allow us to catch up on the past seventy-two hours.
I listened to Alex, and she listened to me. There were our
usual brief exchanges of smiles. I thought she recognized
my smile had a touch of sadness in how my lips took shape,
a remnant of our recent fight. We didn't talk about our
recent fight or the few days, we didn't speak. I suppose
neither wanted to rehash an issue we knew would never
get solved, a recurring theme in our relationship.

I never questioned our love. Not that night at dinner, or on
the rooftop of the Luncheonette, thirty-something years
before. I also knew that Alex wasn't even close to making

the changes I wanted her to make so that we could share more of our life. The pattern was exhausting, a constant source of emotional tension that threatened to tear us apart.

After dinner, I sat up, with my heart heavy with unspoken words. Alex, sensing my unease, reached for my hand. "Hey," she spoke softly, "I am sorry we go from zero to sixty sometimes." I nodded, my voice barely a whisper, "I just want to be able to talk, but it seems to me you don't." She took my chin and forced it towards her, her touch a mix of tenderness and frustration. "Hey, are the kids still leaving on Friday for Chicago." She changed the subject again, but I didn't want to press her and start an argument. "Yeah, their flight is in the late afternoon." Her eyes lit up, and she raised her eyebrows. "What's going on?" I asked, my voice tinged with a hint of longing for a deeper connection.

She told me that customers had offered her their beach house. "It's ours for the week if you can make it happen?" The proposition hung in the air, a sudden burst of excitement filling me up. I was shocked and thrilled at the thought.

I knew that was exactly what we needed to reconnect. "You can get away from the restaurant? Who is going to run Iris, and whose house is it?" She took both of my hands in hers. "Some customers. I don't think you know them, but they have a house in Cherry Grove, and Maggie will be me, and Randy will bartend." Randy was a reasonably new hire. I asked, "Maggie is running the show, not Sophie? Oh boy, she must be pissed. And you think Randy is ready to run the whole bar?" She was direct and clear about how it was going to go. "Randy will work the bar with Sophie. Rae will seat and help out servers. Maggie looks good in a dress and she knows everybody. She will do fine managing. I trust her completely." Oddly enough, I wondered why I didn't feel as trusted as Maggie. I tried to put the negative thoughts out of my mind.

"Okay, so give me details on the plan. I can go, I suppose. I have some work for the Tribune, but Justine will let me work from wherever as long as I can write and meet deadlines. I think I can swing it." We planned our get-away. We would spend the night at the Iris on Friday after closing and leave early the following day to catch the ferry. I knew I had a lot to accomplish in a few short days. We signaled for our waitress. Laura brought the check, and Alex placed down her credit card. "You got the tip?" she asked. I slapped down twenty-five dollars and we both rose from our chairs. It was nearly eight o'clock when my text sounded. Alex and I were standing by our cars in the parking lot. It was from Jesse.

Where are you? I am dropping the kids off???

I responded immediately:

It's fine. I will be home in ten minutes; the kids will be okay alone for a few.

"I gotta go, Alex." She looked around and took my left hand in hers. She leaned in, and we gave each other a quick kiss. She smiled. I smiled. She said, "Em, let's take this week and make it epic!" I shook my head and replied, "Yes! Let's!" I hurried into my car and headed home.

I arrived home. Jude was clearly in a rotten mood. His upcoming weekend plans had fallen through. He walked into the kitchen, cracked open a Sprite and sat next to Sami at the table. "Sami, you took my phone charger, didn't you?" Sami adamantly denied the accusation, "No, I didn't, Jude!" Jude got up and the chair slid inches away. "Well, ya know what, Sami? You always take my stuff and I am sick of you in my room and taking my stuff."

The house went from one hundred percent calm to an uproar of loud voices. Sami began to cry. I had to step in. "Jude, you are out of line! Who do you think you are speaking to your sister like that?" He walked past me and mumbled, "You always stick up for her!" He retrieved a red plastic cup from the cupboard. He filled it with ice and stomped out the front door. I followed him. I was aggravated and shocked at how angry he was with his sister for no reason.

"Jude, what do you think you are doing?" I demanded he explain his behavior. "I am throwing ice cubes because you two are so annoying." I watched him clutch each cube and hurl it on the blacktop driveway in rage. He arduously launched another. I sauntered to his side. He looked at me. I dunked my hand into the cup and tried to grasp a cube. "Give me one," I ordered him. I took the ice cube from his hand. I threw it to the ground with all my might and watched it shatter into slivers. "My God, that felt good! Jude, give me another." Jude handed me another and three more after the second request. He quietly observed and when I was finished, I let out a deep sigh.

"Did it feel good, Mom?" he asked. I replied, "Yeah, maybe it did." He took an ice cube out of the bucket and studied it close to his eyes. It began to melt between his thumb and middle finger. He shouted, "Girlfriends, suck!" He threw the cube and it broke into pieces. Jude offered the bucket of cubes into the air with extended arms. I grabbed one. "Laundry sucks!" I said, and I threw the cube away hard. He laughed, took a cube, held it up, and said, "Dad, not living here sucks!" I grabbed another ice-cold cube and held it up before hurling it to the ground and repeated his sentiment, "Divorce sucks!"

Jude studiously looked at me. He carefully chose an ice

cube. He held it up and slammed it down, "I am so mad!" I nodded my head in a vertical up-and-down approval while I reached my hand into the cup. I never looked away from Jude's deep green eyes. "We're going to be okay, Jude!" And I gently slung the cube to the floor. Jude handed me another cube, "Can you go again, Mom?" he asked. I tossed that cube with less fury, and it didn't even crack on the blacktop drive.

Jude handed me another. "I love you, Jude, and I am sorry you are hurting! Did you and Cassie…" I cleared my throat, "Did you guys break up?" I held the cube in my cold fingers and watched it melt. There was a silence, and I realized it may have been his turn. Jude took out a cube and held it in the air. He turned his body towards me and I grabbed it. I popped it in my mouth. Jude frowned momentarily. He could not help to laugh at me. He put his arms around me and I grabbed hold of him tightly. I dropped the melted ice and pulled him close. I did not let go until he did.

"Let's go inside," he said. "My fingers are about to fall off." I said, "Mine too! Maybe we can put on mittens and talk inside, yes?" Jude started to cry. He said, "Mom, my heart is broken. I truly loved her." I didn't tell him that although it was his first heartbreak, it probably wouldn't be his last. I felt his pain.

Sami watched by the front door but never came outside. She pushed the door open as we approached and Jude walked in. I followed behind. "Sorry, Sami," Jude whispered. "It's okay," Sami replied.

Later that night, after Sami fell fast asleep, I knocked on his door. I sat on his bed. He told me how awkward school had been since he and his girlfriend broke up after over a year of dating. He looked like Michael after Audrey broke his heart but with darker hair. He told me that he missed her even though he knew the relationship had run its course. It was the first time we spoke about Alex, as he referenced experiences about Cassie and asked me if I ever felt the way he did. I asked him about the ice cube thing since that was the first, I had seen him do that. He remembered a camp friend from years earlier who told him he threw ice cubes on his driveway when angry. He figured he would give it a try.

We both hung out on his bed. I felt as if I was spending time and having a conversation with a similar version of myself, trying to push through when life just sucks.

That was the night I came out to my son. It was the most honest conversation I had ever had with one of my children. He told me that he wasn't shocked and always had a hunch that Alex was more than just a friend. He asked me, "Is that the reason you and Dad got divorced?" I told him it wasn't and explained that sometimes two people aren't meant to stay united forever, even when they love one another. He told me the kid who told him to throw ice to the ground also had parents that got divorced. He said he often didn't want to leave on weekends to go to Jesse's. He told me it wasn't because he didn't love, his dad. He said his life was more straightforward with me and the divorce was probably a good thing but really inconvenient for him.

Our divorce disrupted his life and Jude explained to me that is why he hated divorce. He also told me he was grateful that we got divorced as he witnessed most of his friends living in unhappy households with parents who probably should not have stayed together but did and kept trying when clearly their marriages were falling apart. He told me those friends were miserable.

I answered all his questions honestly, and he told me he loved me no matter what. It was another pivotal moment in my relationship with Jude; I have never forgotten it. I stayed until he fell asleep. I watched him sleep for over an hour before kissing his forehead and closing his door almost all the way. I was worried about Jude.

Chapter Seventeen

That Saturday, it was just the two of us. I had one week free of parenting for the first time in over six years.

I sat on the queen-size bed and crouched over my laptop while she applied her mascara. "Alex, why do you wear mascara to the beach?" She held the brush, glanced through the mirror, and answered, "Because I do." I smiled, and she continued her application.

We were both excited to start our vacation. It would be the first time Alex and I would spend more than a weekend together. I was hoping to discuss our future and make a plan. The years were rolling by.

Our connection was deep and unique. It was what kept us together in our own magical courtship, but Alex and I fought as hard as we loved. She would never say when she and I would settle down together for more than a weekend or a dinner on Valentine's Day. We had lives to live. We fell in and out of patterns being apart instead of working on what would bring us together.

"Hey, Em! Are we ready? It's getting late." I popped my laptop closed. "Yes, one minute. I forgot my brush." Alex was pretty patient with my last-minute, forget-me-nots and the lengthier time it took me to prepare myself for an outing. She rolled her eyes and mocked with loving sarcasm, "Where we're going, sweetheart, you won't need a brush… or a bra."

I hurled my bag onto my shoulder. Alex and I pretended to hip-check each other. Our usual game to get out the door first. I won!

The thought of the kids traveling on a plane to Chicago without me was terrifying. I knew it was good for the kids to see their paternal grandparents, but out of sight did not mean out of mind. I thought of them every minute of every day.

I was also looking forward to an entire week with Alex. We spoke very little on the ride to the ferry. The iTunes shuffle was booming through Bluetooth. The windows and sunroof were fully open as we drove eastbound. We arrived with time to spare, and I settled onto an outside barstool. Alex leaned over the bar. She ordered two Margarita's, and we sipped them slowly.

"When is the next ferry?" a man beside Alex asked. She replied, "Twelve-twenty." He said, "Thank you." I was so excited, "Alex, I am thrilled with the forecast," I said. She was equally as happy. "I know! I was praying for sunshine. I can't believe we have an entire week away from everything." We tipped our glasses together. We simultaneously spoke one word, "Cheers!" It was amazing to be so close to home but feel worlds away.

The Grove was ultra-intriguing. It would be my third time there. I had never been for the first *forty-something* years of my life, although it was always only a twenty-minute ferry ride away.

Franco's boat took us to Ocean Beach; that was all I knew about Fire Island. I heard about the *gay* Fire Island but never desired to visit. The first time we went to Cherry Grove, I thought, *the gay is everywhere*. As if... I wasn't. It was hard to acknowledge myself as one of *them*. I didn't know I was gay for *forty-something* years. Years later, I was more comfortable. I saw Wanda Sykes walking with her wife. I laughed, remembering one of her stand-up routines about being married to a man.

We settled into our new digs. The house was quaint with outstanding décor. We climbed the outdoor stairs to sit on the top deck. I stared out to the ocean and thought, *this is where I want to be and with whom I want to be with.* Alex stood peering over the railing. She leaned into a backbend, holding onto the rail, and with her head upside down, pointed and said, "We should get out there, huh?"

I walked over, cradled her head, and kissed her upside-down. We went inside, grabbed our bags and set out for our first day on a beautiful beach. I was thrilled. When I was with Alex, no matter where or what we were doing… I always felt joy in the freedom.

She waved and shouted, "Come and bring my phone." I pushed myself up from my beach chair. I reached for her phone and felt the burning sand on my feet. She grabbed her phone from my hand and turned her body behind and close to mine. "Smile, baby." I couldn't help not to. It was a perfect selfie. She kissed me, returned the phone to my hand, and ran into the ocean. I watched her joyously dive into a wave. I slid her phone into my shorts and watched the surf fall over and around my legs. My feet sunk further into the sand with each ripple. I began searching for hidden treasures and found sea glass along the shoreline. The shells and sand sifted through my hands as the tide came in and washed out. One piece was green and moments later I found another, red. I knew it was sea glass because I had seen jewelry made from it. Both were smooth and miraculous. The red was harder to come by, so I felt lucky to have spotted one.

A young man walked naked to my right. I wasn't attracted to him, but I thought his lack of inhibition was very sexy. I could not help to notice him. He was casual as he entered further into the ocean than I would have dared. He dove through a wave, emerged on the other side, and flipped his hair over. He was beautiful. He exited the ocean as freely as he entered, bare and unreserved. Alex paid him no mind, though she swam just a few feet away. The sunset showed itself too soon. The sun dropped to the edge of the water. The same stunning crimson and coral as my trusted memory served me from the rooftop of the Luncheonette. That day, I was thirty-something years older and so was she. It was bittersweet and wonderful.

We spent a beautiful week, forcing me to open my mind to a world full of people I would have once deemed freakish. There was a lesson I could learn from one or all of them. Our week was more perfect than I could have imagined. We met new friends and saw shows. We read books and had dinner outside. Alex was right; I hardly wore a bra. It was beach living in a nonjudgmental society. It was the most relaxing vacation I had ever experienced.

In between our perfect, scarce time together, my concern was mounting. I wanted more from the relationship. I had two children, and it didn't seem Alex understood they were part of the package deal. I didn't hide them. It wasn't as if I was some stranger, she met on Match.com and I casually mentioned on our sixth date; *By the way, I have two kids.* On our last night in this peaceful environment, I asked her how we would take this to the next level. Her hands were folded in front of her. I reached out, and she offered me both hands.

"Hey babe, I want our worlds to merge more." She pulled her hand away. "And there you go again, Em. Only you can ruin this! Our last night!" She was aggravated and I tried to calm her. "I have no intention of ruining anything. I thought it was a great time to have a serious conversation." She was combative, "Well, I don't." She looked away and said nothing. She would not allow the hard conversations. "Alex, what are you afraid of? Yes, I thought you'd choose me over the restaurant. I thought you would love Jude and Sami and come watch them grow with me. I thought the restaurant would become ours, not stay yours. I felt that we were going to share our lives."

Her blank, silent stare was enough to make my insides turn. With every word she didn't say came the answers to the many questions I already answered myself. I concentrated on her silence. Alex wasn't interested in total commitment. She was a fortified castle surrounded by walls and she only let me in when we had time off from our family, our jobs, my children, and real life. The conversation went nowhere and the wordlessness was torturous.

"Are you having coffee?" I asked. "No, perhaps you haven't noticed my sunburn and I'm freezing. I just want to leave." We said nothing on the walk home and didn't hold hands. Alex fell asleep early. I went outside and gazed at the stars. The next day we left and again didn't speak for over a week.

Love was something I believed would propel us forward. Thoughts swept in my head like a sandstorm. Perhaps, Alex loved me but never intended to share a life raising Jude and Sami with me. I silently pondered. I wanted more, and she seemed content with us, sometimes. I just didn't get it and I wasn't happy with her half of commitment to me. After each fall-out, I carried sadness. Burdens to bear inside the deepest part of me. I needed more but I wasn't ready to lose her.

What was starting to define us as a couple were beautiful overnights in luxurious bed and breakfasts, where being gay was completely acceptable and we could hold hands in public. It seemed easy to experience love, romance, and undeniable connection away from real life. Her hand on mine as we drove with the radio turned up, the windows down, the sunroof open and about thirty hours of space and time to concentrate on only each other.

Alex relaxed and left Iris to her sisters and under-dressed hostess to take care of a slower Sunday dinner crowd. We were in and out of shops, enjoying an ice cream cone or lobster overlooking the Atlantic waters of Eastern Long Island. Alex bought clothes that would hang in her over-stuffed closet with tags, like so many other never worn garments. She always bought something for me as a parting gift on returning to our realities.

She stood on her driveway, grabbed my left shoulder and

touched my arm, through the car window. "Please hold onto this. I love you." I would reply, "I love you too." I would close the window and look at her standing, waving in my rear-view window and my heart would cave a little more each time I drove away from a person I never wanted to be away from. I was at my wit's end and tired of my double life.

After that extended period of being away, I knew Alex and I would never work however, I wanted and continued to convince myself we would. We didn't reconnect or leave Cherry Grove any closer. In fact, we grew farther apart. It was still hard to come home.

I was only home for an hour before the kids returned home from Chicago. I was elated when they walked in the door. I missed them more than my greatest moments with Alex that week. Their smiles and hugs made me forget our worst moments. Jesse and I had a brief and cordial exchange at the doorstep as he placed two knapsacks down and went back to his car to retrieve the two suitcases. I was sure to pick up Jude's duffle and simultaneously inch Sami's bag towards the front door. "I can help," Jesse said. "No prob Jess, I got it." I wasn't ready to invite him in. The one time I did, he looked around the house as if he was taking inventory counting the contents of what he left behind and what I had that he didn't. He always made me feel I took away a life that he wanted, one that he signed up for and thought was his forever. In some ways, I knew I made a mistake, but the mistake turned out to be the best thing that happened to me. Not for Vivien and Franco, not for Jesse, Jude or Sami, but for me. It was the best mistake I ever made. I was finally free but with two of the greatest kids any mom could ever have hoped for. I felt like the luckiest, unlucky mom in the universe.

Since the divorce finalized, I never had coffee with Jesse. I wanted to but it just didn't happen. All the years that I wanted to smoke a joint and watch a documentary, he didn't. All the years I wanted to make love and talk about everything, I suddenly had nothing to say. We were so different and yet at one time he fit so perfectly into my family unit. Jude gave Jesse a hug and told his dad he loved him. Sami jumped into his arms and asked her father if her new jumpsuit was in her suitcase before heading inside. He procrastinated on his departure. I stood there and it all felt so awkward.

"So how was your week?" he asked. "It was fine. I missed the kids. How are your parents?" He had a look that I didn't recognize, and I knew the questions I had dreaded for years were about to come. I knew the answers I had rehearsed for years would not come. "So, did you go away with Alex?" I didn't know whether to answer him truthfully. I wasn't sure I was ready to out myself and I was certain he didn't deserve to know where I was and with whom. Nonetheless, I replied, "I spent some time with Alex, and I spent some time working." He crossed his arms. He dug one hand under his arm and the other hand clenched his forearm. "Emily, what the fuck is going on with you?" For all the times I imagined an honest conversation pursuing between us, I had never imagined it starting with *what the fuck is going on with you*? I immediately became defensive. The rehearsed words never came but I unleashed a complete impromptu reply, "You think that question will get you the answers you need? Do you? You're asking me to give you the out, Jesse? You are asking me to take the blame for every fail in this marriage. We lived on the surface for so long. You were comfortable there; I wasn't! I won't let you give me an honorable discharge from this union because you know Alex represents love in my life. So, you want an answer? You think you deserve to hear it from me?"

He stood there perched with his still folded arms and a distasteful expression. I continued, "I asked you every day for so long, too long… to give me what I need or try to. What would be enough for me to stay and try to love you forever? You refused and you mocked me. Told me that lyrics and books are silly and real life is work and money and things. You made more time for Franco and Michael and nights of cigars and Patron than you did for me, your wife! You were more concerned with porn and your ego than you were finding your own truth, finding a life for us. Are you asking me how I spent my week or are you asking me who I am?" He said nothing.

There was a brief period of silence. I continued, "I am the same person you married and had two beautiful children with. How I spend my time and whom I choose to love is none of your concern. I love and will love many, in many different ways. I will not close my mind to Alex, who came into my life and brought me so much of what was always lacking. I will not look for a label burned on my skin. I am Emily. I'm done fighting and I'm done explaining myself to you. You've lost the right to ask me anything." He stood there with a smirk of narcissism. "I am not surprised." He chuckled, "I always knew there was something wrong with you. You're a dyke and that's probably why I never wanted to fuck you!"

I didn't feel hurt. I felt a calm flow through me. I opened the storm door and was about to lock it behind me. I turned back and said, "I am sorry. I am also not sorry. Been meaning to tell you that and probably would have years ago but you decided to board the revenge train to hell before I had a chance. I think I know how you feel, and I am certain you have no idea how I feel. You feel I blind-sided you? I didn't, Jesse. I should have known when you punched through the wall in our first few months of marriage after our fight about who the fuck remembers?

After ten years I just couldn't pretend anymore we were… what we weren't. He unfolded his arms. He saluted me like a five-star general, turned and walked away. *What a dick*, I thought!

I grasped my stomach. I slammed the door and locked it behind me. I was hoping the kids did not hear our exchange and yet every part of my being figured they did. I walked into the house and leaned over the kitchen sink and felt like I wanted to vomit. I missed and wanted Alex to knock on my door and beg me for my whole heart, which she already had. That would never come, and I had to embrace the idea of being free to choose whatever and whomever came into my life may be liberating. My mind was spinning. Finances were still a mess. My kids were what I kept my eye on, in between my chaotic state and I remained present knowing and anticipating the changes on the horizon.

Chapter Eighteen

I needed desperately to see Mara. She was one of my few friends who knew about my relationship. We didn't speak regularly as my friendship with her annoyed Alex. Every relationship I had outside of Alex and her sisters annoyed Alex. She wanted me all to herself and only when it was most convenient for her. She was the most insecure, assured person I had ever known.

I had come out to Mara about a year and a half after Alex and I started seeing each other. I did it over lunch on one of her visits to New York. I did it by reading her a story that I wrote about Alex. She was so worried I would tell her I had some fatal disease. She was relieved. She was compassionate and understood. I subsequently came out, to many people through those years. Charlotte, Vivien, and Franco many months later. They were the most complex truths I had ever talked about out loud. Alex was mostly mad and never supportive when I told her these conversations ensued. She thought I scheduled these conversations and none of them I did. They happened because I was ready to explain my weird and crazy behavior to those who loved me most.

I was terrified those days and let fear and guilt infiltrate my core. It's a scary thing to live within those emotions. Learning not to care about what others think was the most challenging part of my journey.

I spent endless nights on the phone with Mara explaining my confusion and conflict. It was difficult to accept that what I wanted and what I knew truly made me happy wasn't necessarily what was easy or made my parents most comfortable. When I walked arm and arm with Jesse, people smiled adoringly, and so did my parents. When I walked with Alex, people looked at us like we fell short of the American Dream.

I loved him, and I loved her. Jesse gave his whole self to me, but our love fell short. She gave her whole love to me and for a long time that seemed more important, but her whole self was less obtainable.

I picked up the phone. "Mars, Can I come to New Hampshire? I need lobster and I need you." I started to cry. She welcomed the idea immediately. "Why not this weekend? And why are you so sad?" I wiped my tears, "I am just questioning everything Mars. I am struggling. My whole life was blanketed in a world of show. Alex and I are not doing well; I'm fighting with Vivien and Jesse. I feel like a failure in every aspect of my life." She immediately stopped me. "Emmy, becoming one's authentic self is tough. In some ways, it must have been easier to live on the surface, as you call it." I agreed, "Yes, Mara, it was! I have hurt so many people on my journey to find my true self. I never meant to do that." She understood and replied, "I just think you need to forgive yourself and understand that the lessons will keep coming hard and strong until the universe teaches us. You are going to be okay and I'm here for you. Get to New Hampshire. We will decompress and figure it out over a lobster."

Jesse picked the kids up late Friday afternoon and I jumped into my car and headed to Mara's. I made it in a record four-hour time. I arrived around nine in the evening and of course my guest room had clean sheets and Mars had a bottle of red waiting at the table. I walked in and she hugged me for as long as I needed. Her husband Ben went to retrieve my knap sack and then he dismissed himself to the den to watch football. Her house was beautiful. The loft hallway upstairs was made for high ceilings and an open layout. She paid a third in taxes and had four times the space. I wanted to move there and start anew.

We sipped wine and tried to solve my worries. By midnight

we were so tired, and we went to sleep. The next day Mara
and I took a ride to a hiking area. We talked and brought
peanut butter and jelly sandwiches for our lunch. I told her
how things were just a mess with Alex. I told her about the
fight we had two weeks prior and how we hadn't spoken
since. "Mars, Alex wailed out on me. I stared her down and
asked her three times... What? My insides were screaming
and kicking, and I wanted her to give me the damn truth.
And you know what she said? She paced silently and
said, Em, I didn't have children by design. I have my nieces
and JJ, and I have, I have... well, I have the restaurant. She
said she didn't see how this could work. She said I came
back into her life like a gusty wind and was one of her
greatest loves. Oh, and then, I asked her how many great
loves of her life she's had. And Mara, she did not like that
question either. She was so defensive, said Seriously? You
disappear for decades and ask me about my loves?"
I continued, "It became too much for both of us. We loved
in secret. It was a whirlwind of what was supposed to be or
almost missed, wasted time, and perhaps too late. She went
into psycho mode and once she screamed and yelled so
much and hurled a Poland Springs bottle at me. I stood up
and gathered my things. She watched me closely. I wanted
to hear her say don't go and I knew she wouldn't. I left. I
felt hollow. My soul is drained. It's a feeling I can't wrap
my head around. Oh Mars, I know I must get back to me
without her and then there is Jesse and the kids; they are
constant reminders that he did, in fact, exist. I want to hate
him but still I can't, and I almost have no reason to."
Mara was appalled at Alex's anger and asked if the water
bottle hit me. I told her it didn't, but it did chip the
sheetrock. Mara made me understand that Alex was
probably never going to move in my direction. She knew
Alex from decades past and thought she was very
controlling. She was right and I had to accept that the

relationship was not healthy for me. We spoke about Vivien and Mara really believed that the gay thing wasn't the problem for Vivien, but Alex was.

Mara became my lifeline. We spoke often about our struggles and helped each other solve problems. She helped me on the hardest days. New Hampshire was the best therapy because there was no fake between us. With her I could discuss anything, and the stress began to disappear. We had a fun night and no serious conversation when we returned home. We played cards with Ben and her daughter, Loreen. We ate and laughed and kept it light. I went to my room and started packing my bag for my next morning's departure.

I heard my phone buzzing on vibrate and there was her name and picture flashing. I answered, "Hi Alex," I said. "Where are you and why haven't you called me?" Her tone was the same argumentative tone I had grown accustomed to and hated. I was quiet. "Hello?" She asked. "Hello?" I replied and she heatedly inquired, "Where the fuck are you now?" I pressed the red end button and continued to pack my bag. I didn't do that to irritate her. I had to save myself from elevating blood pressure and I just could not deal with her screaming or worse, her silent disapproval about what I chose to do when she chose to abandon me, again.

I found myself watching a tennis match from center court. My head would turn right and left, and I would see Jesse and I would see Alex. Everything she gave me, he never did. Everything he gave me, she never would. I was in pain missing my old life with no hope of starting a new one that would be good for me and my children. Every one of my struggles were still ever-present.

I returned home from New Hampshire. There was still a colossal void in my life. I failed with Jesse, with Alex, and it was still undetermined how well the kids would do as they grew into young adults. I drove home for more than five hours in traffic with no radio. Just me and my thoughts.

I realized I valued everything Alex said to devalue me, and her words were tattooed all over me.

Jude and Sami were with Jesse. He was hanging out with the old friends we used to hang around with because Jude or Sami were in similar activities and growing up with their kids. I always wondered why or how they could remain friends with Jesse. They clearly chose him over me. They made plans conveniently when it was his every-other-weekend or I had other engagements. It was years later, when I had lunch with one or two of those friends who told me they were sorry and may have misread Jesse and perhaps, misread me way back then. Some of those relationships fell through over the years, some stuck around or reappeared years later, but while it was all unfolding, it felt utterly isolating. Everything boiled down to a field of possibilities, and I felt mine were few.

Chapter Nineteen

Sitting at the kitchen table on a quiet afternoon, my home phone rang. I glanced at the caller-id which read, Davie Green. He said he was coming in from San Francisco for three weeks and his girlfriend would come a few days later and he told me I had to meet her too. I was both anxious and looking forward to seeing him. We hadn't spoken for years, and I wondered why he was returning to New York to make a point to spend time with me. We were close neighborhood friends but we hadn't been in touch for years. I wasn't at my best and had gained too many pounds to feel great about meeting him or anyone after so many years.

I would have to convince him I was okay in person, which would be another challenge. We planned to meet up and I agreed only because I was sure after meeting Davie alone, I would cancel the second visit wherever he expected to have dinner with him and his girlfriend of five months.

Davie asked me to meet him in the old neighborhood joint on the strip. The name had changed, but it was still an old dingy bar where we had our first drink together decades earlier.

I walked in, and there he was. He still looked like my thirteen-year-old friend from Haypath Lane. Suddenly, all my doubts of time gone by and how I may have aged disappeared. He stood up as I approached, and his arms embraced me and took me off the floor in a swirl of love. "I have so much to tell you, Emily! You have no idea how much you have come to mind these years. And now something so enormous has happened to me!" I looked at him and studied the years. "Dave, this is crazy. I feel like so much time has gone by and changed…." I lowered my voice, "…this dingy bar hasn't changed, though?" My eyebrows rose to my forehead. I continued, "Are you finally rich and famous, and you wanted to come in person to tell me you haven't forgotten about me?" He laughed heartily. "Emily, I am not famous, but my sister and I are finally signed with an agent in LA. That means nothing too famous yet, but we are opening for a few bands who are starting to hit the charts in a big way." I exclaimed, "Oh my God, so you are here because you didn't forget me, I mean, just before you are about to become enormously famous?"

He took my hand, squeezed it, and said, "You know, you were my first crush, but you never knew that. It was a great neighborhood, and our friendship was always the one I missed the most." I looked at him, "That's a huge compliment, but I am not ready for a heavy reunion of any sort; my life is somewhat... well, busy and complicated and...." He interrupted me and took out his phone. "Look at these two?" I looked at a picture of me and my roommate, Bonnie, from college. I stared at the picture. The bar was dark, but I knew exactly who she was at first glance. "That's my roommate from Florida, and how do you have a picture of us on your phone?" He had a glowing smirk of happiness and didn't answer me immediately. "Dave!" I proclaimed, "How do you have this picture?" "Emily, I met her a little over five months ago at a gig in California! She came out to meet up with friends and I was gigging with Laura. We met that night and hit it off. I learned she was your college roommate the first time she invited me to her place for dinner. She had a picture of twenty people with WPB shirts, sitting on a lawn, and you were in it." I was in complete disbelief, "Get the fuck out of here? Are you kidding me, for real?" He beamed, "Em, I wished I visited you in college because she's the best thing to ever come into my crazy life." I could not believe it, "Dave, this is nuts. I remember taking that picture. We were all orientation leaders preparing the field for the

incoming freshman rally. This is crazy! You are dating
Bonnie Jensen?" He said, "You could not imagine walking
around her place and seeing you next to her in that
picture!" We spent the next four hours with each other and
a bunch of White Russians. I told him about Jude and Sami.
He told me about his sister Laura and their music.
We sat in the strip bar next to the laundry mat that was still
open from six in the morning til midnight, seven days a
week. The Luncheonette had been sold years earlier, and it
had been turned into a pizzeria. The frozen yogurt place
closed. Tom's travel agency and Mack's card store became
a spacious gym. The post office remained, and so did I and
my long-time friend, who ran into my college roommate
and fell in love. *How unreal that the universe brings us
back to those who we were never meant to leave*, I thought.

I told Dave about the shift and transformation. He was
supportive. He told me his roommate was gay, and so was
everybody else in California. We laughed, and I asked him
if he remembered Alex from the Luncheonette. He vaguely
did because he moved soon after I met her. He recalled,
"When us kids started growing up and fleeing the confines
of our hood, I came home one day to get more of my stuff,
and I was in the back of that white, beat-up van my father
gave me." I interjected, "Oh my God, we smoked pot for
the first time in that wreck." He winked, "And the second,
and third...." We laughed out loud, and he continued,
"Well, that day Alex pulled up and was yelling at you, and
she was really loud and I was going to walk across but
thought it was none of my business, so I didn't."
I admitted, "Dave, she's still like that. It's so beautiful at
times, but we fight too much, and who wants that in a
relationship?" He agreed, "You just answered your own
question, Emmy. Back then, I just found it odd that she
behaved more like your *girlfriend* than, ya know, just a

girlfriend."

I told Dave about our reunion and our toxic and confusing relationship. We talked about my divorce, his father passing away, and all the ups and downs life had offered in the decade-plus since I had last seen him.

He said, "One day, you will feel when enough is enough, and you will walk."

I still wasn't ready to lose her. Since our days in the Luncheonette, we had been inseparable, and I felt life was offering up a second chance to get it right. I had never felt for anyone what I felt for Alex, and I may have known deep down that she was always more than just a friend.

The evening Dave and I spent together in that rundown bar reminded me of who I was before Jesse, Jude and Sami, and Alex. I was wrapped up in a moment that felt so conversant. It was perfect, and it was the beginning of reconnecting with myself at a time when it was absolutely detrimental for healing to begin.

I was finally putting perspective on everything. I was thrilled to have spent time with him and looked forward to meeting up after many years with Bonnie. We shared many great times for two years at West Palm before she transferred to a smaller school in California. She studied nursing and secured a job in a hospital down the block from an outdoor bar that Dave and Laura played twice a week. I thought, *What a big world and a small one.*

I hadn't seen Alex in weeks. We had a text exchange that placed all the blame on me and for the first time, I had to go silent. Letting her go was agonizing. I missed her, but I was calmer and emerging. My friends took up some of the time I used to loathe alone, which was good. I wasn't convinced we were over, but memories kept reminding me why Alex would never fully commit to me and the kids. The conflict was getting so old, and no matter how much I loved her, I knew our differences would ultimately cause our demise.

I took myself to the local diner and sat by myself, noticing people. The ones who ate alone in small booths like me. The ones who sat silently as the years of their couple-hood left them without much to say. The ones who took turns talking while the other took a bite of their French toast, while chewing proved to be a perfect time to listen, and then swapped roles as the other enjoyed a forkful of their omelet. The world was turning, and I was okay to be alone for the first time in a long time. Being with oneself, *what a concept*!

Dave told me to meet him and Bonnie at a fun Mexican restaurant, and I was excited to see them. I still was in disbelief that Bonnie was dating my childhood friend. I pulled into the lot and saw her exiting her car. I rolled down my window and screamed. "Yo, Bonzo!" I parked, and we headed toward each other. She practically leaped into my arms; we hugged and smiled. "Oh my God, you look amazing," I told her. She was beautiful. Long blonde hair and always in great shape. We stopped our embrace and held each other's hands in front of us. She told me I hadn't changed a bit, and I told her that was a lie. Just as we started walking towards the restaurant, Davie pulled up. "Hey, you two, wait up!" We chatted while waiting for Dave to park and join us.

Through the corner of my eye, some hundred feet away, I saw Alex alone in her parked car staring at me. Bonnie sensed my distraction and looked her way. "Who is that?" she asked. I shook my head without turning to her, "That's my girlfriend." I answered. Bonnie tried to peer through the reflection on the windshield. Alex put the car in drive, drove away fast and furious, and turned left. Bonnie looked at me in shock, "Maybe, you need to make her your ex-girlfriend? My God, if looks can kill!" I kept looking into the distance, and whispered "Yep, you got that right!"

By now, Dave had caught up and witnessed the whole thing. "Tell me? Is that Alex?" I shook my head up and down, "Yep, that's Alex?" Bonnie said, "Oh no, that was Alex, as in… *Alex*, who you were friends with when we were at WPB?" Dave gave Bonnie a kiss hello and then insisted, "Okay ladies, let's take it inside; it appears we have much catching up to do."

We all started walking to the door, and Bonnie asked, "Why was she here spying on you? Dave opened the door and waited for us to enter. "Let's get a Margarita, and I will Splain Lucy." Bonnie burst out in laughter as she and I watched all the re-runs of I Love Lucy many nights in our apartment, sharing a pint of ice cream. She loved the show and got me to like it too. We followed the host to a booth, and Bonnie stated, "When the Margarita gets here, let's start with… um, when you hopped the fence?" I replied, "You only want to know because you wanted Nick back in the day, but he was all mine." Dave waved his arms like a referee, "Okay, we will have none of that." Bonnie grabbed his hand and said, "There is some truth to Nick being a hottie but since you came along, I want nobody but you, sweetie." We all sat down, and Dave ordered Nacho's Supreme and three Patron Margaritas.

My phone vibrated, and I glanced at the text. Alex was angry, and I knew she pulled over moments after she sped off.

The text read:

How can you?

I read the text and put the phone down. Dave grabbed it off the table. "Hey Em, let me answer this kooky bitch!" I grabbed my phone. "Dave, Stop!" He retreated into his corner and released my phone to the table. "I am not happy with her behavior, but you guys don't know the whole story, and I'm surely not going to try to make you understand the last thirty-something years in one night." I was upset, and clearly, they saw the change in my upbeat self that first arrived. My phone vibrated again and again. I did not pick it up. I did not look at it during dinner and though it was hard to concentrate and be fully present, I did the best I could.

Bonnie and I told Dave countless stories about our college days. Some secrets remained, and I wondered why Bonnie and I had also lost touch after so many shared memories. They seemed like the perfect couple, and I was happy to have them both re-enter my life. I knew after our nachos and our endless conversation, our friendship would last the duration of our lives.

I got home and read the texts that Alex had sent:

5:45pm Wow, wow, wow. Doesn't take you long to jump right back out there, huh!

5:48pm Weeks of no contact, and it makes sense you would just be out on a date and up to your same old stuff. Tequila and the party are all you were ever into, Emily. I kept wondering if you would ever text.

What a fool I have to EVER think you ever cared about me at all.

6:02pm Too busy to text back, I see. Long first date or is it a third or fourth?

6:38pm I've given you everything, and you quickly move on. Just like that! What a fool I have been!

I finally replied:

10:02pm Hey Alex – pretty hard to give you anything when you aren't accepting of anything. If you only knew who that was – maybe it was bouncy Bonnie – ya think that can be true?! If I was going to date her or anyone, that would have happened decades ago, but of course, that's what you would surmise.

She texted back:

10:38pm Okay, so who was she?

I immediately answered:

10:39pm Seriously, you disappear and then accuse me of being out on a date and expect me to think you would understand that I met a friend out for dinner, and wtf – why were you there – are you following me? What kind of relationship built on trust is that?

She continued:

10:41pm Trust? You don't know the first thing about trust, Emily – you are always running off trying to get drunk with old friends and new friends that obviously you've met in the last few weeks... go get it, party girl!

I am not sure why I entertained the nonsense, but I replied again:

10:45 Alex – quit it! You have exploded and retracted so many times. The more you left, the quicker I learned that you would just leave again. Your name-calling is unacceptable, and that thing about me being jealous of your sisters is preposterous. Maybe they should pick your next girlfriend, Alex. I am so tired of this!

The text fight continued, but I put my phone down for a while. I skimmed through a barrage of insults and ridiculous rhetoric. I ended it with one last reply.

11:38 Alex... I've always wanted a life with you. After all these years... well after a few incidents these last years... I don't believe you are in a place of acceptance. I am who I am... You had your relationship issues, and I have had mine - it was what it was. And you blaming me... look at your choices, Alex. Look at your surroundings and stop judging mine. You left so many times for days, weeks. You called me horrible names and do it repeatedly. I would be a complete zero to accept that. So, we are done now... Get yourself happy and healthy, and I promise to do the same. I'm rooting for us - together or to each our own. Either way... I love you forever.

Alex never replied to that text. If she had texted back or called and said one thing differently, I would have dropped everything and driven to wherever she was. A defining moment and my entire life could have changed. I thanked the sky above that didn't happen. While I was so worried that I wasn't ready to move forward, it was really her who wasn't ready. It wasn't until four months later that she texted me to wish Sami a happy birthday but by then, it was too late. I wasn't going back! My life and confidence had taken shape.

I fluffed my pillows, and I lay down in the dark. I fell asleep, not quite believing it, but I figured I would never see, talk to, or laugh with her ever again.

Chapter Twenty

The days and weeks, and months that followed were sometimes as hard as the days of my divorce. I was alone again, and I was a sad sack of suds. I tried hard to be in no-contact mode, and eventually, I got through two consecutive hours without Alex on my brain. I delved into the kids and the home front. I began spending time cleaning and organizing every single drawer and closet in my house. When those projects were tackled, I started to take walks, and it wasn't until months later that I could turn on the radio and listen to music again. Often a song that reminded me of the many weekends with Alex, I would have to immediately switch stations or stream a podcast, anything to take my mind off her.

I didn't realize that my period of grievance was actually coming to an end, and I was beginning again. I spent much time thinking about my family and reconnecting with friends. Most of my friends were in their forties, facing tragic moments when they became orphans. I witnessed them come to grips with their lives being forever changed without their parents, which made me want to spend more time with Vivien and Franco.
I had more time to spare and wasn't running off to meet Alex. I loved my parents in such different ways. My relationship with Vivien was real and complicated. My relationship with Franco was less emotional and uncomplicated. My mother was more of an essential in my life, and I loved Franco like he was a superhero. Either way, I knew I would miss them both when the time came to say goodbye.

Vivien liked it when I was established at home with the kids. She noticed Alex did not have a presence in my life after a month or so. Franco never noticed. One afternoon we sat at her table outside, enjoying the view. "Is it over?" she asked. I replied, "Yeah, and my heart feels broken."

My mother hated to see me hurting, but relieved, I thought. "You will pull through this!" I didn't go into depth about when it ended or why. I knew my mother thought I was better off without her, and in the end, maybe she did know what was best for me. I changed the subject quickly, "Mom, I notice Dad's forgetting a lot," She didn't hesitate, "Oh, Em, he's always been like this." I looked right into her eyes. "Viv, he's worse than whomever he has always been. He's older." She interrupted, "I am too. I am older too. When will you and Michael start worrying about me?" She almost yelled it out as if it were a painful cry. I wanted to tell Viv to have patience. I wanted to tell her I saw her aging but less rapidly. I spoke gently, "I will worry about you when I must. I will worry right now about him. And I will take care of you both forever." Vivien tried hard not to buckle in emotion, so she winked and then whispered, "Core Four." I told her I loved her and headed home with bittersweet, heart-filled gratitude that I still had parents to visit.

The kids were growing and needed less of my time. Jude was driving, and Sami worked after school part-time. I started writing and freelancing again. The freedom and the money felt good. I was still struggling, but it became easier every day I pushed through.

I saw my neighbor gardening one day. She reminded me of a younger version of myself. A similar pac-n-play that Sami used to play in when I planted fall Mums, from the same St. Christopher's sale at the same elementary school her daughter attended.

Her younger son amused himself on the grass a few yards away. His name was Graham. I said hi to her husband, Henry, who was tall and handsome. He casually held a 2x4 in his left hand as he mentioned the wall he was building inside. Our exchange was brief and friendly. I walked away with memories of some part of my life with Jesse. I still missed those days.

Alex and I never spent a day shopping for shrubbery at Home Depot. She had little interest in that.

I no longer had a husband who would hurl a big bag of soil onto the orange flatbed cart. I no longer had Alex, who would sit on a beach with me and let me talk about anything I wanted to talk about.

While recognizing I missed some of my past, I had insurmountable enthusiasm for my future. My divorce forced me to delve into so many areas of my unknown self. I felt emotions in parts of me I wasn't aware existed, and I had to feel and make sense of a whole new set of emotions. The tide changed and instead of swimming against it, I was learning to let it carry me through. The universe had a plan, and I knew that. I knew my original plan A wasn't the universe's plan B. I began to own my choices but still kicked and screamed along my walk.

Years later, I was sure Alex saw the pictures posted the day I married Stevie. Though I didn't post much on social media, Stevie did and often tagged me. Somehow, we were not in contact and yet still connected. Oddly, neither of us blocked one another, but it didn't matter. I still hated Facebook and yet never quit.

Jesse and I shared spirits and even danced together at our kids' weddings. That was something I never thought could happen when I was *forty-something*. He finally remarried a girl named Emily. That was quite a dichotomy too. I only saw them together a few times and he appeared happy. Jesse and I have these arbitrary texts from time to time. We never really became the friends I thought we could after the divorce, but it felt good to not be enemies. I always thought I could reach out if I needed him, but I never did. I think he always knew if he needed me; I too, would jump to help him out in any way possible.

I decided to think of Jesse as someone I used to love instead of someone I learned to dislike. I decided to accept Alex's choices and not dwell on why she made them, however accept our relationship had to come to an end. I decided to revel in the glory of my ever changing and growing children who were, in fact soaring to heights beyond my comprehension in terms of heart and soul, and good judgement. I was a witness to them making choices for themselves and, those choices were pronounced. It was amazing and I was proud I had something to do with their happiness and success.

Waving goodbye to my neighbors, I heard my phone buzz and answered. "Hey Mars! What up, girl?" She said, "My sweet friend, I have a proposition for you." My curiosity peaked, "Well, let me in on it," I beckoned. "LBH has a room with clean sheets for you!" Her words were both clear and unclear. "Mara, what the hell are you saying?" She clarified, "Em, I was supposed to go this week and meet up with my sorority sisters - remember I told you?" I nodded, not that she saw that through the voice call, but she knew I remembered. She continued, "So Marge and Stevie will be there, but Em, you need to go in my place. You're the one to replace me, and Lord knows you need some peace, girl. Go find it with my dearest friends at LBH. I have to stay here and take care of Dad." Sitting outside on my deck, I looked up at the stars.

"Mars, I don't know Marge or Stevie, and without you, I mean… I don't know if that's my peace." Mara didn't seem to hear a word I spoke. "Emily, remember that day you passed the fourth level in Jungle King?" I said, "Hell yeah, the highlight of teenage summer, nineteen-eighty-something!" She said, "Em, I know this sounds crazy, but I had an epiphany the other night. This visit to Maine will take you to the next level, the fifth level! It's also a great place to write and wrap up the ending of your book. I know you will love Marge and Stevie and they will love you. I interrupted Mara, "Is that her real name?" She replied, "Yes, her real name is Stevie, like Stevie Nicks, and she is as cool too!" I immediately inquired, "Can she sing?" Mara laughed again. "It's so good to hear you laugh, Mars. Please hug and kiss my second Dad." I was sad, and the silence over the line told me she was too. She cleared her throat, "Em, I'm not ready to lose him, but please tell me you will help me get through this!"

I reassured her truthfully in my promise, "No way I ever let you float out of my life again. You're my best friend forever, Mars!" I heard her take a deep breath. "Em, go to LBH and be me. Meet my two friends who are my family, like you. I will need all three of you to get me through this." I heard her tearing up. She continued, "Go bond with them so you can all pick me up from the floor that day. Please, Em, sleep on it?" I felt all the pain of my nine-year-old best friend who lost her mom and was coming to terms, *forty-something* years later with losing her dad. "Mars, I will go. I will be you! I will meet Marge and Stevie Nicks!" She was laughed again. Then, she said, "Babe, gotta go! Take care of you! Pack your bag for an epic LBH retreat. I will call Marge and Stevie and tell them you are joining in, and you won't regret it, Em!" I drove to Maine ten days later.

My thundering Spotify playlist drowned out my off-key vocals. I sang out loud and silently rejoiced in the complete newness of liberation. I was content and fulfilled and oddly, I was happy to be on my way. I prayed for Mr. C and Mars. I was halfway there and made it aboard the ferry, which alleviated about three hours of driving time. I stared out into the water and thought about everything, and I thought about Alex. It had been eight months, and neither of us spoke a word. *Is this truly how it ends*, I thought?

I finally arrived at LBH. I could not believe the sight I recognized and the smell of the air I had thought I never paid attention to when I visited thirty-something years earlier. It was familiar, and I wished Mara was there so we could remember the lake together.

I turned the wheel to park, and my tires crackled along the pebbled driveway. I knew it was Stevie sitting on Aunt Millie's weathered deck steps. I stepped outside, stretched, and began my walk to the front porch. "Hi Stevie," I said to a complete stranger. She seemed to be waiting for me. She had magic in her smile, "I'm not Marge, so yep you got it right, Emily!" She said with conviction.

I noticed everything about her in an instant. "It's nice to meet you," I said and extended my right hand. She was stunning. She lit up the lake, and she lit a wick inside me that had been long blown out.

"You must be tired?" she asked. "I replied, "No, I am thirsty, need to pee and... any food in this joint?" She popped up, and I noticed her some more. Stevie was a force, and I was immediately attracted to her entire being. "Hell yeah, Mara sent us steaks, and we were just waiting for you to throw them on the grill. Marge made sides. Come and eat, friend!" It was a warm welcome, and I stared at Stevie as she led the way into Aunt Millie's, *Little*

Blue House. I stopped on the threshold and took a deep breath. I paid attention to the historic smell of the home and the same rotary phone on a small antique table in the tiny foyer, where Mara would stand and talk to me for a minute before running off to the lake so long ago. Stevie stopped and turned to see why I wasn't close behind. "Did you know her?" My eyes welled up enough for her to notice. Stevie stepped towards me, and I shook off my sentiment. "I did know her. I was her guest for a week and a phone friend after that, every year Mara came. She was extraordinary." Stevie stopped short of me by three feet. "Millie was extraordinary, and so is Mara. And here we are, and Millie would like that, and so does Mara."

Those were the exact words I needed to hear, and Stevie said it with compassion. I was paying close attention to her as we continued out the side door. My sights set on Marge, holding a glass of white wine with a few ice cubes to her lips. She bounced out of the Adirondack. "Emily Netti, in the flesh!" I smiled, "In the flesh!" I repeated. She jumped up and gave me the kind of hug that Mara would have loved to witness. The lake, in the background was beautiful.

Our threesome was delightful. Stevie managed the fire pit that wasn't there decades before. Marge made drinks and cleaned up the empty plates of fresh corn on the cob, broccoli casserole, and succulent steak perfectly marinated and cooked to a warm pink center. We enjoyed talking and we all loved the faint sound of country tunes playing from Marge's Bluetooth speaker. I missed Mars. "Let's call Mara ladies," I said. Stevie stood up and pulled an iPhone from the back pocket of her cut-off jean shorts. Her thighs were tan, and her white t-shirt barely slid up over a sterling silver ring just to the side of her belly button that glistened when the light hit it. I noticed everything about Stevie and appreciated everything about Marge. I was excited hoped Mara's epiphany about a *fifth level* was real. Either way, I knew I was supposed to be at LBH with my best friends' best friends.

Early the next morning, I wiped the sleep from my eyes. I was quiet in Aunt Millie's kitchen. I carefully studied the sameness in her coffee mugs and cupboards. I was in a time capsule of my twelve-year-old self. The little homesick girl I was, and nearly four decades later, I was there again. I recalled so many memories. LBH was unique. It was the last place I had been before growing up into a more mature adolescent. I didn't know I'd be back ever again. I made my coffee in the Keurig, also not there thirty-something years earlier, and set out to the lake to sit on the edge of the dock.

I heard her footsteps and used all my strength to not look at her approaching with her distinctive smile. Before I turned my head to see her, I said, "Good Morning Stevie." She sat with ease in a position close to me on the dock.

I wish she had landed closer. She was assured and sexy. I noticed all her beauty and looked for flaws. I saw none.

The decision to pack a bag and head to Maine changed my life. Marge read a million books and didn't like to leave the house, so Stevie and I had time to sit and talk for hours about our lives. She taught me how to fish and after we caught them, we would throw them back into the lake. She was very outdoorsy and while we walked, she talked about camping and fig trees. She told me about how she takes care of her pool, and I loved listening to her talk about how she was raised, what her family was like, and how she became a quiet conqueror.

As I figured I wasn't good enough for her or someone like

her, I never pursued more than a friendship, and neither did she, but when I arrived home from LBH, I felt a renewed sense of self and spirit.

Smiling with memories of a peaceful and surprisingly fantastic weekend, I made a right onto my familiar paved block. My tired eyes suddenly awakened when I saw an orange, four-door Jeep in my drive and was surprised Jude was home from college. I left all the bags and grabbed only my car key. I coded in my front door and saw him at the kitchen table. I froze at the sight of my son and his visit that he didn't tell me about. My eyes filled with pure happiness, "Mom, hey, nothing like your meatballs; I hope you weren't planning on these for your dinner because I ate them. How was your trip?" I was delighted and surprised, "Hey Jude," I said, "My trip… well, I may have fallen slightly in love." His smile reminded me of a little boy with long jet-black hair, only it was not as long. It was very short and neat, but just as black. He responded, "Really, who is she?" I said, "Myself." He mocked, "Well, that's great, Mom, but damn, I was hoping you met someone! You deserve all the love you gave to me and Sami, to just kiss you back." He slid out of the chair and walked quickly to me. He put his huge hands on my shoulders and pulled me close. I was elated. "How did you learn how to speak so eloquently, Jude?" He said, "I learned it, from my mom." I hugged him briefly, and as he started away, I added, "By the way, I did meet someone, though. I may have fallen in…umm…very big *like*, which was really something," I giggled. He raised his eyebrows twice.
"Hey, ya never know what's waiting around the bend, right Mom? And if it does pan out for you, I hope she loves on you hard, till forever." I told him I liked him popping up for a quick home visit. Jude ate another helping of meatballs,

while we talked about his girlfriend, his life and busy schedule. He told me he was going to take a ride and visit Vivien and Franco. I told him I was going to shower and go to sleep.

I called Mara and told her that my time in Maine was better than the fourth level of Jungle King. I never told her I had a crush on Stevie because it was just a quiet fantasy on the way home, and I didn't want it to get back to Stevie. I trusted Mara completely; however, from my conversations with Stevie, she was near ending a relationship of over fourteen years. I knew she needed space to figure that out before I chimed in. I did tell Mara she was right about it being the best place to finish my book and I was researching and reaching out to everyone I knew who could help me to get it published. I wasn't sure I would be completely joyful about everything, but I felt joy about most things that were happening around me.
I knew inevitably things would change again, and I knew I would be able to adjust to those changes without anxiety, without drama and with my whole heart intact.
Mara was excited for me but asked, "So now what?" I laughed, "Truthfully, I think I did the easiest thing... I wrote a book. Now to get it published! The good news is that a friend I've worked with, Justine from The Tribune, called a publicist friend of hers for me. Her name is Trudy, and I have a meeting with her soon. I am nervous and excited!" I was grateful to Justine for an opportunity to learn from Trudy how to get my book out there.

I told Mara I would be swamped in the weeks to follow. I asked about Marge and Stevie every time Mara and I spoke on the phone, and she said they often asked about me too. Mara said the four of us would eventually reunite in Maine, but it was difficult due to our conflicting schedules and busy days.

On a separate occasion, I was more honest with Bonnie about everything that didn't happen in Maine but how it made me feel. I told her that if I ever met someone again; a woman I could fall in love with, I had hoped it would be someone a lot or exactly like Stevie. When I knew that our Maine reunion wasn't going to happen that summer, I contemplated reaching out to Stevie but I was still unsure of her situation and didn't want to complicate anything for her. As noble luck would have it, Stevie texted me, a few months after I arrived home from Maine.

I'm house and dog-sitting for some friends on Long Island next week. Wondering if that makes it possible to see you and you to see me? We can talk like we did on the dock in Maine, and you can meet Cooper.

I read her text twice before replying:

Hey Stevie. So nice to hear from you and yes, I would like that! Where on Long Island will you be, and who is Cooper?

She tapped back: *Ha-Ha*

The dog... lol. You do like dogs, right? Because my entire opinion of you will change instantly if you tell me - you don't.

I tapped back: *Ha-Ha*

Yes... OMG Yes! I love dogs! People, not so much! Did WE NOT talk about dogs in Maine?

She replied:

I suppose not. We still have much to talk about. How close are you to Oyster Meadow?

My answer:

Not far. I will call you tomorrow, and we can make a plan.

Oyster Meadow was only a thirty-minute drive from my house. I arrived, and Stevie showed me around. Cooper was the cutest two-year-old Maltese I had ever met. It was amazing to see Stevie too. She was as comfortable as she was in Maine. She asked me if I liked Sushi and told me there was a great place around the block we could walk to. She placed Cooper's blanket on the couch and grabbed a milk bone from the cupboard. She gave Coop a kiss and a gentle pet and out we went. We shared a California roll, some Saki, and other appetizers. Three hours later, we walked home laughing with no lapse in conversation.

Cooper jumped off the sofa and greeted us both. The house was charming, cozy and put together. We sat outside until we felt the chill in the air and light rain started to fall. Our hot coffee woke me up though it was getting late. Stevie walked me to the door. "I had a nice time tonight, Stevie. How long are you in town for?"

She didn't answer, but she leaned in and kissed me. My lips met hers. "Is this our first kiss?" I muttered. She whispered, "If we're not counting the kisses, we've shared in my imagination the many times I saw pictures of you that Mara showed me." I tried hard to believe she had ever dreamt or had even a mere thought of kissing me the second before that first kiss, but I relished her words, and her voice soothed me. I breathed and returned to her soft lips with a slow-moving tip of our tongues. "Why didn't you kiss me in LBH?" I asked, then she asked, "Why didn't you kiss me?" And her lips met mine again. It didn't feel like it was a first kiss. It felt like a familiar sweetness. The intimacy was overwhelming and wasn't ordinary for me or her. It was the sweetest thing.

We took each other into the bedroom, and I felt her heart beating as our naked bodies tangled and touched. She was magnificent, and I did not want to be anywhere else in the world. She knew exactly what to do, and I closed my eyes and enjoyed every second of what she so effortlessly delivered.

I stayed with Stevie until the early morning hours. I looked up from laying my head on her bare chest. "I need to get home. I'm so late." She knew I didn't want to go, and I knew she didn't want me to. I stood up and looked for my clothes. Her eyes stayed on me as I sloppily and quickly tried to dress. A small beam of light shone through the window. It allowed me to study her silhouette, and I knew it would be forever etched in my mind, like Reb's baseball cap.

I hoped I would get to see her again. I wished and felt it was understood that we both would entertain the notion of a likeness encounter and perhaps I wished for more than just another. She walked me to her door. "I still have a situation, which is why I didn't reach out sooner, but it has a shelf life" she said. "I figured," I said, and I held her cheek with one hand and my other hand simultaneously reached down her side to find hers. I grabbed her small soft hand. She eased into squeezing my fingers. I felt a grasp that spoke louder than any words I had ever heard or believed.

I recognized Jude's ringtone immediately. "It's Jude," I announced as I hunted through my bag. I grabbed it and pressed accept. "Hey, bud!" Jude was concerned, "Mom... Are you okay? It's so late!" I pressed speaker. I wanted

Stevie to hear Jude's voice. I am not sure why I did. I thought she could know more about me if she listened to my almost twenty-year-old son asking me where I was at two in the morning on a rainy summers' night. She still had a beaming smile and unhurriedly let her fingers slip away from my gentle grip.

I told Jude I was okay and would be home soon. Stevie and I kissed like teenagers for another minute and then I left. She stayed at the door until I backed out of the driveway into darkness.

On the ride home, I thought endlessly about how unforgettable our evening was. I wished I could have known if she felt as euphoric about everything that had happened between us. Life served up some phenomenal hours. I also thought about the worry in Jude's voice. The same concern he heard in my voice from the moment he could listen. He became a man overnight, and he worried about his mom.

So many thoughts entered and exited my unencumbered self. My life was shaping into a magical journey of joyful experiences, and I thanked the universe for sending me a bit of excitement and tranquility.

It was my time of living after a time of great sorrow. I felt freedom and strength. I was no longer lonely, yet I reveled in my time alone. I resolved the love and failure I experienced in my life. I was happy in my own lane. I felt like every day was brand new and could bring blessings that I could never have imagined. I had time to become and find myself. I was living a genuine life for the first time.

The peace and love in my home between Jude, Sami, and myself was a gift. I promised myself I would never take peace and love for granted. I understood that my life was a blessing, and the transition wasn't about me becoming someone else. It was quite the contrary, and I felt comfortable in my skin. It was about making my own life, taking my power back and being grateful for an hour that wasn't confusing, hard, or a reason to complain. I opened my mind more and more, and the gifts kept coming.

I had hardly stepped into my home foyer when Jude met me at the door. His long arms engulfed my entire petite self. He said, "I'm glad you are home, Mom." I held onto him for a bit longer than I usually would. "Jude, I love you and am glad you are home too." I didn't let go until he did. It reminded me of the days when he was a toddler and hung onto my neck for dear life. He let go but kissed my cheek, "Goodnight, Mom. I'm glad you are staying out late, living again, and having fun. I have to get sleep; I am driving back to school in the morning to move my stuff to the new apartment." I smiled and asked if he would have help. He said, "I got it covered." I went to bed. I felt like a million dollars. I tucked myself in and fell asleep smiling; I felt like Sleeping Beauty.

It took a little while, but eventually, Stevie worked on figuring out how we could become a committed couple. She knew I wanted that, but I didn't ask for it. It came easy, like everything for Stevie and I did. We didn't have to work for it, but we always honored it. My love for her was enough for her to take steps forward. I was amazed she chose me. And… love came again, and it came in many moments as the days trickled on. Life moves. People move. After love, we can and often will fall in love again. And the love is never the same. It's different. Sometimes it's healthier. Sometimes it's poignant. Sometimes it takes us further than the love we've experienced before. We take our lessons and experiences and rise to another level of love. That is what happened to me, and I hoped from the very little knowledge I knew of Jesse's life and of Alex's, that was precisely what I wished for them both.

Stevie became a regular. She began spending less time at her home in Connecticut and more time at mine. My children saw me happy for the first time since they could process what happiness may look like. She just fit into my life and theirs. I didn't think I would ever feel ready to give and receive again, but we had chemistry and commonalties. We existed in a place of no inhibition, no fronts. She would never ask me to wear lingerie, nor would she judge me if I did. She just loved me. The extra pounds, the visible wrinkles, and the visible and invisible scars; She accepted all of my less-than-flawless qualities. She told me I was beautiful, and on days I didn't feel beautiful, I still felt I was enough. I didn't feel ordinary, and I didn't feel lost. She helped me believe again.

Time was moving fast. Vivien and Franco were holding their own but growing into their late eighties. I was finally feeling younger and liberated.

Stevie came with us to Aruba on a few occasions before Vivien and Franco served up the sad news, they were contemplating selling our beloved beachfront after forty-something years. They were considering downsizing to a smaller condo somewhere in Florida and planning to keep their Long Island house so to become full-fledged snowbirds. As pensive as I was knowing visiting Aruba would never be the same if not on our beachfront; I wondered if I'd ever go back after it sold. I knew the travel was too much on my parents and I knew we would not be able to accompany them in the years ahead. Jude was soon to finish college and Sami was growing into her own and a tad bit away from calling me her *BFF*.

Time was just moving at a rapid-pace and I think that's when I was having the most fun.

Chapter Twenty-One

I woke up in a deep sweat. I wanted to jump back behind the lens. Reb was there, her cap worn to its side. It was vast and cold, with rounded paved cement on the floors. There were enormous cameras on tripods with wheels, huge lights mounted on heavy metal ceiling grids, and the freezing studio. I searched for a sweatshirt even though the set felt warm. There was Alex behind and inside the lens, a sort of unqualified camera operator. I wasn't sure why she was there, and I couldn't get to her from behind the thick round glass. I felt myself in a mirage of some reality, but through that crystal clear glass, she looked extremely far away, and that distance made me feel safer and strong. I thought my presence was concealed. Somehow, Alex knew I was on the other side.

I knocked on the lens, and Alex came straight up close and peered at me. I glanced back at Reb, "How do I get there?" I wanted to know. Reb said, "Why would you leave the set? You are free now. You saw so much of your life through a lens." I answered her, "Well, the lens sees what I point it at," I said with conviction. She replied, "But here on the set, you can see the full view, and people can see you." I was in full view on the set. I knew so many people were watching back in the control room, running the entire show, and yet only Reb and I were there in the studio. I felt like many people were watching me, judging me but not saying anything. Reb was trying to make me comfortable even though I wasn't. There was no lens to hide behind. The lights in the studio were hot and bright.

I felt awkward. I silently begged the universe to *put me back behind the camera that lets me see out, and others never look in. Let me write or record the story, and not be in the story.* Reb smiled as if she heard my silent sentiment. "Hey Reb," I said, "The view inside the viewfinder was sometimes beautiful. I barely noticed, not noticing anything but that parochial vision." Reb shook her head and said, "You might want to think about staying here on the set and in the light." I said, "It's hot in here!" She said, "Sometimes it is." I pointed to the camera, "People do tend to entirely believe what this captures and records. Then there is editing and polishing, and the story becomes my perspective of the story I want to tell. Reb asked, "So you want to live a surface or edited, polished life; a Facebook life or a real one?"

Alex kept knocking inside the thick glass, and the sound became deafening. She was angry and losing patience. I could not hear her speaking, but the knocking was piercing, and her expression commanded me to come off-set and back behind the lens where she was. *Come back right now! I am here.* I kept looking through the glass lens to see Alex on the other side, but she was small and distorted. Reb was in plain sight, with her cap worn to its side. The bright lights were all present and clearly would let me decide as she pointed to how and where I could go back and crawl through the glass or stay in the light and sweat it out. I did not jump back behind the lens. I finally saw Reb again, even if it was in a dream. I woke up in a deep sweat.

Stevie pulled the hair away from my brow, "Good morning, beautiful." I barely opened an eye and muttered, "Good morning, beautiful." She felt my forehead, "Emily, you are sweating. Are you okay?" I opened both eyes, "Yes, I am. I had a weird dream." I glanced at the big numbers on the green digital clock across our room. "Oh jeez, Stevie, we gotta get up." She said, "Um, yeah, that's why I tried to wake you for the last twenty minutes." She paused and asked, "Ya know, babe, we have a few minutes if you want to tell me about your dream?" I looked deeply into her eyes, "You are my dream. Let's get ready for this wedding.

We gotta boogie!"
We kissed and sprung out of bed. I started the Keurig, and
she jumped into the shower.

The big day came in a hot minute. Charlotte's sister,
Jaclyn's wedding festivities was about to begin. It was
time for me to wear a lacey bridal dress and walk proudly
into a room of two hundred with Stevie on my arm who
would sport her black, flowing jumpsuit and sensible shoes
in the middle of the dance floor as comfortable as Pat
Benatar rocking out to a crowd of thousands. Authentic
Stevie in her own skin and out since her early twenties, she
did not ponder or juggle with her true self. I fell, big-time
in love with her for that, which was only one of her many
other enduring qualities. She knew I did ponder and juggle
because we discussed everything and often. She never got
upset that my mindset on the topic was quite different than
hers.
It would be a long weekend with the rehearsal dinner, the
next day's morning prep with the girls in the bridal room,
and then the pictures, ceremony, and reception.
Jaclyn and I were friendly and enjoyed family holidays
throughout the years. Still, I was shocked when she and
Layla were engaged years earlier, and Charlotte gave me
the heads-up that Jaclyn planned on including me in her
bridal party. Layla was in the Air Force and stationed in
Iraq, which postponed the wedding more than once, but
years later, it was about to come to fruition.
Stevie and I settled into the upscale New York City hotel
that afternoon. I ran to the door. Michael slid into the foyer,
making my hair messy with his big hand cupping my head.
"You're here!" he said with excitement. I hugged him, and
he shouted to Stevie, who was unpacking across the room,
"Let's go, kids! Get it together and meet Charlotte and me
downstairs for a drink in ten." I pushed him out of the foyer

and told him Stevie and I needed at least a half hour. Stevie interjected, "She needs a half hour! I need a cocktail! See you in ten, Mike!" He gestured *bye* and he left.

I walked over to Stevie and put my arms around her. She pulled me in and held me tight. "Thank you for being here with me, babe," I whispered in her ear. She gently kissed my shoulder. "Nowhere else I'd rather be," she replied.

I told her my dream that morning was about a giant lens and how we see things through our own tiny ones. I told her that I hated Facebook but will probably never quit. She paused and asked, "Em, did I out you on Facebook?" I chuckled and appreciated her heartfelt concern, "Babe, I hadn't thought about it like that, and maybe you did. Hey, I followed suit and posted a profile picture of us. So there! You have my answer!" She beamed with dimples that made anyone in her presence happy. I added, "After I did that, I will have you know that Michael told me about the few distant cousins that texted him and asked if I was playing for the other team?" I laughed. "Oh my God, Em! You didn't tell me that! What did he text back?" I took her hand in mine. "Michael asked them if their brothers or sisters were playing for the other team. And some, I suppose he just never answered. I won't know for sure. After all, I never asked Mike for the details because I don't care." She said, "I'm sorry." I said, "Nothing to be sorry about. I love you." Stevie kissed me and I kissed her back. Then she pushed me away, "C'mon, let's go, sexy." I said, "k, give me five." She waited patiently while I freshened up and changed into my rehearsal dinner clothes. As I applied some light makeup in the bathroom mirror, I thought about how I would not have been ready to attend such an occasion three years back when the wedding was supposed to initially occur.

Three years earlier, I hadn't even come out to Michael. I came out to Charlotte before Vivien, Franco, or Michael, and although Charlotte promised she never told Michael, I suspected she did. I knew he started acting differently after she told him, and she used that conversation to get closer to him in their failing marriage with nothing else interesting to talk about. I knew she told her sister, Jaclyn because Jaclyn was gay and called me immediately after hanging up the phone with Charlotte about me *coming out*. We often chatted via phone in my earlier days of struggle and Charlotte didn't even know how close we were at that time. That is why I was in her bridal party I guessed and I was honored to have been asked. As the years passed, Charlotte became very closed and private. I was sad that our relationship fell apart and I think I knew why, but I never spoke to anyone about it.

I don't think my family and close friends were utterly shocked when I finally came out. However, I always felt until I said it out loud that it wasn't their business to come to conclusions. I was very unsure of my sexuality, throughout my on-and-off-again relationship with Alex. Jesse wasn't even a part of my life unless the kids mentioned him in passing when they were having dinner with him or attending a backyard gathering. My thoughts and feelings also evolved when they did tell me small snip-its, about his life and I always smiled and silently wished him well.

I know Jude and Sami loved him. Part of me never stopped loving him, and I liked feeling that way too. He was good to them and I believe he did his best throughout all our hardships, as did I.

The photographers and video crew at the wedding were all my friends from freelance days in local television. I orchestrated the recommendations to help Jaclyn and Layla set up trusted vendors to capture the days' memories. I had only come out to some of those friends and colleagues in recent months, and others I hadn't seen in many years. It would be the first time they would see me coupled with a woman and not the husband some had met a handful of times, decades earlier. I still wondered what they would think, peering through their camera lens and witnessing this tremendous life change I had chosen with my partner of three years, Stevie Ann Nittola.

She grabbed my hand as we exited the elevator into the busy hotel lobby. "There are four bars in this place," she inquired, "Where are we meeting your brother?" I grabbed my phone to glance at Michael's text. "This way, hon." As we approached the bar, I spotted Charlotte's mother and father, Marnie and Ronnie. "I kissed them both, congratulated them and introduced Stevie. "We have heard so much about you, Stevie. It's so nice to meet you," they said and shook her hand. I guess Charlotte or Jaclyn told them about Stevie because I was confident Michael didn't. I wasn't sure they even knew my story, but it appeared that most who did weren't concerned as much as I thought they would be. People talk about that over dinner and then move on to the more essential things in their own lives. Years earlier, the fear I put myself through worrying about what people would think and say was almost paralyzing.

That day it didn't matter who knew, who told them, or when. I was finally with the right person and with her by my side, I felt confident, released and loved beyond all measure. It was a tremendous awakening and a fantastic feeling. I finally came to understand that it was up to me and only me to accept myself and the life and the person I truly loved. And it was the way she loved me that helped me to do that. It was unlearning so much of what I had been taught to believe in the world and time when I grew up collecting *spiders*, as Vivien called them.

We had a great late afternoon. We met up with Mike and

Charlotte, and soon Jaclyn, Layla, and a small and cheerful group of all their closest people convened. After a quick drink at the hotel bar, we all sat at a tremendous table and enjoyed the food, the chatter, and the reunion between the friends who knew each other well and the few who had just met.

Layla stood up with her Prosecco in hand, and Jaclyn hit her glass with her silverware, and the room grew quiet. "I want to thank you all for being here with us after so many postponements. And I want to thank Jackie too for her patience and…" she looked down at Jaclyn, "I love you, Jac." Jaclyn looked up at her and winked with a loving smile, and Stevie placed her hand on my thigh under the table and squeezed it ever so gently. As Layla talked about when she and Jackie first met, I closed my eyes momentarily and vividly remembered running to my phone the ten days before I met Stevie when Mara called me and blurted out, "LBH has a room and clean sheets for you!"

Layla continued, "This moment right here, right now, feels so perfect. So, here's to all of you for this perfect day, and here's to you, my love, and till tomorrow when we continue and start again in our new iconic life together!" We all held our glasses up. "Cheers!" Jaclyn's eyes welled up.

I slept soundly in Stevie's arms that night, and we woke up with excitement and nervousness. It was Jaclyn and Layla's big day. It was about to begin, and we were a huge part of it. Stevie and I would do everything possible to make it great for them.

Michael sent a limo to pick up Vivien and Franco that early afternoon. He kept telling Charlotte how our parents were stressed about getting into Manhattan. When Charlotte stopped listening, he came and told me. "Dad is really being difficult because I got them a car. I could not have made it easier!" I listened because I knew that was really all Michael needed. "Hey Mike, Dad would have preferred driving his car into NYC. It really has nothing to do with you. He's just annoyed that he is getting old." Michael kissed the top of my head.

I said, "Hey, I'm in a dress and about to walk down an aisle, and I kind of hate this, so let's feel worse for me right now and not Mom and Dad in a limo, in traffic." He smiled, "Okay, Emmy, don't trip down the aisle and I will go fetch Viv and Franco from their fly ride." I could not help to laugh, "You do that! And I'll try to wear this dress the entire night. Not sure what's harder?" I rolled my eyes. He said, "Both!" I said, "Huh?" He said, "I mean… everything is hard lately." I said, "Mike, I have to prepare for the ceremony rehearsal. Go get a drink, get Mom and Dad, and watch your sister-in-law get married." He walked away and looked back at me with an unfamiliar face. Things between him and Charlotte had been declining since their union began, but never the same since the one morning he came staggering to my doorstep many years earlier.

That day the rain had just stopped, but the day was still gray. I peered out my window and was glad it was a Saturday. I dragged myself to the bathroom, trying hard to pee and creep back into bed before my brain realized I was awake. The doorbell startled me a short hour later. I jumped out of bed. I didn't want the kids to wake up, so I rushed. I saw him through the textured blurred glass. I unlocked and flung open the door, "Michael?" I asked. He looked tired. I immediately noticed the dark, black circles under his eyes. He stepped inside, "Em, I'm not feeling right. Em, I need water. Get me water, and I gotta sit down." I was shocked

and never saw Michael in that state. I rushed to the fridge and clutched a bottle of water. Michael was already sitting in the den. "Mike, what is going on? What the fuck?" I popped the cap off for him and he took hold of the water,. He guzzled almost the entire bottle. "Em, I was at a dinner last night, and that douchebag from Walter & Thompson was there. You know, I'm sure I talked about that asshole?" I was worried. Michael was slurring his words and hardly comprehensible." I think Charlotte is have an affair with him? Do you think that is possible?" I immediately replied, "No! Mike! I don't think that is happening. Though, Charlotte distanced herself from me these past years and I feel like I hardly recognize her."
He said he felt the same. He said that Charlotte never cuts him a break and their lifestyle isn't easy to maintain and that is why he still had to work long days and sometimes nights too.
I interrupted, "What happened? And are you drunk?"
He confidently admitted, "Um, yeah Em, I'm a little drunk. I think my wife is having an affair." I couldn't believe this was happening, "I don't like any of this! Where is Charlotte? Why are you here at 5:30am on a Saturday?" Michael swigged the last drops of his water. He shook his head, "Em, if you are going to ask this many questions, I can just go home and let my crazy wife, the one who thinks I am cheating on her, interrogate me… and she will for the next several weeks." I sat across from him on the loveseat. "Michael, are you?" He answered, "Hell no, though I asked if she was! Some guys I know from downtown courthouse told me they saw Charlotte at the bar with that guy and Charlotte doesn't go to bars. So, I asked her if she was there?! She adamantly denied it and then turned the tables accusing me of being out to dinners all the time. Emily, it's part of my job to wine and dine clients. I tried to tell her I have never cheated on her and yeah, I

could have Em… I could have a lot but I never did!" He took a breath and explained everything to me most credibly.

I was shocked Michael came to me. I asked him to fill in the timeline. "Michael, it's six in the morning; Where have you been since the meeting and after you knew she locked you out?" I felt like Vivien interrogating me, in her pajamas, when I was speeding home on my bicycle from the strip when I was running late.

He described his day at work and the phone call he made to Charlotte to ask her to meet him for a quick cup of coffee before he had to go back to work. She agreed and when she got there, Michael asked her if she was having an affair. She was appalled by the question and told him how she got all dressed up thinking Michael wanted to spend quality time with her. She thought since Mike knew she loved coffee, perhaps he was trying to be romantic and tell her he had the rest of the day off and planned something as a surprise. He told me how she went crazy and eventually left the coffee shop upset. Charlotte demanded if he wasn't home within the hour, she was deadlocking the doors and flipping the kill switch to the entrance gate.

I listened to Michael, and I was convinced that his narrative was accurate. He said he took a cab back to his office because he had an important meeting at seven for dinner with clients who flew in from Europe. He went home after his dinner and Charlotte did in fact lock him out. He showed me his recent calls, "Look, I called her like fifty times and she won't answer my calls. He figured he'd give her time to cool off and went back to his office. He was upset and exhausted and fell asleep on the sofa in his plush office. He went home after four in the morning, and he was still locked out. He decided to drive to my house.

After an hour or so, Michael fell asleep on my sofa and I draped a blanket on him. I returned to bed once I knew

Michael had enough water and seemed peacefully asleep and breathing regularly.

A few hours later, young Sami stood in my doorway, "Um, Mom, do you know that Uncle Mike is on our couch?" I sat up in bed and answered her, "Indeed, I do. Go say hi and turn the coffee machine on, please." Michael stayed, and I cooked a big breakfast. It didn't take long for the kids to dress and head outside. I was happy they had parts of what was so wonderful in my childhood. Our neighborhood was filled with kids, and there was always a swarm of them riding bicycles, playing in the yards, or swimming in backyard pools.

I was cleaning up the kitchen, and Michael was yelling on the phone before he clicked end and slammed it down on the table more than once. I pulled the kitchen faucet forward, and the water shut off. I turned to face my brother. "Mike, please work this out with Charlotte. Divorce is ugly, and unless, well…." I didn't finish my sentence, yet I began another. "Michael, just go home and work this out with your wife."

Michael gazed at me. It felt like he had a question, and I knew it might be one I wasn't ready to answer. "Em, What really happened between you and Jesse?" I let out a breath and sat across from him at the table. "I'm not sure I have all those answers, Mike." We both sat quietly for a few moments. I hadn't come out to anyone at that time and I truly wanted Michael to be the first I did tell.

I asked him if he remembered when Vivien and Franco dressed us up and took us to church. He said he did and wanted to know why I was asking. I explained, "One day after Mom asked me to slip off the knitted cap that her Aunt Josie made for me in that terribly cold church, I think I felt something, and until recently, I never knew what that feeling was." My brother sat up and was paying close attention. "I think I was about four or five, so you were about nine? I remember the thick and massive wooden headers above me. I noticed the man on the cross; the organ resonated and echoed. I remember wanting to leave." Michael said, "Who doesn't want to leave Sunday Mass, even still? The twins hate it." I chuckled, knowing Charlotte was responsible for making their family attend weekly mass. Had it been left to Michael he probably would have opted out of being a loyal catholic like I decided the year after Sami made her first communion. "Anyway," I continued, "I sat in the cold church, slipped off my white knitted cap and looked up at the headers above. I hated it, but Vivien and Franco kept taking us there every Sunday. I remember you would stand next to Vivien, and I would stand on the opposite side beside Franco. That was the rule after that one time in church you snapped my knee sock, and it hurt so bad." Michael made a sad face but laughed, "Sorry, Em." I continued, "That morning, I tugged on Franco's shirt. A giant to me, glancing down with a stern smile and a finger over his lips, whispered, "Quiet, not now." I behaved and knew when mass ended, I would surely forget the many questions I wanted to ask when I had to be quiet. Maybe, I knew something then. If I had ever paid closer attention to how my insides felt certain moments in my life, whether in church or anywhere else, I would have known why I cried in mass decades later watching Sami and Jude sing in the choir during family mass."

Michael was so confused, "Emily, what does the way you felt in church when we were kids have to do with my question about you and Jesse. I don't get it." Jude entered the front door and grabbed a bottle of water from the fridge. "Mom, we are all going to Luke's." He ran his fingers through his wavy black hair. "Okay," I said. "Sami is with you too?" Jude answered yes, high-fived Mike and fluttered out the door.

Mike smiled as Jude walked back outside. "He's a good boy, that Jude," he said. I nodded, "I got lucky, Mike." He said, "Your kids got lucky too. You did a good job through all the stuff, Em."

Life was shifting, and it was shifting back to the core four more than ever. I knew I had to be there for Michael when it seemed Charlotte disregarded him as nothing more than a provider of built-in pools, fine art, and riches.
Mike's phone rang again, and his face strained when he shouted, "Are you kidding me? You locked me out of my own house?" There was not much silence in between when Michael said, "Hold on," he said. He grabbed his jacket and said, "I gotta go, Em!" He walked out the door while pleading with Charlotte to stop yelling at him.

I never came out to him that day though I was trying to. The story about church was supposed to lead to how I always knew there were times in my life I didn't feel comfortable in places where I was supposed to feel safe; And I never knew why.
I thought I questioned my faith as a young girl and later cried at Jude and Sami's elementary family mass because I finally understood that I never really did question my faith, but my faith, my church and some of its members would one day, question me because of who I fell in love with. I would pray for strength. My words came out wrong when trying to explain all of it to Michael, and our interrupted conversation after Jude walked back inside and Charlotte's continued calls after numerous hang-ups before Mike left, ruined the flow of our talk.

"You got this, Em!" he said before the rehearsal began. "I always thought you got real, lucky when Stevie came into your life, but I never told you... she's even luckier." He

winked and left to wait outside for our parents' limo. That
was the nicest thing he ever said to me.

I watched Layla walk up the aisle as I stood under the
beautiful canopy filled with fresh bouquets of white roses
with white and green baby's breath. The guest's heartfelt
grins and eyes were all glued to her.

She looked so calm and blissful. Lena would stand by her
when she reached the end of the aisle, and then Stephanie
and Cari. Funny, I had only met some of them the night
before, yet I felt we'd been friends for a lifetime.

Stevie snapped pictures from her chair in the second row
of the aisle. Vivien, Franco, and Michael entered a little
late and sat a few rows back because traffic was terrible,
and they just made it in time to witness the ceremony.

Marnie looked on adoringly as Jaclyn and Ronnie were the
last two down the aisle. Charlotte stood next to Jaclyn, I
stood next to Charlotte, then Fran and Laura. It felt like
the most loving and nonjudgmental room in New York
City. The ceremony was sentimental, funny, and over in a
blink. The reception began, and the twelve-piece band had
the crowd up since the energizing grand entrance.

I left Stevie dancing with Layla's maid of honor, Lena, and
I stood by the room's edge. My heart was full, and I looked
up with a silent thank you to whomever might have been
above listening to my absolute humble reminiscing when I
met Stevie at LBH in Maine.

I watched Jaclyn and Layla kiss as the lyrics and the music
brought their lips closer.

Michael came over and waved a vodka and cranberry with
a lot of ice and lime in front of my face. "Why are you
hiding in the corner?" I took the glass out of his hand and
took a big gulp."

"The thing is, my favorite brother, I am not hiding at all. I
am looking at the bigger picture and the whole set. I can

see it way better than Ethan over there," I pointed to my friend, the videographer, peering through his lens. Michael said, "Um, Em, that guy is a photographer, and you are a guest. In fact, you are an important bridal party, peep." I said, "Wow, Mike, I'm pretty sure you don't know the difference between a videographer and a photographer." He sarcastically asked, "Is there?"

I was about to respond with disgust. He then stated and asked, "Ya know you were always a little weird, Em but wanna go tear it up?" I took my brother's hand, and he led me to the dance floor.

After a few spins with Michael that Stevie observed, she and I naturally gravitated to each other, and I was dancing with my partner and two women who were just married and with most of our elderly parents, and my entire self was loving the vibe. *Wow, Emily, you really came full circle*, I thought.

Hours later, Charlotte was in the far corner chatting with her cousin while Michael was still twirling around some of the young girls on the dance floor. Vivien and Franco sat at their table talking with the other seventy or eighty-something-year-olds. But whoever was there, and no matter their age, all we felt was a room filled with joy.

The only people who never wanted this day to end more than me was Layla and Jaclyn. They took it in and went for it full out. I was proud of Jaclyn because she and I talked about how nobody would choose this. She said to me numerous times, "Em, nobody wants this. Nobody wants to be gay or would choose it. It's a harder life, but when you're a girl and you wake up next to someone you just want to hug, and it's a girl… you have to admit or come to grips with the gay thing." That conversation was more than ten years before her wedding day. It really resonated with me when she spoke those words and again that day, I remembered. I thought about how far both of us had progressed in owning every bit of our journey and developed our non-apologetic, out-loud lives.

Chapter Twenty-Two

We walked through the store to the front entrance, where there was a white party tent and a table with a few chairs where I would sit, and Trudy would bounce up and down for the three-hour event. There was a billboard of me on an easel and the front cover of *"Until We're Forty-Something."* A line of people showed up to meet me, and I was overwhelmed. It was a dream come true. Trudy was a fantastic publicist who worked tirelessly to arrange all of it.

Jude came with Haley. They were adorable. Haley had a chic floral dress, and Jude wore dark jeans and a belt that complimented his tucked-in collared shirt. I missed Sami. I wished she and Aydin could have been there, but I knew it was an expensive flight and an ordinary Tuesday in most people's lives. Aydin couldn't get off work, and I understood as much as I was disappointed. Dave and Bonnie promised to come for the last bit of the book signing and join in for dinner with Stevie's brother and sister.

Michael also was meeting us at dinner and told me he was picking up the bill for all of us. He told me Charlotte wasn't feeling well and she wouldn't be able to attend. Stevie was there the entire time, standing about twenty feet from the white pop-up tent, sipping a little champagne and waiting while I shook hands and signed copies of my book for hours.

I kept looking at her off to my side, supporting me. I loved the moment I was in and I looked forward to the dinner we would all share when this surreal dream came to an end. There were about ten minutes before the signing promotion would wrap up. I looked up, and there she was. I excused myself and ran to hug her. Sami was glowing and I reached

down to touch her big belly. "I can't believe you came!"
I said with tearful eyes. She was so beautiful and said, "No
way I would miss this, Mom! You did it and I am so proud
of you!" I hugged her and my son-in-law, Aydin. Jude,
Haley and Stevie approached to greet Sami, and I told them
I loved them and had to finish my engagement.

At dinner, I studied all of them and listened with pure intent
to all the stories and reveled in the laughter. I was living
my best life, and I felt so much love. I was so grateful
sitting next to Stevie and all of our family. She understood
my creative crazy and my true being. I built a life with a
love that was perfect for me, and I didn't try so hard to be
perfect for her. She dared me and I was never angry she
did. Stevie reeled me in too. Stevie was the only person
who loved me entirely.
I never saw Alex again, but I saw her from time to time in
my dreams like I saw Reb, with her cap always tipped to its
side.

After our beautiful dinner, reliable life resumed.
Jude was off painting, learning, and enjoying his life
traveling abroad. I missed him greatly though he popped in
and out of my life like the free soul he was born to be. Sami
married a minute after college graduation and was rooted
too far away, even though I was the first to get the text
picture of two lines on a stick. My grandchild was soon to
come, and I was beyond elated. Sami was never the least bit
scared about any of it and grew into a beautiful, loving, and
competent woman.
She said Stevie and me could visit and stay as long as we
wanted once the baby arrived. I told her I would stay
forever, which didn't scare her either. After the baby's
arrival, I told Stevie we may have to move to Chicago
though I knew we never would.

Stevie and I live a simple life but a good one. We have dinner out twice a month and spend more money on our two glasses each of pinot than the food we usually share. Those nights are the best. But our other nights at home, when we take in or cook for each other are unsurpassed too. We have each other and our dog, Monti. He loves Stevie the most. Seems crazy, but I love that too! I found a blessed life and am thankful for each day I live it. A breath of fresh air. I am pretty sure she didn't change me. I am sure I changed because she loved me. She loved me through all the stuff others couldn't.

Sami gave birth to Peyton Thomas and another perfect little bundle, Paisley Gerise. Jude eventually married Haley and had three boys, Colson, Kye & Tristan. I had my fabulous five like Vivien had some decades before.

Grandchildren really do content the heart. And so it goes, I thought. They are the light of my life and contented my heart in ways nothing else had ever. I am still sad and always will be that Vivien and Franco never met their great-grandchildren. Vivien could have offered them more love than anyone. I wished she could have taught them by sharing her stories and experiences, witnessing many suns and moons. But I will teach them that, carry on some *core-four* stuff and tell them about her often. I will also tell them about Franco; they will learn honor from stories about him.

Michael tried to keep the family holidays going but fell short as Charlotte disappeared into herself. Mike never left her, and she never left him. I still talk to Mike but Charlotte, not so much.

After Vivien and Franco went to become my guardian angels, I guess there really wasn't much of a reason to get together as much. I miss the old days sometimes, but not enough to try too hard to make them come to be again. Without my parents, the holidays are hard enough and I don't see the point in making those days harder. Stevie supports me and we make our life decisions together. We play it all by the seat of our pants. We talk and take each day as it comes. We plan less and do more. No matter what a day brings, I know we face it together every morning and end it together every evening.

I am in love with her, and our commitment and devotion to the life we built is honored and appreciated.

Not sure the exact day that I finally knew I would be okay. I finally just knew it. I still missed parts of Jesse and Alex from time to time. I still had moments when I reflected on memories from my past, but none were painful. I knew Stevie felt the same but was less vocal about it. I still had my regrets and some mistakes to be accountable for. I began becoming whatever it was Emily was supposed to become. I stopped blaming Vivien and Franco. I stopped wanting closure with Jesse or Alex. I stopped resenting everyone who had wronged me or misunderstood me. I stopped wondering if I was the perfect mom. I stopped regretting years that I thought were stolen from me.

I just began to love myself, my life, my growth. I learned to honor my existence, in my tiny corner. I stopped talking and miraculously I started to hear.

Eventually, I accomplished everything I wanted to become and thought I'd be the day, I sat and stared at Reb in *Video and Imagery for Young Adults*.

I was a daughter and a sister who worked in freelance production studios all over Manhattan, Long Island and states across the USA. I was an editor, wife, mom, and author; And I did all of that from the walls of my home; in a small studio, in a pair of ripped Levi's. Maybe Mrs. Thurman never understood my essay or how I pictured my life when I was in the sixth grade.

Stevie taught me to receive it when it is given and just say thank you. I share my life with a woman who accepts and respects our lives and roles. We flow together and each in our own independence. Stevie loves me exactly the way I am, and while nothing in life is perfect our time together is ideally very close to what I always searched for. What I always thought could be *our version* of perfect.

I witnessed Jude and Sami teaching their children; my grandchildren about all the people that came before, taught, raised, and loved them. I feel blessed to see personalities and traits passed on. I see Vivien in all of them. I mostly see Franco prevalent in Jude's son, Kye and I can't wait to see them grow and wonder who they will become. I get to witness the best of our immediate *core-four* family traditions still ever-present, and I know they will continue long after I am gone too.

There is the bittersweet where the love will always be. That is what makes life so beautiful. No matter how you get it, where you feel it, or how it comes into your life… Love is universal, and love is what makes life's moments mean something.

I see Jesse these days, and he looks okay and happy enough. Weathered, like me. Regretful and unsure, like me, and sometimes happy, just like me. How are any of us supposed to feel? I don't know how Jude and Sami have weathered my storm.

Essentially, what I do know is the world hands out both sadness and euphoria like candy. We all learn – we all become. We all evolve, and the best of us take all the worst, and we find our way. I learned that life is a gift. Everyone I have met or known was a gift and a lesson. I learned purpose.

I just didn't learn this, *Until I was Forty-Something*.

www.ingramcontent.com/pod-product-compliance
Lightning Source LLC
Chambersburg PA
CBHW041929090426
42744CB00016B/1988